IF I SAY 'YES, I EXPECTED IT,' I'D BE LYING
IF I SAY, 'NO,' I'D BE LYING TOO.
OBVIOUSLY YOU KNOW HOW GREAT HE IS.
ON THE OTHER HAND YOU SAY, 'HOW CAN HE BE
DOING THIS?' HE WAS GONE THREE YEARS.

SOURCE: BRETT HULL, DALLAS STARS / SPORTS ILLUSTRATED (MICHAEL FARBER)

LEMIEUX IS THE ONLY GUY
WHO CAN MAKE THE PUCK
DISAPPEAR FOR A SECOND.
HERE'S THE PUCK NOW – OOPS,
WHERE IS IT? HE STILL HAS IT.

SOURCE: JACQUES LEMAIRE, COACH MINNESOTA WILD / SPORTS
ILLUSTRATED (MICHAEL FARBER)

GREAT HOCKEY PLAYER,
GOING TO BE DOUBTS.

Y TO DO IT.

MOMENTS IN HOCKEY (BRIAN KENDALL)

HOCKEY IS CONSTANTLY READING.
EVEN THOUGH THERE ARE SET POSITIONS,
IT'S ALWAYS CHANGING. WHEN HE PLAYS, THOUGH
IT'S ALMOST AS IF YOU HAVE TO IMAGINE YOURSELF
IN A DIFFERENT POSITION. IN YOUR HEAD
YOU'RE RUNNING THROUGH A LOT OF THINGS, TRYING TO KEEP UP
WITH HIM, THE POSSIBILITIES, AND HE JUST SLOWS IT DOWN.
HE'S ARRANGING EVERYTHING.
HE'S BRINGING YOU INTO HIS GAME.

SOURCE: BRIAN LEETCH, NEW YORK RANGERS / ALEC WILKINSON, ESPN.COM - ESPN THE MAGAZINE

MARIO WAS THE MOST AMAZING PLAYER I EVER HAD
BECAUSE HE VERY SELDOM COULD PRACTICE.
HE HAD HODGKIN'S DISEASE ONE YEAR, THEN CAME BACK
AND WON THE SCORING TITLE. HE HAD TO PUT TOGETHER
FIVE OR SIX POINTS A NIGHT
WHILE THE OTHER GUY (PAT LaFONTAINE) WAS PUTTING
AWAY TWO OR THREE. IT WAS AN AMAZING FEAT.

SOURCE: SCOTTY BOWMAN, COACH DETROIT RED WINGS / TORONTO SUN

MARIO LEMIEUX **OVER TIME**

66

I DIDN'T REALLY KNOW HOW MUCH

MARIO LEMIEUX **OVER TIME**

CHRYS GOYENS | **FRANK ORR**

I LOVED TO PLAY HOCKEY UNTIL I STOPPED.

TEAM POWER
PUBLISHING INC.

ÉDITIONS DU
TRÉCARRÉ

REICH PUBLISHING & MARKETING

MARIO LEMIEUX
CAPTAIN, TEAM CANADA, SALT LAKE CITY 2002

When I retired as a hockey player in 1997, I never imagined that I would have an opportunity to be involved in another book project. So it has been a unique pleasure to be part of an effort like this, to share my thoughts about my career and especially my recent comeback with the many people who have supported me over the years. It is a thrill for me to be back on the ice, and I think this book will reflect that.

I would like to thank all of the fans around the NHL – and especially those in Pittsburgh – for their unwavering support of my comeback as a player.

This book is dedicated t the people closest to me, the people who have made great sacrifices to enable me to continue my career – my parents, my wife, and, of course, my children.

My parents, Jean-Guy and Pierrette, were totally supportive of my hockey career from the first time they helped me tie my skates back home in Montreal. I couldn't have achieved anything without them.

My wife, Nathalie, always has been at my side, providing love, support and advice. During my medical problems, she was the best and most attentive nurse I ever had. We are having a wonderful time together raising our four children – Lauren, Stephanie, Austin and Alexa – and watching them grow.

I also would like to thank my agents, Tom Reich and Steve Reich, for their friendship and guidance. And a special thanks to my fellow investors in the Penguins, our sponsors and supporters, and the many civic leaders who stepped forward to keep hockey alive in Pittsburgh.

Mario Lemieux
Pittsburgh, PA
September 2001

JOINTLY PUBLISHED BY

Team Power Publishing Inc.

Trécarré Inc.

Reich Publishing & Marketing Inc.

PUBLISHER

Allan Turowetz

EDITOR IN CHIEF

Chrys Goyens

CONSULTING EDITOR (PITTSBURGH)

Tom McMillan

CONSULTING EDITOR (TORONTO)

Frank Orr

CREATIVE DIRECTOR

Julie Desilets

ART DIRECTOR

Nathalie Michaud

CO-ORDINATOR | RESEARCHER (PITTSBURGH)

Mike Reisinger

CO-ORDINATOR | RESEARCHER (MONTREAL)

Geneviève Desrosiers

GRAPHIC DESIGN | COMPUTER GRAPHICS

Julie Desilets, Nathalie Michaud, Brigitte Boudrias

PRINTING | BINDING

Transcontinental Interglobe Inc.

SCANNING | PREPRESS

Graphiscan Inc.

CATALOGUING IN PUBLICATION DATA

Goyens, Chrys, 1949-
Mario Lemieux: Over Time
Issued also in French under title: Mario Lemieux, le Magnifique
Co-published by: Trécarré Inc. and Reich Publishing & Marketing Inc.
Includes bibliographical references.
ISBN 2-89568-036-1

1. Lemieux, Mario, 1965-   2. Pittsburgh Penguins (Hockey team)
–Biography.   3. Hockey players–Canada–Biography.   4. Hockey players
–Unites States–Biography.   I. Orr, Frank, 1936-   II. Title.

GV848.5.L45G69 2001   796.962'092   C2001-902818-0

Legal deposit, fourth quarter, 2001
National Library of Canada
Bibliothèque nationale du Québec

DISTRIBUTION IN CANADA BY:

H.B. FENN & COMPANY LTD.
34 Nixon Road, Bolton, ON
L7E 1W2 CANADA

DISTRIBUTION IN THE UNITED STATES BY:

UNIVERSE PUBLISHING
A division of Rizzoli International Publications, Inc.
300 Park Avenue South, New York, NY
10010 USA
via St. Martin's Press, NY
ISBN 0-7893-0663-8

PRINTED AND BOUND IN CANADA IN SEPTEMBER 2001

TABLE OF CONTENTS

— TOM ROONEY

It was an Orwellian Christmas — gray, bleak and cheerless.

Santa Claus had left lumps of coal in the stockings of dot.com millionaires all over North America and the No. 1 carol of the season was *"How low can they go"* — a limbo-like ditty that chronicled the travails of telecom giants like Nortel, Lucent and Cisco. In some cities, the Christmas music was muffled by a succession of blizzards, making it impossible to get around. In others, unseasonably drab without a hint of flakes from the sky, the holiday lights downtown fought a losing battle to inject color into the season.

Entertainment stocks were flat-lining everywhere, as well as sports teams and leagues. Basketball's television ratings were down, the NFL was undergoing a lackluster season, Vince McMahon was promising dynamite with his XFL in February, and NHL hockey was in the blahs. Even Bing Crosby sounded vague.

Gary Bettman was driving into his office in Manhattan when his car phone rang.

"Gary, it's Mario. I have some interesting news."

As he listened, the NHL Commissioner somehow kept his vehicle pointed Manhattan-ward, a huge grin illuminating his features.

For the rest of the holidays, the Christmas songs were Christmassier; Hanukah ditties had more life to them. Fans across the spectrum of North American sports had one subject on their lips, and sports talk shows, normally in holiday hiatus, were the animated forums of interchange they were supposed to be.

In Pittsburgh, and other cities around the league, fans checked their schedules and flocked to the box office, snapping up NHL tickets bearing the word "Penguins". "Will he" or "won't he"? — these people were going to be there to judge for themselves.

In press boxes, cynical sportswriters, who had seen, heard or lived it all, whiled away pre-games and game intermissions in idle speculation that had only one subject, The Big Guy. Everywhere, red circles pinpointed December 27. Mario Lemieux was back; game, most definitely, on.

MARIO LEMIEUX **WAS BACK;**
GAME, MOST DEFINITELY, **ON**

Mario Lemieux, just six days past his 19th birthday, strides onto the bandbox that is the Garden ice for his first official shift in the National Hockey League. There are 14,451 Garden faithful packed into the venerable rink at 150 Causeway Street to celebrate the Bruins' season opener. Beantown's rabid fans are also here to see what the fuss is all about. The entire NHL is aware of Pittsburgh's No.1 draft choice, the super-sized center from Montreal who is touted as the next Gretzky.

Controversy has followed Mario Lemieux his entire hockey life, one in which he was ordained as a sure-thing NHL superstar from the earliest days. Scotty Bowman, then coach of the Stanley Cup champion Montreal Canadiens, made a special trip to take in a peewee game of the then thirteen-year-old Lemieux's Ville Emard Hurricanes. Four years later, Le Magnifique was the best player not playing in the National Hockey League and a member of the Canadian Junior team, an all-star team of top players in the three Canadian major junior leagues and best players from U.S. Division I (NCAA) and Canadian university (CIAU) ranks. His game clashed with the defensive orientation of coach Dave King's squad, and Lemieux came away from the experience disappointed and bitter. When Team Canada came calling the following year, he demurred, and when suspension from his own league was threatened, Lemieux took junior hockey to court and won. He stayed home that Christmas, continued playing for his Laval Voisins, and went on to set a scoring record in the Quebec league.

That June, sitting in the stands of the hallowed Forum, a few miles from his home, he heard his name called as the first pick of the 1984 Junior Entry Draft. Controversy erupted when he refused to acknowledge his new team and don a Penguins sweater. A Penguins fan, watching on TV back in Pittsburgh, allegedly barked: *"I ain't signin'* (a season ticket contract) *until Lemieux does!"* Mario signed soon thereafter, and was an instant hit at training camp that September.

Moments after his No. 66 banner was taken down from the rafters of

the Mellon Arena, with his four-year-old son Austin a fascinated on-ice

observer, Mario Lemieux, 35, lines up against Toronto's Mats Sundin for

his first National Hockey League face-off in more than three-and-a-half

years. The entire hockey world is watching. Strangely enough, Mario

Lemieux felt the first twinges of ice envy on the day in 1999 when he found

himself farther removed from his playing career than any time since he

retired. That day, he became owner of the team he had helped save several

times already.

THIRTY-THREE

AUSTIN LEMIEUX   GUY LAFLEUR   WAYNE GRETZKY   TOM GREA

PENGUINS
0
PLR PEN

7:34
PERIOD 1

LEAFS
0
PLR PEN

SHOTS 0
TIME OUTS LEFT 1

JumboTron
SONY

0

0
SHOTS
TIME OUTS LEFT

UPMC Sports Medicine

LEMIEUX
66
1984-1997

SECONDS

H · CHUCK GREENBERG · TOM REICH · DARIUS KASPARAITIS · JAROMIR JAGR · JOHN

While fellow NHL governors and partners were congratulating him for the business coup that would guarantee the Penguins remaining in Pittsburgh, Le Magnifique, resplendent in pinstripes, couldn't help but dwell on unfinished business of another kind; on the ice.

"I can't really explain it, but I think the seeds for my return to playing were planted on the day that I bought the team. It might have been because I was involved with the team on a daily basis around the players at home and on road trips and being a part of making decisions for the organization..." his voice trails off, the serendipity of the situation still resonating.

Becoming owner and president of a National Hockey League team is probably the most definitive slamming of a door on a playing career possible. Yet, *"I just felt that my place in the organization would be more useful on the ice. At this stage of my life, being only 35 years old, there's not too many years left, so you might as well do it when you're able to do it and while you're young, and that was a big part of my decision."*

I THINK
THE SEEDS
FOR MY **RETURN**
TO PLAYING

00:00 | 00:07 Although the Penguins had previously announced that Mario would play wing while he worked himself into playing shape, he stands at the center circle of Mellon Arena as referee Bill McCreary prepares to drop the puck. Joining him on the wings are two Czechs, young Jan Hrdina and All-World right wing Jaromir Jagr. McCreary drops the puck, Sundin sweeps it to his right and it skitters towards the boards to Mario's left. Mario follows it into his defensive zone where Darius Kasparaitis flips it high into Toronto territory and beyond the end line for an icing call. This time as the Pens line up to the left of goalie Garth Snow for the face-off, Mario is on the right side and Hrdina takes the draw. THE COMEBACK IS SEVEN SECONDS OLD.

WERE **PLANTED** ON THE DAY THAT **I BOUGHT** THE TEAM

|Mario Lemieux|

Two great hockey players loomed large in Mario Lemieux's decision to return, Wayne Gretzky and Guy Lafleur. His forced retirement had gnawed at Mario when he attended Gretzky's last game at Madison Square Garden in 1999 and, like the Great One; he wanted to leave the game on his own terms.

"Wayne had the opportunity to say his goodbyes to the hockey world in a real and meaningful way, and I felt that I needed something like that," Lemieux said.

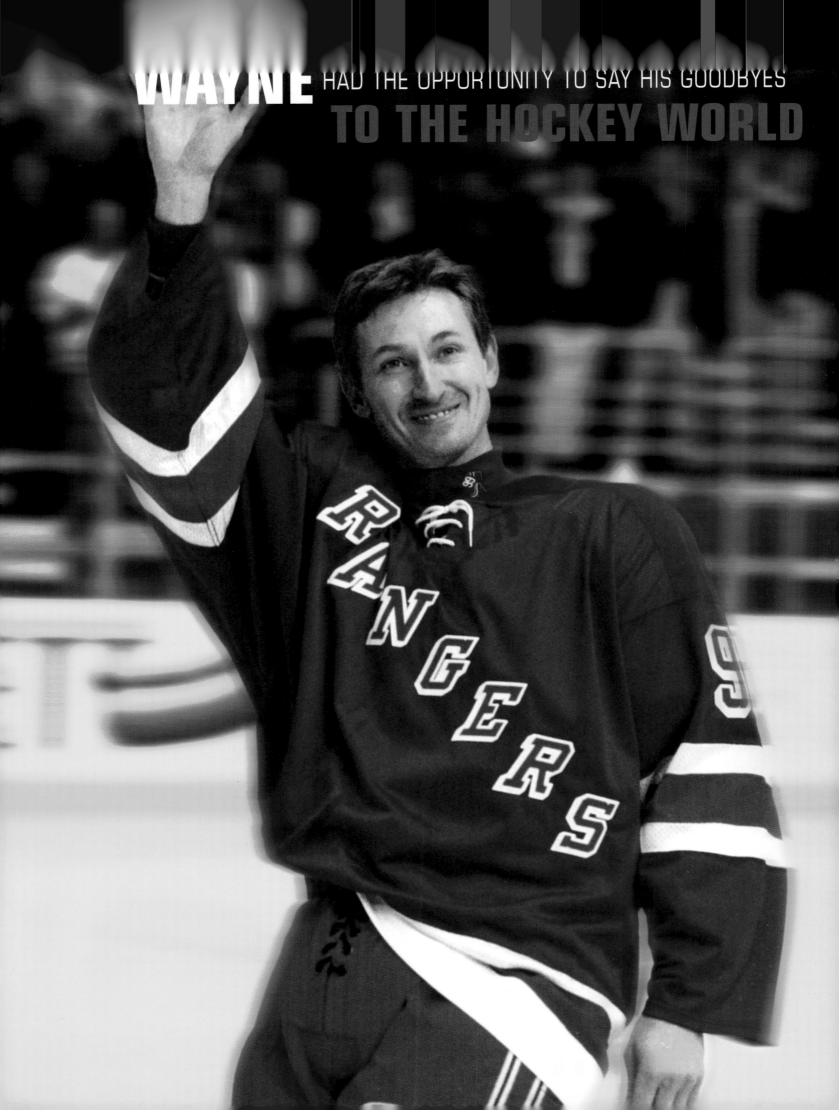

WAYNE HAD THE OPPORTUNITY TO SAY HIS GOODBYES
TO THE HOCKEY WORLD

IN A REAL AND MEANINGFUL WAY,

AND I FELT THAT I NEEDED

SOMETHING LIKE THAT

|Mario Lemieux|

Was he dissatisfied with his original exit at age 31?

"It was tough to leave when I did, but I had to," he reasoned. *"My health wasn't very good. I was struggling with my back quite a bit and my cancer had really taken a toll on my stamina overall... being fatigued all the time and not being 100 per cent. That really played a major role in my decision to retire at a young age."*

As time went by, he began to feel better, rested, and deep down somewhere, the itch began.

The other influence was Lafleur, and his *retraite manquée.* Growing up in Montreal in the 1970s, Mario was swept away by the Canadiens' six Stanley Cups in a decade and the blond superstar who led the way. *"Guy Lafleur was my idol from way back,"* Lemieux said. *"He was the best player in the world and the Canadiens were winning Cups every year it seemed. I had the opportunity to meet him when I was about 12 or 13 years old, and that's something I still remember to this day."*

Mario, Mom and Dad pose with Guy Lafleur at a hockey banquet.

11

What Lemieux remembered, too, was that The Flower's retirement coincided with his debut NHL season, and that Lafleur's return to pro hockey at age 37 in 1988 was inspirational to fans and players alike.

"When you do something like this, you need the support of a lot of close friends or it will be very difficult to achieve, and I think many people helped Guy when he finally decided to return," he said.

Lafleur had quit in frustration after his role was changed on a team in transition. As the Canadiens could no longer maintain the hyper-offensive style that had characterized their four-straight Cup swing in the late 1970s, they were forced to adopt a more defensively oriented game. That didn't suit their superstar, and his goal totals were halved, matching his decreased ice time.

"It's difficult when you're used to scoring 50 or 60 goals a year, and all of a sudden you have to change your game and play more defense than offense," Lemieux surmised. "Everybody asks why you're only scoring 25 or 30 goals a year, not realizing that you're not playing as many minutes or getting the power play opportunities you once got. I'm sure that was frustrating for him and a reason why he decided to retire early."

Both players had issues (confidence, dedication, continuity) to resolve, and only would return after a healing process was completed.

00:07 00:20

Hrdina takes the face-off and Kasparaitis scoops up the puck and swings behind his net, heading up the right wing. As he crosses center ice, he backhands the puck softly into the corner in the Toronto end. This allows his fellow forwards to crash the zone at speed, and forces the Toronto defensive pairing of Dimitri Yushkevich and Danny Markov to scramble for possession. Just as they reach the puck, Jagr barrels in on the right side and Mario enters the zone on the left wing. THE GAME IS 20 SECONDS OLD.

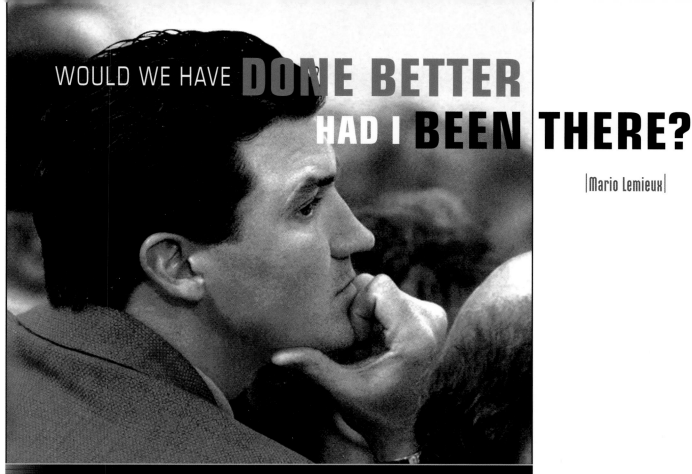

WOULD WE HAVE DONE BETTER HAD I BEEN THERE?

|Mario Lemieux|

As the itch to return grew, Mario Lemieux's day-to-day business dealings on behalf of the Penguins served to widen the gap between him and any attempt at returning to the ice.

For all of the 1999-2000 season, he was immersed in a version of a work-training MBA course, learning the ropes in the front office and the suites of the National Hockey League.

Yet, as his collection of pinstriped suits accumulated and he became more comfortable in his leather chair in the CEO's office of the Pittsburgh Penguins, his antennae began to quiver and point to ice level as each day passed. The team's playoff run in April 2000, taking a 2-0 series lead on the road over the Flyers and then returning home to start a 0-4 winless slide, tugged at the Hall-of-Fame center. The questions

he mulled over were the obvious ones: *"Would we have done better had I been there?"* and *"Could I have taken the pressure off some of our stars and helped us finish off Philadelphia?"*

He found himself sitting high in the seats of Mellon Arena, watching team practices and pondering his future, often, he admitted, when he had no reason to be there. No one else in the building gave a second thought to his presence or guessed at the questions roiling in his mind.

No answers were forthcoming in the off-season, but as the summer passed and the team prepared for another training camp and another campaign, the itch became more persistent. Still, everything was internalized; no one in his family or his immediate circle of friends and business associates broached the subject.

Tom Reich, Mario's agent, is much more of a friend than a business representative.

Mario and a pair of friends and business associates, Tom Grealish and Chuck Greenberg, were out to dinner one evening, a common monthly occurrence as both were intimately involved with Lemieux's business dealings, Grealish as head of the Mario Lemieux Foundation.

Dessert was a special treat that evening as Lemieux let his companions in on a secret: He was going to attempt a playing comeback and would begin training within days. A day later, agents Steve and Tom Reich joined the Inner Circle and were sworn to secrecy. It is a testament of the closeness of these parties that no hint of Lemieux's intentions would surface for almost eight weeks.

"These are special persons to me," Lemieux said. *"They were surprised, but as good friends they were very supportive. They asked me a lot of questions, whether I thought about it thoroughly, which I had. They backed me up and thought it was a great idea."*

The news exploded on the sports world like a bomb. On December 7, *USA Today* posted the news on its Web site, and sports radio stations in Pittsburgh, Toronto and Montreal ran with it immediately. There were no other stories in the NHL until Super Mario confirmed the story at a news conference four days later.

During the two weeks after the confirmation of his comeback, and for several months after his return to the ice wars, the "new" Mario Lemieux would politely answer the same questions in each "new" NHL city: Why the comeback?

THEY WERE
~~SURPRISED~~ BUT AS
GOOD FRIENDS
THEY WERE **VERY SUPPORTIVE**

|Mario Lemieux|

The correlative questions included: Are you back to make Jaromir Jagr (whom, it seemed was pouting throughout much of the first half of the season) happy? Do the Penguins need to sell more seats? Is the team in trouble financially?

Veteran Vancouver writer Tony Gallagher combined the response to two questions in his theory: *"Lemieux is coming back to protect his investment,"* he wrote, *"and that investment lies with the world's best player, Jaromir Jagr."*

By nature, sports journalists are a cynical lot. Even though Jagr was the league's leading attraction and, arguably the most exciting player—Pavel Bure fans notwithstanding—ticket packages sold at the 16,958-seat Mellon Arena numbered under 9,500. Still, in the team's first 13 games, attendance was up from the previous season by almost 1,000 per game at 15,223.

They quickly ascertained that Lemieux's announced return had caused a stampede at the Box Office, as available tickets for the remaining home games in the 2000-01 season were snapped up. Super Mario's influence hit the road with the Penguins, as the team played to full houses all across the league.

The Arena says hello: The Mellon Arena is lit up in a special way on December 27, 2000.

The most important statistic, several writers speculated, had nothing to do with attendance in the current season but, rather, in 2004 or 2005 when the Penguins would have to replace the 40-year-old Mellon Arena with a new facility. With Mario Lemieux on the ice, instead of in the owner's box, the process of financing the new building would be easier to undertake, they reasoned.

Lemieux fielded the question as team CEO.

"We certainly need a new arena here to remain competitive, to have a successful franchise," he said. *"Hopefully, down the road we'll have one. That's certainly in our plans, but this had nothing to do with me coming back to play. There are team issues, health issues, competition issues and family issues."*

In order, the Penguins (team issues) were close to competing with the league's elite, and adding a Hall-of-Fame center might be enough to put them over the top.

SWOOSH, THE COMEBACK

While the physical and mental pressures of The Comeback were his alone, Mario Lemieux's return to game action in the National Hockey League was no solo act.

Accompanying Le Magnifique was a back specialist, an agent and, of course, a brand new equipment endorsements deal.

Call it Swoosh, the Comeback.

"Nike didn't do hockey when I retired; I was a primary spokesman with Karhu (Koho-Jofa) back then, and I had been for years," Lemieux stated. In the interim, Nike became the largest manufacturer in hockey products when it bought Bauer, a Canadian manufacturer of repute.

NIKE BECAME THE BRAND OF CHOICE FOR MARIO LEMIEUX WHEN HE RETURNED TO PLAY HOCKEY... AND GOLF.

"I knew Karhu vice-president John Pagoto had moved to Nike and a week or so before the first game against Toronto, we called Nike and asked them to display their Nike Bauer professional line to us," Lemieux added.

The demonstration, which included a fitting, was arranged and shortly thereafter the name of Mario Lemieux was added to an impressive athletes' stable that includes such thoroughbreds as Tiger Woods, Michael Jordan, Mia Hamm and Vincent Lecavalier.

"We weren't sure which way Mario would go," said Duke Stump, vice-president of Brand Management for Nike Hockey. *"We had just introduced our Nike Quest Gamereadyfit™ line of hockey products, and the timing couldn't have been better for us, especially if he decided to go with us."*

Within weeks, cover stories on Lemieux in *The Hockey News* and *Sports Illustrated* were "swooshed" to the max, with Nike's world-recognized symbol prominent on Lemieux's helmet and his new gloves (team sweaters are manufactured under separate, team contracts).

"The negotiations went very quickly between John Pagoto, John Slusher, who is our NHL representative, and Steve Reich, Mario's agent, and we were happy to usher in what we see as a win-win situation for everybody," Stump added.

GOLF IS A SECOND SPORT FOR NIKE SUPERSTARS MARIO LEMIEUX AND MICHAEL JORDAN.

"Another point of interest with Nike for Mario was our broad range of products. For example, his love for the game of golf and annual participation in the Celebrity Professional Tour, and the sweep of our Nike Golf products, were a natural fit.

"We already have Tiger Woods and David Duval, yet the endorsement of a celebrity golfer like Mario Lemieux, a regular on the CPT alongside John Elway, Mike Schmidt, Michael Jordan and the like, had us extremely excited."

Lemieux picked up his brand new lightweight Nike skates in Denver during All-Star Weekend, and pronounced them *"probably the best I've ever worn. They're tight around the heel, which is important when you skate, and they seem to have helped my skating."*

"The agreement signed, for which no figures have been made public, calls for Mario to wear our equipment – skates, gloves, helmet – and also to endorse Nike apparel, footwear and golf balls, throughout the rest of his career," said Stump.

Mario was in the best health he had enjoyed since the 1980s (health issues), and felt that he would be able to play at a high level (competition issues) that included regular season, the Stanley Cup playoffs and the 2002 Olympic Games. Canadian hockey agreed with him, and Mario was scant weeks into his comeback when Team Canada general manager Wayne Gretzky named him captain of the Canadian Olympic team.

Ironically, his role with the Canadian team will pit him against Pittsburgh executive vice-president and general manager, Craig Patrick, who is general manager of the 2002 Olympic team, and who is the man who works closest with Mario Lemieux on a day-to-day basis with the Pens.

Another hot issue for the press was Lemieux's return to the Penguins' dressing room. What kinds of problems would he cause for the coach and the players, just by simply appearing in the room? How hard would it be for a rookie forward to find himself dressing for a game beside the highest officer in the company?

Darius Kasparaitis is a spirited defender who is adored by his teammates.

It was up to the inimitable Darius Kasparaitis, defender and Clown Prince, to provide the answer to that sticky question.

"When he walks through that door, he isn't the team owner or Boss any more," he said. *"He's going to be a player just like the rest of us, and that's how we're going to treat him, because when he puts on the sweater, he's part of the team."*

Jagr, who was rumored to be out of sorts that December, greeted his former linemate's pronouncement with humor.

"Jaromir's slump played a small part in my desire to come back, but I sat down before a game when he was struggling and I told him we were trying to get some players (to work with) for him, and I told him I was thinking of coming back," Lemieux said. *"He was obviously very excited; he had a big smile on his face. He said: 'You can't do it; you're too fat.'*

"I'd been training about a month at that time. I just explained to him that I thought that I could come back and play at a high level and I wanted to come back and play with him again. That was the extent of our private preparations for my return."

Later, it would appear that the humor in their relationship would disappear, a strain that perhaps was the result of the incessant trade talk swirling about the huge Czech.

The "new Mario," a more forthcoming person who now appeared more comfortable with the media than at any other time in his career, gained sympathy from some quarters of the media and the sports public with his next answer.

"First and foremost was something very special to me, the fact that I was in a position to give my son Austin some special memories," he said.

Family issues centered on young Austin, who was born a year before Mario retired. Even more significant were the circumstances of his birth. Austin was a premature baby and the weeks leading up to delivery were touch-and-go for Mario and Nathalie Lemieux.

YOU CAN'T DO IT;
YOU'RE TOO FAT

|Jaromir Jagr|

Mario spent hours and days by the bedside of his wife, and Austin Nicholas Lemieux made his entrance on Sunday night, March 24, 1996. Two nights later, an emotional Mario expressed his relief and love for his infant son the best way he knew how, with a five-goal, two-assist explosion in an 8-4 win over Wayne Gretzky and the visiting St. Louis Blues.

As a toddler, Austin went everywhere with a cut-down hockey stick in his hands. He became a rabid Pittsburgh fan who worshipped Jaromir Jagr. When family and friends would recall his father's on-ice exploits, young Lemieux had trouble understanding that Dad once had triumphed on the ice.

Lemieux admits that the best aspect of his comeback was announcing the move to his wife, parents and siblings, and then to his children.

"The first thing we told Austin was that I was going to go back and play with Jagr," Mario recalled. *"Obviously he was very excited about it, but I don't think he knew exactly what that meant until the first night when I stepped on the ice and played my first game. He is enjoying this and it is very special. After the games he comes down to the dressing room and mingles with the players. I think it's great for a kid to be able to do that at a very young age."*

Austin Lemieux looked up at his father on December 27.

All kidding aside, the biggest thrill is Dad's, watching his experiences reflected in the smiling faces of his children.

A special time was the NHL All-Star Game in Denver, where Austin rubbed shoulders with the children of other league stars. *"It was very, very special. I didn't have any kids until I was 27 so that was something that was missing. I'm glad to have had a chance to do that with my kids."*

00:20 | 00:30 Hrdina forechecks and forces a quick move by the Toronto defenseman. A weak clearance is intercepted by Jagr at the right half-boards and he automatically throws the puck where he knows Mario Lemieux will be... behind the net, and a bit to the right of Curtis Joseph. This allows Le Magnifique to use the goal as a screen for a Toronto back-checker, and also gives him an angle to clear the pass in front of the net to an oncoming Penguin shooter. THE GAME IS 30 SECONDS OLD.

WE **WOULD GO** FOR A
MINUTE-AND-A-HALF OR TWO MINUTES,
TAKE A MINUTE BREAK, AND **DO THE NEXT ONE**

|Mario Lemieux|

It is easy to announce a return to play, but Lemieux made sure that he would be ready when he stepped onto the ice for the first time in four years. He embarked on a homemade training regimen, riding an exercise bicycle hard and working on various exercise machines for several weeks to prepare for his comeback. Mario weighed 250 pounds when he began his physical regimen, and aimed for a return to his playing weight of 233.

In early November, former Pittsburgh teammate Jay Caufield (1988-94) answered the phone.

"I called him up and told him I needed a skating partner and somebody who would train me for the next couple of months. He never asked any questions; he said whatever I needed he was there for me. That's the sign of a good friend, for him to be able to be there every day for me."

Owner of a company that distributes special terminals to stores and outlets that monitor age-restricted products like liquor and tobacco, Caufield was renowned with the Penguins for his off-season preparation. A former football and hockey player in college, he put himself through a challenging physical program every July to prepare for September training camp.

"Mario knew the work I had to do every year just to get myself ready for the new season, and that several teammates joined me every summer." Although retired, Caufield still works each off-season with former Pens Mark Recchi and Rick Tocchet.

Early morning Boot Camp at the Island Sports Center, a semi-outdoor practice facility, began immediately, and there was no soft-pedaling the comeback attempt. For an hour, Mario Lemieux underwent a program of what hockey players call gutbusters, a series of very intense skating drills with multiple repetitions.

JAY CAUFIELD WAS NOT A TRAINER; HE FUNCTIONED AS

Nobody ever outworked Jay Caufield, which is why the former Pen was the best choice to help Mario Lemieux return to playing shape.

"We would go for a minute-and-a-half or two minutes, take a minute break, and do the next one," Lemieux said. *"It was very demanding and that's something that I obviously needed after three-and-a-half years of not skating. We went right into it and struggled the first couple times. I remember the first drill, I had to go back and forth five or six times and after three times I had to stop because my legs were not moving anymore."*

"Jay Caufield was not a trainer; he functioned as my training partner, doing all of the same exercises as I did and that made it a lot easier for me to keep going," Mario acknowledged. The first plateau came two weeks into the program; when both men were able to acknowledge a definite improvement.

"We had a program; we started at Point One and really wanted to get to Point Two and so on, and each day we would gauge where we were. It was encouraging to see progress. I don't think I could have done it without Jay. I started off about 17 pounds overweight, about 250 after having played at 230-233 in my prime. As my conditioning came back, the pounds fell off."

MY TRAINING
PARTNER

|Mario Lemieux|

MARIO LEMIEUX'S vaunted return is a runaway success. Mario assists on Jaromir Jagr's goal 33 seconds into the contest, and then scores the first goal of his comeback on a one-timer at 10:33 of the second period. The game's first star, 66 totals three points in the contest.

TORONTO 0   5 PITTSBURGH

There was method to the madness. *"I needed to come back and play at a high level from the start; that was important to me,"* Lemieux said. *"My ultimate goal was to be better than I was when I retired if my health permitted. The Mario Lemieux who retired almost four years ago played in a body debilitated by injury and cancer. The time off healed a lot; it was just a matter of getting myself back in game shape and I had a lot of confidence that I could do that."*

Caufield understood the mental and physical aspects of the training program.

"Special athletes like Mario Lemieux, Wayne Gretzky and Michael Jordan, who are far above the rest of us, need to stay there," he said. *"It was evident from the start that Mario was not going to come back as half of what he once was.*

"We were a little more than two weeks into the training when he felt comfortable and confident enough to announce his comeback to the world. As it was, we skated together on Christmas Eve and on December 26, the day before his first game back."

00:30 | 00:33

Mario receives the pass and swings around out front, simultaneously flicking the puck into the Toronto crease. Hrdina is tied up by Markov, but the Toronto left winger takes his eye off Jagr for a fatal second. As he had shoveled the puck toward Lemieux, Jagr left his spot on the right boards and drove to the net. The puck that just misses Hrdina lands on his blade and is immediately directed into the net, under Cujo. At that second, Hrdina and Markov crash into net, dislodging it. Is it a goal? Or was the net off its moorings when the puck crossed the line? Welcome to the new National Hockey League, Mario, where pucks cross red lines and referees dash to the phones to "call it in" to the video goal judge.

As Mario Lemieux rounded into playing condition, the question of the shape of play in the National Hockey League was a major preoccupation.

Late in his pre-retirement career, Mario had very publicly castigated the league and its policy makers for adopting a very lax attitude towards fouls in the game, especially stickwork that fostered injury and impediment of the opponent. When he moved into the front office and the league governors' meetings, his criticisms retreated behind closed doors, but went straight to the ears of those persons who could make a difference.

Zero tolerance for stick fouls became official league policy, and veteran official Andy Van Hellemond, a stickler in his career as one of the league's top referees, was hired before the 2000-01 season to enforce this strict diktat. Facilitating the crackdown was the introduction of the two-referee system, with one behind the play to catch much of the retaliatory stickwork that plagued the game.

"I thought they had improved this part of the game, especially from upstairs," Mario said, as he discussed the decision-making process that led to his return. *"It's a different story especially when you play the game. I think the game has changed tremendously and it is better than it was when I retired. I think the referees are calling it a lot closer, giving the opportunity to the stars to display their full potential and I think that's the way it should be. I also think that the game is safer with the slashes to the hands and upper body handled strictly. There's less of that, a little bit more respect for each other.*

"The other side of it is that the rinks have gotten so small; players are so big now compared to 10-15 years ago, especially since they combine size and skating ability. They are so mobile that there's not much room out there."

A couple of minutes elapse as McCreary leans against the boards at the penalty box, talking on the telephone. He returns the receiver to the minor officials, puts his helmet back on, and points to center ice. GOAL. A caucus of smiling Penguins converges on Mario Lemieux. The first point of The Comeback is in the books.

At his retirement, Mario Lemieux's career scoring statistics were frozen at 613 goals and 881 assists for 1,494 points in 745 regular season games played (and another 70 goals and 85 assists for 155 points in 89 playoff contests).

Another, more telling statistic, was the 272 regular-season games missed due to injury and serious ailments that plagued the first twelve years of his career.

Upon his return, it took all of 33 seconds to re-activate his NHL account, and light a fire under a National Hockey League in the doldrums. Better still, he would go on to play 43 of his team's remaining 46 regular season games, and then play three rounds into the playoffs.

MARIO LEMIEUX, INSTANT IMPACT, 2000-01

33

It was a typical snowy Saturday in the St. Lawrence Lowlands, that geological

dip in the Laurentian Shield whose fertile soil breeds superior athletes

in the Hockey Triangle of Ottawa, Quebec City and Montreal. At hundreds

of outdoor rinks, the sounds of pucks on rickety, weather-beaten boards,

skates, sticks and scraping snow shovels would echo loudly one moment,

and then retreat, muffled by the intensifying snowfall. One sound could not

be muffled; the high-pitched glee of pre-adolescent boys who lived for,

and on, the rink, rising and falling with the tempo of the four or five shinny

games in progress.

LE PRODIGE

## CHAPTER 2

PIERRETTE LEMIEUX . JEAN-GUY LEMIEUX . ALAIN LEMIEUX R

2

At indoor rinks across the Triangle, teams divided into single age levels only would play in organized, hour-long increments, with designations like atom, mosquito, peewee and bantam. Here, outdoors, class and age distinctions blurred as boys played up or down to their skill level, and everybody kept an eye out for *les petits*, four- and five-year-old beginners who tottered through the traffic on shivery pins. Games were day-long affairs and there were no scoreboards to keep track, but everybody seemed to know the score.

The *patinoire* behind St. Jean de Matha church on Rue Dumas was one such bubbling cauldron of hockey intensity on the day that four-year-old Mario Lemieux traipsed after big brothers Alain and Richard on his first trip to the rink.

Dressed in the uniform of the day, hand-me-down sweater and hockey pads (mis-matched), toque and a well-used pair of skates previously worn by an older sibling, his eyes shone. He would finally become a *joueur de hockey*, a player. He would finally join his brothers in that sacred rite that marked his passage into official Montreal boyhood. They were letting him out of the family basement, his Field of Dreams until that moment.

MARIO WANTED A

HOCKEY STICK
IN HIS HANDS,

AND A PUCK
AT HIS FEET

[Fernand Fichaud]

JEAN-JACQUES DAIGNEAULT   MARC BERGEVIN   WAYNE GRETZKY   SCOTTY BOWMAN

Brothers Alain, 9, and Richard, 6, as had generations of older brothers in hockey-mad Canada, tied little brother's skates, supervised his first steps on the snow-encrusted ice, and then were lured away by hot shinny games with their peers. Young Mario was left to maneuver gingerly through the traffic, leaning on his stick for balance as he propelled himself across the rink in choppy V-steps.

Earlier that summer, he had taken part in a special hockey school sponsored by the St. Jean de Matha organization, one of 13 hockey teams in Montreal's District 1.

"We ran a hockey school for all of the boys in our organization across the St. Lawrence River in Laprairie (a South Shore suburb)," said Fernand Fichaud, who was Alain's coach and would become Mario's first hockey coach.

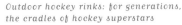
Outdoor hockey rinks: for generations, the cradles of hockey superstars

Coach René Tailleter celebrates a championship with two Lemieux boys, Richard (left) and Mario (lower right).

"We had this rickety old bus and we were shuttling kids back and forth to the rink all day long."

Instruction for the "pre-atoms," ages four to six, consisted only of skating and the most rudimentary puck-pushing exercises. The toddlers were given chairs to lean on for balance and set off across the ice with their first hockey steps. Most boys latched onto the chairs for dear life and were weaned off them with difficulty.

"Mario lasted about one session," Fichaud said, *"and then he ditched the chair. He wanted a hockey stick in his hands and a puck at his feet. And then he wanted a goalie to shoot at. The first time he pushed the puck towards a net with a goalie in it, he tried to deke him. It was what we call in French, du jamais vu, none of us had ever seen such a thing. By six, he would shift easily from leg to leg and put the puck over the goalie, that is, when he wasn't over-matching the goalie with his shot."*

MA, YOU HAVE TO SEE MARIO

|Richard Lemieux|

After his initial on-ice experience at the hockey school, Mario turned to the cradle of Quebec hockey superstars, the outdoor rink.

Several months later, with snow swirling, *Maman* Lemieux, Pierrette, wife of Jean-Guy and mother to this brood of budding superstars, watched her sons leave for the outdoor rink and returned to her daily chores before joining the boys.

The patinoire behind St. Jean de Matha church was the geographical center of Ville Emard, a west-end Montreal district adjacent to the suburbs of Verdun and LaSalle; fertile hockey territory situated a stone's throw west of the hallowed Montreal Forum. Less of a district and more a village, Ville Emard was Lemieux territory, with as many as 70 relatives living within a six-square-block area surrounding the church, where everyone in this urban village was baptized, confirmed, married and buried.

Here, the village raised the hockey player and Mario, on his first visit, would be in good hands.

"I went to the rink several hours after the boys, bringing them sandwiches because they weren't going to waste time coming home for lunch," Madame Lemieux reminisces.

"Since it was snowing so hard, I sat down in the cabane (the ubiquitous rink cabin generally large enough to hold a pot-belly stove and twenty or so skaters coming and going) *and I enjoyed a quiet cup of coffee.*

OTTAWA **3** PITTSBURGH **5**

Instant history in Game Two of the Comeback as Jaromir Jagr registers his 1,000ᵗʰ career point, and MARIO LEMIEUX his 1,500ᵗʰ. Mario has a pair of goals and assists against the offensive-minded Senators.

2 DECEMBER 30, 2000 GAME 38

"Eventually, Alain and Richard came in to dry off and warm their feet and eat their sandwiches, but no Mario. I wasn't too worried."

She sat quietly, enjoying the *ambiance*, and then picked up snippets of conversation from various skaters, coming and going from the rink. "You should see that little kid out there. He won't stop, up and down the rink, up and down, with his hockey stick and puck, and bugging some of the bigger kids to play in their game."

Richard entered the *cabane* for a cup of cocoa. "Ma, you have to see Mario."

Mother and son plodded off to rinkside. There, skating up and down the ice, falling often but always bouncing right up, was little brother. His cutoff stick was pushing a puck and he was already stick-handling, moving the puck side-to-side to avoid traffic and maintain control. Alain, the eldest, spotted his mother and skated over to the boards.

"He picked up his stick, found a puck, and away he went," he said. The best player in his own age category, Alain's eyes were shining with pride, and amazement.

Maman Lemieux shook her head, shrugged some snow off her shoulders, and headed home to prepare supper for her boys.

PIERRETTE & JEAN-GUY LEMIEUX

On a sunny winter day, *Maman* Lemieux holds court in her kitchen at *6700 rue Jogues*. Photographs and other mementos are spread on the kitchen table as she is engaged in animated conversation with her visitors.

Jean-Guy Lemieux, a distinguished gentleman in his early 60s, a retired construction worker, sits quietly in the corner taking everything in with his customary good humor. It is immediately apparent that Mario Lemieux has inherited his mother's looks and his father's shy demeanor.

"Salt Lake City? Mario will be the second famous Lemieux to play there," she smiles, proffering a yellowed news clip of older brother Alain in the livery of the Salt Lake City Golden Eagles of the Central Hockey League, the top farm team for the St. Louis Blues in the early '80s. "When Alain played there, he was their top scorer and they nicknamed him The Count. When Mario plays there during the Olympics, there might be some CHL fans who will remember that."

ALAIN LEMIEUX WAS THE FIRST OF THE LEMIEUX BOYS TO PLAY IN THE NHL, FIRST WITH ST. LOUIS, AND LATER WITH QUEBEC AND PITTSBURGH.

She is in her element. After an almost four-year absence, her youngest son has returned to the National Hockey League as a player, something "I always felt he should do. Mario had much more to give, and I prayed that he would come back. We would talk on the telephone, and I would ask him, 'when are you coming back, Monmario?'"

Monmario, my Mario, the words run together as she recounts how the family discovered that her youngest, and his Prodigal back, was returning to the hockey wars.

"Mario phoned from Pittsburgh in early December and asked where Jean-Guy and I were going to be on Jean-Guy's birthday, the fifth. I said we were going to Richard's for supper and he said he would call us there. When he called, he said 'I'm coming back to play, Maman,' and I started to cry. Jean-Guy took the phone and Mario gave him the news as his birthday present. We were all crying."

Shortly after Mario's comeback, the other Icon of Canadian hockey, Wayne Gretzky, general manager of the Canadian Olympic team, announced that not only would Mario Lemieux take part in the 2002 Games, he would be Canada's team captain.

"It's all too much," Maman Lemieux says, as she surveys the world from Lemieux Hockey Headquarters. Unlike The Great One, whose tottering first steps were filmed on a backyard rink by his coach and father Walter, a Canadian hockey icon himself, the Lemieuxs left the tutoring of their sons to a series of coaches and instructors.

PIERRETTE LEMIEUX WITH HER YOUNGEST SON, BACK IN THE DAYS OF ICE SKATING IN THE HALLWAY OF THE FAMILY HOME

When *Maman* and *Papa* weren't at rinkside taking in the exploits of their three sons, they were in the family kitchen, discussing hockey.

"Alain was a very, very good hockey player, you have to be to make it through Major Junior and all the way to the NHL," Pierrette recalls. *"And Richard was very good too, but he didn't have the hunger for it. He was interested in other things."*

And then came Mario, the hockey equivalent of winning the Loto when the jackpot has been accumulating over several weeks.

The common theme with Jean-Guy and Pierrette Lemieux, almost two decades after their third son was the No. 1 pick in the Amateur Entry Draft, is sheer amazement at how such a talent could be bestowed on their son.

"God works in mysterious ways," she says. *"We have seen hundreds, thousands of good young players, and enough of them came from this area, but from Day One, Mario was special and everybody knew it."*

And then she shrugs her shoulders and picks up another photograph with a story to it.

"Don't stay out past suppertime, you don't want your father coming to get you, and don't forget to bring Mario home with you," she teased her two eldest. In future days it would not be easy to separate Mario from his beloved rink.

"Believe it or not, from that first day people were talking about Mario and his abilities in hockey. They've never stopped talking about him since."

The summer school in Laprairie was not Mario Lemieux's first indoor hockey experience. Ever since he could walk, he was playing "knees" hockey with his older brothers in the basement or front hall at *6700 rue Jogues. Maman*'s piano made a perfect goal, with the keyboard serving as the horizontal bar and the side legs as the goalposts.

"We used cut-off sticks, plastic ministicks we got at tournaments, wooden spoons, you name it, and the puck would be anything from a shaved tennis ball to a bottle cap, ping pong ball, whatever," Mario remembered.

"The games were ferocious and I don't know how many times my Mom had to replace the ceiling tiles, dented and shredded by pucks and sticks, especially when we celebrated goals like NHL players."

Christmas at the Lemieux house was a very decorative season.

One apparently apocryphal tale of Lemieux lore had one of the parents carrying in buckets of snow and tamping it down on the runner carpet in the front hallway, so the brothers could skate indoors at home, on a "rink" that was 20 feet by three feet.

"Absolutely true," Mario smiled. *"Mom did it for two reasons; so we could skate, and because the snow would help clean the carpet. It wasn't great skating but it worked,"* he added, saying that he had never heard of any other parent doing the same thing.

The Lemieux parents, like many others in their working-class district, did all the small things to ease the road of their children to hockey stardom.

"My Dad used to take us to practice at five and six in the morning; he was up early to take us on road trips to go play all over the province, including the peewee tournament in Quebec. He was always there, my Mom as well. Alain and I were very lucky to have parents who were very supportive in everything we did. They were a big part of our careers."

There were new skates for the three boys every year, and other pieces of equipment when needed, even though Mom and Dad would make do with the same wardrobe year-in, year-out.

WASHINGTON 2   3 PITTSBURGH

Mario has a goal and an assist against the stingy Capitals and sets up JAROMIR JAGR with the game-winner midway through the third period. It is Pittsburgh's third straight home win.

41

3 **JANUARY 3, 2001** **GAME 39**

CHAMPIONS
City of Montreal
1972 ATOM "A" 1973
HURRICANES

I'M GOING TO BE AN
NHL PLAYER AND MAKE MONEY
FOR **PLAYING HOCKEY. IT WILL BE**
MY JOB, TOO

|Mario Lemieux|

"Hockey meant everything to our family, and Mom and Dad would make sure that it was the first priority, even over school," Mario recalled. "They were proved right, as two of us would make the NHL in the long run."

Aspiring to an NHL career came early in the piece, as well. A five-year-old Mario had a special conversation with his father Jean-Guy one night when the senior Lemieux returned home from his construction job.

"Mario understood that I went to work to make money to feed my family," Jean-Guy recalled.

Where did the NHL players he saw on TV work when they weren't playing hockey? Mario wanted to know.

"They work at playing hockey, they get paid money for it like I get paid money in my job," Papa answered. "That's their job."

Mario has yet another multiple-point night, his fourth in a row, with a goal and a pair of assists, but defenseman ERIC WEINRICH's two goals propel the visiting Canadiens to victory, the Pens' first loss since the return of 66.

MONTREAL 4   PITTSBURGH 3

"That's it then," his youngest son replied, "I'm going to be an NHL hockey player and make money for playing hockey. It will be my job, too."

Precocious or not, Mario Lemieux never deviated from his five-year (old) plan. "That's all I wanted to do from then on, which wasn't that different from many of my friends and teammates in the lowest levels of hockey. But I never changed my mind. It wasn't like saying I wanted to be a cowboy, fireman or policeman. I meant it."

During the winter, Mario had a daily routine. He would return home from school, drop off his books, grab a sandwich and an apple and head for St. Jean de Matha, and four or five hours on skates until eight or nine in the evening. Then it would be home for supper, bath and home-work, and off to bed.

Hurricanes teammates Jean Fichaud and Mario Lemieux

"I was skating four or five hours a day, and way more on weekends, and it was the most natural thing for me," he said. "I've always felt most at ease on the ice, as a result."

Sometimes homework didn't get done, but little pressure came from *Maman* Lemieux on that front. "Mario was always very good in school. It would seem that he wasn't doing anything and he'd come home with marks in the mid-8os," she said.

"That's the way he always has been, and he'd never changed; he's a perfectionist and he has a habit of going away and perfecting something out of sight of others, and only showing what he can do to others when he can do it very well."

Fernand Fichaud had the same recollection of a young Lemieux.

"For many years I would read journalists describing how inaccessible Mario was over the years, how people couldn't get close to him and crap like that," he said. "What they never understood was how shy and modest he has always been, ever since the beginning. Mario was always the star of our teams, all the way up the levels of hockey, and as the star and best performer, he would routinely receive Best Player medals at hockey tournaments.

"He never wore the medals or carried the trophies around. He would fold them up and give them to his mother. He didn't want to stand out from his teammates off the ice. He was a regular guy and a teammate, even though he was the most talented player in his age group in the entire country. And, as for his talent, nobody worked harder in practice than he did."

PITTSBURGH 5 3 WASHINGTON

Mario Lemieux has a pair of assists in his first away game since his return, but the star of the game is center MARTIN STRAKA, who scores three to put away the Capitals for the second time in five days.

JANUARY 8, 2001
5
GAME 41

I WITNESSED HIS
FIRST DAY ON SKATES, AND EVEN THEN
HE HAD SOMETHING
NOBODY ELSE HAD

|Fernand Fichaud|

Mario and long-time coach and friend Fernand Fichaud celebrated when the Penguins' captain brought the Stanley Cup home to Ville Emard.

Decades later, journalists and other observers entering the security gate at the Forum in Montreal were taken aback by the sight of the superstar of the Pittsburgh Penguins deep in animated conversation with a gray-haired gentleman at the security gate.

"Mario would never come to town, here or at the Forum, without dropping in to say hello," smiled Fichaud, a security co-ordinator with the Montreal Canadiens for almost a quarter century. *"It's not the same at the Molson Centre because I'm located far from the press and players' gate, but he still finds time to talk to me.*

"I witnessed his first day on skates, and even then he had something nobody else had," Fichaud recalled. *"Hands, moves, shot, head and later, size, it all came together in an unbelievable package."*

Asked to select several enduring memories gleaned from many years of watching the rise of a superstar, Fichaud admitted defeat.

"From the very beginning, Mario was making highlight plays every game, and as he got older and better, there were more such plays. It is almost impossible to recall one highlight over another. There are some things that stay with you, though. Like the time Mario came onto the ice with the team trailing by three goals and when his shift was over, we were up by one. But it all runs together."

I WAS ALWAYS MUCH TALLER THAN THE OTHER KIDS

|Mario Lemieux|

Mario Lemieux and teammate Marc Bergevin of the Ville Emard Hurricanes. The two would wear black-gold-and-white together in the NHL.

Still, when Mario was barely six years old, he beat a path through three opponents, cruised in on goal, and shifted left, and then right, before depositing the puck into the deserted net.

"He's made that move in the NHL hundreds of times, with the same result," Fichaud recalled. On another occasion, an eight-year-old goalie tried to stop a Mario slapshot with his catching glove and injured his hand.

When Lemieux presented himself in front of the net a little later in the game, the goalie skated into the corner of the rink, abandoning his net.

After starting with St. Jean de Matha in atom, where he joined brother Richard's team of eight- and nine-year-olds when he was six, and winning a city championship, Mario moved on to the Ville Emard Hurricanes, a powerhouse in southwestern Montreal.

The Ville Emard Hurricanes, one of the top peewee teams in Quebec in the late 1970s

Joining him on the team were future NHLers Jean-Jacques Daigneault, a smooth-skating defenseman, and Marc Bergevin, a left winger who would play defense in the NHL. Both would play for the Penguins alongside their peewee teammate at one point in their careers.

Mario would play for the Hurricanes before moving up to Midget AAA and, subsequently, Major Junior in Laval.

In Fichaud's recollection, and some faded snapshots seem to bear him out, Mario was not a physical giant in his earliest days in hockey. *"He was a bit above average size until second year of peewee (13), and then he shot up and stayed tall,"* Fichaud said.

Mario demurred. *"Right from the start, I was tall. I was always in the back of the class. I was always much taller than the other kids, but I was lucky in that I never went through a clumsy period."*

Jean-Jacques Daigneault has had a long career in the NHL with several teams, including the Penguins.

This time the hat trick is on the other foot. While Mario Lemieux scores in the first and third periods, Boston's ANDREI KOVALENKO sends the Bruins' faithful home happy with a three-goal effort, and goalie Byron Dafoe stops 20 of 22 shots.

6
JANUARY 9, 2001
GAME 42

Most Canadians in the 1960s and early '70s witnessed the Gretzky phenomenon, the almost daily media coverage of the young star from Brantford, Ontario, who grew up under the glare of TV lights, and appeared on several network shows, including Hockey Night in Canada before he was 10 years old. Although Lemieux could boast similar feats of scoring and playmaking in his era, averaging five or six goals a game, there was little media attention beyond publicity photos with Jean Béliveau and other NHL stars at a season-ending sports banquet.

Wayne Gretzky was a Canadian media darling from the age of nine onwards.

ISLANDERS 3 4 PITTSBURGH

The Pens open a home-and-home series with the cellar-dwelling Islanders with a hard-fought victory, on ALEXEI KOVALEV's third-period game-winner. Mario Lemieux has one assist, on Robert Lang's first-period score.

48

JANUARY 12, 2001   GAME 43

And whereas Gretzky sometimes suffered the slings and arrows of jealousy from both the opposition and, occasionally, his own team, Lemieux trod a quieter path to hockey stardom.

"Jealousy within our team was something I didn't notice, or was not aware of. We had some great teams and won several championships and the players and parents were a pretty unified group," Lemieux added.

"A major reason for that was Mario's character," said Fichaud. *"He was a teammate, period, not a star, and his teammates and their parents knew it."*

The Montreal hockey establishment was aware of his prowess. When Mario was in peewee hockey (12-13 years old) in 1977-78, Scotty Bowman came to watch him play.

"I knew he was in the stands that day," Mario recalled. *"Obviously when the coach of the Stanley Cup champions is in the stands, everybody notices, especially when you're a young kid.*

"I had a lot of talent, right from the start, so I got noticed very early in my career."

The next day, Bowman was quoted in the local dailies: *"I have seen a young man named Mario Lemieux play; He'll be a star in the NHL one day."*

In Mario Lemieux's case, the headlines could wait.

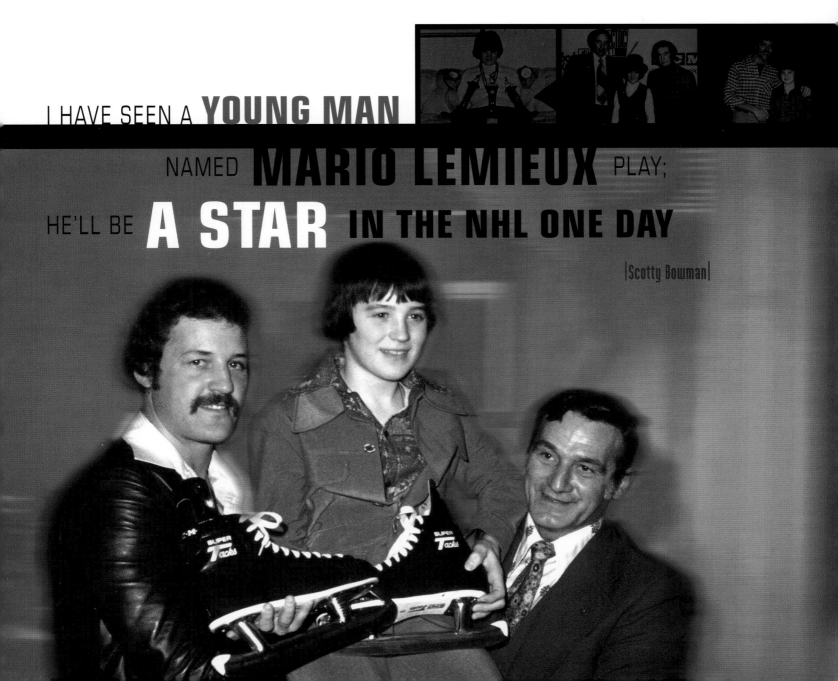

I HAVE SEEN A **YOUNG MAN** NAMED **MARIO LEMIEUX** PLAY; HE'LL BE **A STAR** IN THE NHL ONE DAY

|Scotty Bowman|

BLACK AND YELLOW

ALWAYS WERE THE TEAM COLORS OF PREFERENCE FOR MARIO LEMIEUX

Amateur hockey ends early and abruptly for the very gifted in Quebec.

When Canadiens' coach Scotty Bowman saw Mario play a peewee game and

pronounced him a sure bet for a National Hockey League career, agents and other

actors on the periphery of the sport hovered. Two years later, Super Mario

shared an agent with Wayne Gretzky and was the top-ranked midget player in

Canada. While midget hockey, in Quebec for players 15 and 16, and Major Junior

(up to 20) ostensibly are governed by what was long called the Canadian

Amateur Hockey Association, these categories are anything but amateur.

GOOD NEIGHBOR

## CHAPTER 3

LAVAL VOISINS   GUS BADALI   BOB PERNO   PIERRE LAROUCHE

MARIO

3

From Midget AAA on up, the players are treated like professionals. They play extended schedules, practice for up to three hours daily, and bus all over the province to compete. Moreover, in junior they are paid. Agents, equipment representatives and scouts from many pro leagues are part of the daily entourage.

This entire apparatus was galvanized when Mario Lemieux was drafted into the Quebec Major Junior Hockey League by the last-place Laval Voisins in the summer of 1981. Originally called the National and bedecked in green-and-white when Mike Bossy was setting scoring records, the new team was called the *Neighbors* of all things and the dark blue-purple-and-white uniforms mirrored the city flag of Laval, the next island over from Montreal and the

metropolis's largest suburb. For years, the team had played in a drafty, half-empty barn in the far eastern reaches of Laval Island, next door to the desolate gray, stone walls of the province's most famous penitentiary, St. Vincent-de-Paul.

With the arrival of Le Gros Mario, a second building in the neighborhood would hold thousands captive for a three-year stretch.

I COULD MAKE
MY OWN STATEMENT
BY TURNING

Whereas scant hundreds had watched the sad-sack Voisins founder in the past several seasons, Mario Lemieux would soon have as many as 4,000 screaming fans crammed into the 2,200-seat arena.

For the very best players, those who are projected first-rounders in their draft class, Major Junior hockey is a time to make a statement. Many 16-year-old "all-world" prospects hit a ceiling by the time they are 18 and have three years of this level under their belt, dropping out of the early rounds of the Amateur Entry Draft, if not out of drafting position altogether.

With every contest in junior scrutinized by a phalanx of scouts, fortunes ebb and flow with a week's worth of games.

Mario Lemieux would make several statements during his three years at this level.

The first was establishing a playing persona and the simplest move was a switch in the number he wore on his back. Until this point, Mario had a variety of numbers, 27 in atom and peewee, 12 in bantam, and 10 (like Guy Lafleur, his idol) in midget.

99 UPSIDE DOWN AND
PICKING NO. 66

|Mario Lemieux|

I HAD NOTICED THAT THE OLDER PLAYERS FOLLOWED A REGIMEN THAT COPIED PROFESSIONALS

|Mario Lemieux|

Mario was tabbed as a superstar-in-waiting and his number should reflect that, to say nothing of future marketing possibilities if he could breathe life into the numeral as was expected.

"My agents at the time, Gus Badali and Bob Perno, also represented Wayne Gretzky and he owned the franchise on No. 99," Mario recalled. *"Bob said I could make my own statement by turning it upside down and picking No. 66. Nobody else had the number. It made sense; this would be my number, my identity, especially if I had the career I knew I would."*

In his rookie year in junior, 1981-82, Lemieux scored 30 goals for a hapless team and punctuated his sweater-number decision with 66 assists, leading all first-year performers in the Quebec league. The following September, about to embark on his second junior season and Secondary V (Grade 11), he undertook the calculated decision to quit school to concentrate fully on hockey.

MARIUSZ CZERKAWSKI'S two goals and an assist are the tonic for revenge as the Islanders outlast the Penguins and win the home half of the weekend series. Mario Lemieux scores twice in a losing cause.

PITTSBURGH 5   ISLANDERS 8

"I had noticed that the older players followed a regimen that copied professionals," he said. "They would skate at 10:30 or 11:00 o'clock each morning, often using that ice time to work on things they needed to do to improve, and then play games at night. When I was in school I missed the morning sessions, which I thought could help me. It was pretty much of a sure thing that I would move into the NHL as a career, so school was a secondary issue. While this might not be right for most other people, the decision was the right one for me. From that moment on, I was a pro."

The hockey world came to the same conclusion and several teams began maneuvering for the 1984 Amateur Entry Draft, still two years off. Midway through the 1981-82 season, Montreal traded center Pierre Larouche to Hartford for a switch of draft choices in the Lemieux Draft, or the Franchise Draft, as it had become known. The National Hockey League, and the legions of scouts who followed his every move on the ice, concluded that 1984 would be the most significant draft since George (Punch) Imlach flipped a coin to win Gilbert Perreault in 1970, and Sam Pollock engineered two trades with the Western Division to pluck Guy Lafleur from the amateur ranks a year later.

There were many ironies, among them that these three franchise players were French Quebecers at a time when many in junior hockey denigrated the talent in that province. Pittsburgh's record was good when it reached into Quebec for talent, although tinged with tragedy. Penguins' 1969 draftee Michel Brière from Shawinigan would only play one season before he succumbed at age 20 to injuries sustained in a car crash.

Jean Pronovost followed and scored 317 goals for the Pens over 10 seasons, including 52 goals in 1975-76, but he was long gone from the league. Next up was Larouche, who had set assists (157) and points (251) records in the Quebec league with Sorel Black Hawks, and was Pittsburgh's first-round pick, eighth overall, in 1974. But after three-and-a-half seasons, including a 53-goal performance in 1975-76,

Pierre (Peter in English) was shipped off to Montreal in a weird transaction in which all of the participants (Peter Mahovlich, Peter Lee and Peter Marsh) shared the same first name. Pittsburgh's fortunes waned in the late 1970s and, by the time Mario Lemieux loomed on the horizon, the team was at the bottom of the NHL and in position to qualify for the first pick.

It seemed that everywhere Mario Lemieux went in the QMJHL, Pittsburgh scout Albert Mandanici was in the house. The affable Montreal-based bird dog was under orders from General Manager Baz Bastien to compile the most compete dossier on Lemieux, and he continued this project under new GM Eddie Johnston when Bastien tragically died in an automobile accident in 1983.

"My Mom and Dad shared many a cup of arena coffee with Albert," said Mario. *"He was a very nice, soft-spoken person, and always had a word of encouragement for me. It was his job to report to the Penguins on how I was playing, but he also worked hard to promote Pittsburgh and the team to me."*

"You'll love Pittsburgh," he'd say. *"The fans will love you and you'll get lots of ice time."*

ANAHEIM 2 PITTSBURGH 3

ALEXEI KOVALEV'S two-goal performance, including the game-winner at 1:58 of the third period, propels the Pens to a win over the visiting Mighty Ducks. Anaheim registers one noteworthy accomplishment as the first team to blank Mario Lemieux since his return.

JANUARY 15, 2001 GAME 45 9

ALBERT WAS A VERY NICE, SOFT-SPOKEN PERSON AND ALWAYS HAD A WORD OF ENCOURAGEMENT FOR ME

|Mario Lemieux|

Albert Mandanici, the Pittsburgh scout who bird-dogged Mario Lemieux all over the world of junior hockey, finally got his man.

In year two of junior, Lemieux blossomed with an improving Laval team. In 66 games (there's that number again), he scored 84 goals and added 100 assists for an impressive 184 points, but took a back seat to a diminutive center from Motown in the Quebec league. Pat LaFontaine of the Verdun Junior Canadiens, a Detroit Compuware product, set the QMJHL on fire in his only season in the league with 104 goals and 130 assists for 234 points in 70 games en route to selection as Canadian Major Junior Player of the Year.

Much was made of the Mutt and Jeff nature of the Quebec league's top two players, the darting, quick LaFontaine of Verdun versus Laval's supertanker, and both had their supporters. The gregarious, always smiling LaFontaine, was occasionally held up as an example of what the grim-faced Lemieux could be, if he lightened up a bit. LaFontaine was hot, Lemieux was cold was the consensus, and the Fire-and-Ice show electrified junior hockey that winter.

59

PAT WAS A GREAT ADDITION TO THE LEAGUE,
AND A WONDERFUL

"Pat was a great addition to the league, and a wonderful NHL player for many years," Mario recalled. "His presence in the league was good for me, it was a challenge and helped me elevate my game. I was as excited as the fans were when we played against each other. When he went third in the draft that summer, it was an inspiration for me to have my best season ever in 1983-84 so I would go No. 1."

While LaFontaine was the Player of the Year, it was Lemieux who had lifted Laval from last to first in two seasons, and he would lead the Voisins to a second league title the following year, as well. However, LaFontaine would have the best of their duel in the playoffs and Verdun would challenge for the Memorial Cup, and not Laval.

Players' reputations are fragile things, especially in their pre-professional careers when many outside influences are factored in. That was especially true for Mario Lemieux en route to his No. 1 selection in the 1984 Amateur Entry Draft.

NHL PLAYER
FOR MANY YEARS

|Mario Lemieux|

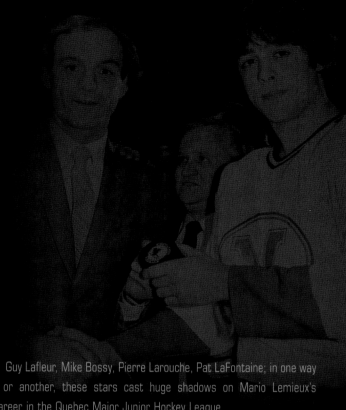

Guy Lafleur, Mike Bossy, Pierre Larouche, Pat LaFontaine; in one way or another, these stars cast huge shadows on Mario Lemieux's career in the Quebec Major Junior Hockey League.

Lafleur and Bossy, two of the best right wingers to play the game, (one or the other was the first team All-Star at that position for every season, but one, from 1974-75 through 1985-86), left a legacy in the Quebec league that drew Lemieux like a moth to a flame: Lafleur's single-season scoring record of 130 goals, and Bossy's scoring records with Laval, Mario's team.

There was a double connection with Pierre Larouche, as well. The slick playmaker with the powerhouse Sorel Black Hawks had set league points records before Pittsburgh reached out and plucked him in the eighth spot of the 1974 amateur entry draft. "Lucky Pierre" then endeared himself to the Penguins' faithful by scoring 53 goals and 58 assists for 111 points in his sophomore season, although he would be dealt to Montreal in his fourth season – and eventually would turn in another 50-goal season for the Habs en route to a more than respectable career of 395 goals and 427 assists.

And then there was Pat LaFontaine, who came out of nowhere – Detroit, actually – to play a single season in the Quebec league and challenge Mario in his second season.

"The funny thing is that my first target, and the last one as things turned out, was Guy Lafleur," Lemieux reminisced. "I say that because Guy was the best player in the world and the Canadiens were the best team and they were winning Stanley Cups; six between 1971 and 1979, the young years in my hockey career.

"It was natural that I would try to pattern some of my play after him, especially my one-on-one moves and shooting power and accuracy, all hallmarks of Guy's exciting talent. At the end of my career in junior, the record that preoccupied me was his 130 goals in a single season," Super Mario recalled. "I managed to break it on the last night of my (regular-season) major junior career."

Many years later, Mario would emulate his childhood hero in another way, by returning to NHL action after a significant layoff and after having been selected to the Hockey Hall of Fame.

"I also seemed to have a pair of connections with Mike Bossy, one of the best pure shooters the NHL has ever seen," he added. *"As my three-year career in junior advanced, it seemed that there was always some Mike Bossy milestone or record facing me."*

The other connection, which both players would sooner not have had, was a history of back troubles.

Bossy, who scored 50 goals in his first nine NHL seasons (nine consecutive seasons – a league record, nine seasons overall – a record shared with Wayne Gretzky), was forced from the game after the 1986-87 season when his back problems overwhelmed him.

"Mike had to quit when he was 30 years old and to lose guys like him who have done so much for the game is difficult for the league. It was similar to Bobby Orr's career being cut short by bad knees; two classy individuals, two great performers, cut down in the prime of their careers."

WHEN MARIO LEMIEUX BEGAN SETTING RECORDS WITH LAVAL, THOSE MARKS HE SURPASSED BELONGED TO MICHAEL BOSSY.

Mario chased Larouche's 1973-74 marks of 157 assists and 251 total points in his final season, and was able to overtake one while falling eight points short of the other. In Mario's third and final season, his totals of 133 goals, 149 assists and 282 total points produced two league records.

"Hockey is a team game, and it was important that our team won, and that's where Pat LaFontaine comes in," said Lemieux. *"We went from last to first in two years and won two regular-season league championships, so our team goals were met. The individual goals were what got me the No. 1 spot in the 1984 amateur entry draft. I remember both Mike Bossy and Guy Lafleur being quoted as saying that they rooted for me to overtake those records, that they were there to be broken."* LaFontaine outscored Lemieux by 50 points in 1982-83, with 20 more goals, (104) and 30 more assists, (130) and he led the Verdun Junior Canadiens to a berth in the Memorial Cup finals, emblematic of the Canadian junior championship.

"Playing against Patty was a challenge that year in junior, as it would later be in the NHL. He did our (Quebec) league proud with his achievements in the NHL and, sadly, also shared the injury jinx with me."

LaFontaine's career was cut short by a series of concussions, the final coming at Madison Square Garden on March 16, 1998, in a game against Ottawa.

Mario Lemieux in action against Team Sweden in international hockey.

In December 1982, in the midst of his second season, the rising star of the Quebec Major Junior Hockey League was invited to join the Canadian team coached by veteran international coach Dave King at the World Junior Championship in Leningrad. What should have been a coming-out party for the giant center of Team Canada turned out to be something else entirely. For all intents and purposes it was a lost fortnight for Lemieux. *"I was homesick all the time, and the food was awful."*

Worse still, Lemieux played a regular shift in the three first games against West Germany, the United States and Finland, only to languish on the bench for long periods against the elite Soviets, Swedes and Czechs. Returning to a regular shift, he exploded in the finale against the hapless Norwegians, swelling his scoring statistic—five goals and five assists for 10 points in seven games—but returned to Canada visibly unhappy with the experience.

King had assessed the defending champion Canadians as strong up front, but weak on defense, and thus decided his group must play team defense all over the ice. Imagine the fallout if a Canadian team had subjected Wayne Gretzky or Eric Lindros to the same treatment.

The lack of respect for Quebec-raised juniors was endemic at the time. King and his staff decided that the giant-sized scoring machine from Laval didn't fit into that system and Lemieux hardly saw the ice in the games that mattered, a strategy that stirred much controversy on both sides of the Atlantic. The Quebec league was long on offense and short on defense, English-Canadian hockey executives argued, and scoring prowess and/or statistics in that league should carry a handicap, Lemieux and his gaudy offensive stats included. They missed the obvious: when Mario had the puck, which was for most of a game, the *other* team was forced to play defense.

63

I WAS JUST
DEFENDING MY RIGHTS

|Mario Lemieux|

The Quebec riposte was succinct: Team Canada was stupid to play "small rink" hockey on the international ice surfaces in Europe. Lemieux should have played more, not less, his backers argued. Lemieux's future sorties into the international arena would make a strong case for the QMJHL argument.

A year later, when the Canadian junior team came calling for the best player in the country, Lemieux slammed the door. Loudly! The embarrassment was keenly felt by Canadian junior hockey.

"I was on the way to a scoring record, and it was my last Christmas at home in what would be many years," Lemieux reasoned, *"So I said 'thanks, but no thanks.' I knew what Christmas at home meant because Alain, who was shuttling from the CHL to the NHL had not been home during the holidays ever since he had left junior."*

By this time, Super Mario was the consensus No. 1 junior in the world, in the midst of a 34-game scoring streak and taking dead aim on the prodigious scoring records set by Quebec junior legends Lafleur and Larouche. On the mid-December day that Team Canada announced its 28-man roster, from which Lemieux's name was conspicuously absent, the Voisins outlasted Hull, 8-6, and the Laval center scored his 63rd and 64th goals of the season, adding a pair of assists.

PITTSBURGH 4   PHOENIX 5

KEITH THACHUK'S second goal of the game, a power-play score at 15:44 of the third, is the winner as the Coyotes come back to defeat the Pens. Mario Lemieux has two assists for Pittsburgh and breaks the 20-point plateau (9-12-21).

10

JANUARY 17, 2001   GAME 46

64

DARRYL SYDOR'S goal 42 seconds into overtime, and three unanswered second-period goals, are the difference as Dallas outlasts Pittsburgh in a wild shootout. Mario Lemieux has one goal in the game, the 10th of his comeback.

PITTSBURGH 5 DALLAS 6 OT

In a show of conspicuous solidarity with their Ontario and Western league counterparts, the governors of the Quebec league felt duty-bound to suspend Lemieux for three league games on December 19, 28 and 30, as well as for the league's All-Star game. They argued that a clause in the standard league contract Lemieux had signed with Laval obliged him to parti-cipate in the world championship if invited. The Lemieux camp responded by seeking an injunction against the league governors in Quebec Superior Court. In less than a week, Lemieux had won his case and was free to con-tinue his pursuit of the league scoring records. *"This wasn't a case of Mario Lemieux being bigger than the league or the game,"* he said. *"I was just defending my rights."*

With a month of play remaining, Lemieux blew by Larouche's total points record of 251, and still had a shot at two other single-season marks: Larouche's 157 assists and Lafleur's 130 goals. On Wednesday, March 14, the Voisins would play host to the Longueuil Chevaliers (Knights) in the last regular-season game for both teams. Going into the game, Lemieux had 127 goals, three short of the record.

Lafleur was asked about his record and responded, *"The Canadiens need a guy like Lemieux to replace me. A player like him would spend his entire career in Montreal. Tell him I wish him luck."*

Player and idol, Mario Lemieux receives the Guy Lafleur award from the man himself.

Lafleur was Lemieux's childhood hero. Wayne Gretzky was a more contemporary idol for the Ville Emard center, part hero and part challenge looming on the horizon. From his first shift in Midget AAA, Mario lived with Wayne Gretzky hanging over his shoulder. They shared the same agents, the same position and a supernatural talent for hockey that had everyone making the inevitable comparisons.

Most significant was a fact that escaped all but the keenest minds in hockey: Gretzky, the only other player who could be compared with Lemieux, had never been drafted. He bounced into the NHL when the World Hockey Association folded and four of its franchises, New England Whalers, Quebec Nordiques, Winnipeg Jets and the Edmonton Oilers, merged with the National Hockey League.

EDDIE JOHNSTON

Ed Johnston is such a rapid talker that one writer claimed: *"E.J. sounds like an old 45 rpm record running at 78."* But as he closes in on the 50-year mark in hockey, from a goalie in Montreal minor hockey to his present job as assistant general manager of the Pittsburgh Penguins, Johnston remains among the best-liked men in the game.

Along the way, Johnston was a highly respected player, coach and executive. He played an important role in the founding of the National Hockey League Players' Association, which made major changes in the workers' situation and altered the face of the game through the NHL's proliferation from six to 30 teams.

EDDIE JOHNSTON HAS LIVED A RICH AND EVENTFUL LIFE IN THE NHL. HE BECAME A CLOSE FRIEND OF TWO OF THE SPORT'S GREATS, BOBBY ORR AND MARIO LEMIEUX.

Johnston had a 17-season, 592-game career as an NHL goaltender with four teams, and was a member of two Stanley Cup championship teams with the Boston Bruins. He went on to coach the Chicago Blackhawks and Pittsburgh Penguins, and served as general manager of the Penguins and Hartford Whalers.

A noteworthy achievement in Johnston's career was the role he played in the hockey lives of two of the game's best-ever players, Bobby Orr and Mario Lemieux. Johnston's guiding of the two extraordinary talents in the early portions of their NHL careers receives rave reviews from both players.

FOLLOWING PAGE 69

Johnston was an established NHL goalie when Orr arrived at 18 to join the Bruins. E.J., as he is widely known around the NHL, took the brilliant young defenseman under his wing and led him through the pitfalls of big league stardom. In his early seasons, Orr shared a house in a Boston suburb with Johnston and other Bruins.

"I was a teenager from a small town and, all of a sudden, I landed in the big city," Orr said. *"E.J. became my friend, roommate on the road, showed me the ropes and pointed out the pitfalls. He made it much easier for me to adjust."*

Eighteen years later, Johnston was general manager of the Penguins, another sad-sack team at the time, when he zeroed in on a precocious Montreal youngster, Mario Lemieux. The hockey world beat a path to his door with offers for the super talent, but Johnston stuck to his guns and claimed Lemieux as the first overall selection in the 1984 entry draft. The big center duplicated Orr's feat in Boston, becoming an extraordinary NHL star and leading the team to two Stanley Cup crowns.

E.J. TOOK GREAT PAINS TO ENSURE THAT MARIO'S FIRST DAYS IN PITTSBURGH WERE COMFORTABLE AND WORRY-FREE.

"I was a kid with little English a long way from home and E.J. went far out of his way to help me get settled in Pittsburgh," Lemieux said. *"He arranged for me to stay with friends of his, a wonderful family, the Matthews, and kept an eye on me, a bit like a parent. We became close friends then and he still is one of my best pals. We often play golf. He's a valuable man in our organization."*

Johnston downplays his role in the two exceptional careers.

"Those two players, Orr and Lemieux, were great from the start," E.J. said. *"I was lucky enough to know them from the debut of their NHL careers, and even more lucky to have them as long-time friends."*

There had been no Gretzky draft, with all of the attendant hysteria that would have enveloped the NHL. There would be a Lemieux draft, however, and the NHL was galvanized in the spring of 1984, with team representatives beating a path to Eddie Johnston's door.

Gretzky would play a significant role when Mario brought down the curtain on his junior career against Longueuil. The Oilers were in Montreal that Wednesday, having beaten the Nordiques, 6-5, the night before and preparing for a Thursday night date with the Canadiens. With a free evening before him, Gretzky and teammate Paul Coffey accompanied Gus Badali to Laval to encourage Lemieux.

The next morning, *Le Journal de Montréal's* front page picture featured Gretzky shaking hands with the new record holder after Lemieux turned in one of the most astonishing offensive outbursts in junior hockey history.

With 3,581 screaming fans out of their seats the entire contest, Mario scored twice in the first two minutes of the game as he directed 10 of his team's 19 first-period shots against Longueuil goalie Daniel Brazeau. At the intermission, teammates were all over their leader in the dressing room.

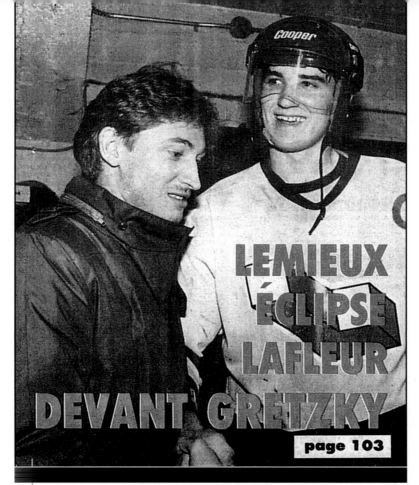

Front page news: Wayne Gretzky and Mario Lemieux on the night of Mario's final regular-season game in junior, were splashed across the cover of Le Journal de Montréal.

"Come on, Mario, the suspense is killing us," quipped defenseman Steve Finn, who would go on to a long career with the Quebec Nordiques. *"Finish it."*

Mario took the teasing to heart and tied Lafleur's mark 78 seconds into the middle period. At 7:14 of the period, he extricated the puck from a scrum in front of the Longueuil net, stepped back to get the angle, and lifted the puck high into the net as the rink exploded. The game was halted as Gretzky came down from the press box and publicly congratulated him as the ovation grew.

"Mario Lemieux will star in the National Hockey League," Gretzky told an overflowing press gallery. *"He dominates with his size, he*

moves the puck well and uses his entire team. That's the only way to work in the NHL where the game is better organized. In junior, sometimes the players are all over the ice. His calmness and ice vision will be even more effective in the NHL."

Once the hoopla was over, Lemieux had added two more goals, for six, and five assists, for 11 points in a 16-4 dismantling of the visitors, a Laval team scoring record. Three years before, Le Magnifique as he was called, had joined a last-place team. On this night, the Voisins were atop the league standings for a second straight campaign, having established four team records: most wins (54), fewest losses (16), most points (108) and fewest goals against (289).

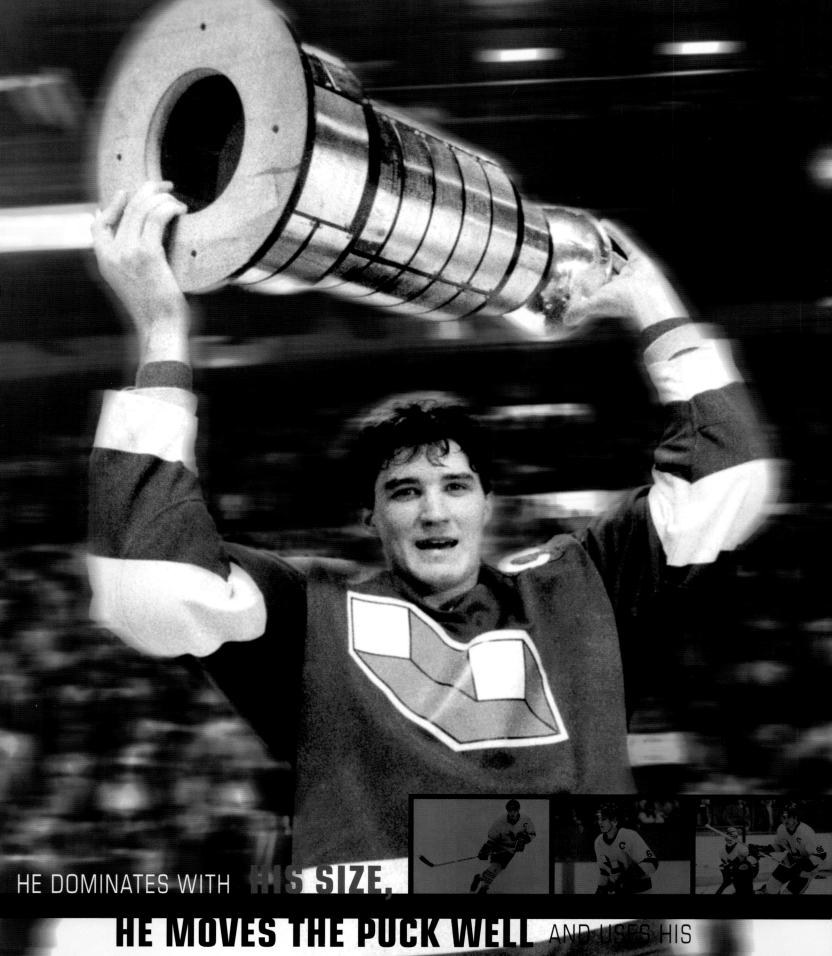

HE DOMINATES WITH **HIS SIZE,** **HE MOVES THE PUCK WELL** AND USES HIS

ENTIRE TEAM

|Wayne Gretzky|

The season over, Lemieux led the Voisins to the league playoff title and into the Memorial Cup, before the team ran head-on into the first adversity they had encountered that year. Laval was swept out of the four-team round robin with dispatch, losing 8-2 to the host Kitchener Rangers in the opener, and then dropping 6-5 and 4-3 losses to eventual winner Ottawa 67s and to the Edmonton-owned, Kamloops Jr. Oilers.

"The Ontario and Western teams are much more physical than Quebec teams," said Lemieux, who concluded the tournament with a sub-par goal and two assists. *"After the first game, we weren't very lucky. I find it frustrating to end my junior career like this."*

His performance in Kitchener would have no impact on his draft position. Ironically, the 67s were coached by Brian Kilrea who had piloted the Canadian junior team that Lemieux had refused to join five months before.

"I don't care what Mario's issues were with Team Canada," Kilrea said. *"He is still, by far, the best junior player in Canada."*

That was confirmed when Lemieux received the Canadian Major Junior Player of the Year award at a special ceremony in mid-tournament, following in Pat LaFontaine's footsteps. Although his team was eliminated in mid-week, Lemieux stayed in Kitchener through Saturday and took part in several promotional events, something which went a long way towards mending fences with the Canadian Amateur Hockey Association.

The last hurdle facing him was the Amateur Entry Draft, June 9 at the Forum in Montreal, three weeks away.

PITTSBURGH 4   0 CHICAGO

GARTH SNOW handles everything the hometown Hawks can throw at him, making 24 saves en route to his third shutout of the season. Martin Straka, Mario Lemieux, Rene Corbet and Robert Lang score for the Pens.

71

JANUARY 21, 2001

12

GAME 48

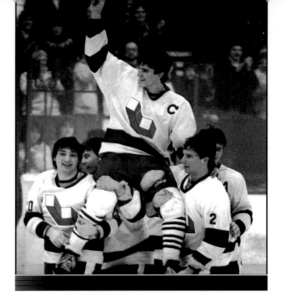

While Super Mario was wrapping up his junior career, Eddie Johnston was fighting off the wolves. The Pittsburgh general manager joined Quebec league scout Mandanici on the road for most of the spring of 1984, often surrounded by his counterparts at arenas around the league.

The former Boston goalie knew what he had in Lemieux and fought off all comers, from without and within.

"Mario Lemieux was the only thing that could keep NHL hockey in Pittsburgh. I was convinced of that," he said. *"If I traded the No. 1 pick, I would receive some significant talent which would help the Penguins in the short term; but Mario was both a short-term solution and a long-term solution. He was going to sell tickets, and he was going to give this very good sports town a superstar in the same mold as Roberto Clemente and Willie Stargell in baseball, and Franco Harris and Terry Bradshaw in football."*

The offers poured in: a package of five or six players, including all three Stastny brothers from the Quebec Nordiques, a promise to *"significantly better anything the Nordiques come up with"* from his hometown Canadiens, as well as all 12 Minnesota choices in the 1984 draft.

"No," said E.J., who also hailed from West End Montreal and had heard of the Ville Emard star for years.

There was more pressure from without. The hapless New Jersey Devils threatened the Penguins' stranglehold on last place. Johnston quickly remedied that, dispatching the team's top defenseman Randy Carlyle to Winnipeg for a 1984 first-round draft pick (Doug Bodger) and a player to be named later (Moe Mantha). He also demoted the team's best goalie, Roberto Romano, and replaced him with journeyman Vincent Tremblay who promptly opened the floodgates, allowing two dozen goals in four games. Pittsburgh finished the season three points south of New Jersey, locking up the No. 1 draft position.

Seventeen years later, a twinkle in his eye, Johnston raised a mild protest when it was suggested that he might have purposely greased the skids under his team.

"Naw, we'd never do that," he smiled.

Then, there came pressure from within.

After a decent start as a member of the group of six new teams added to the NHL in 1967, the Penguins stumbled. Their best season, 1974-75, turned into a nightmare as the team turned in a record of 37-28-15, only to flame out in the playoffs. The Penguins eliminated St. Louis in the first round, and led 3-0 against the up-and-coming Islanders, only to be swept in four straight by New York. Two months later, the team offices were padlocked as the Penguins, drowning in red ink to the tune of $6.5 million, teetered on the edge of bankruptcy.

A group of investors kept the team afloat for two years before turning over the reins to veteran sports entrepreneur, Edward J. DeBartolo Sr., who also owned Major Indoor Soccer League (Spirit) and U.S. Football League (Maulers) teams in Pittsburgh. It didn't take long for him to be quoted publicly and often that *"hockey as an investment stinks"* and the new owner made noises about moving the team to Atlanta or the new Copps Coliseum in Hamilton, Ontario, Canada's Steel City, just southwest of Toronto.

Old friends Mario Lemieux and E.J. share a quiet moment on the ice in 1997.

DeBartolo gave Johnston the go-ahead to change the Penguins' policy of trading away first-round draft picks. He let it be known, however, that in his case he favored a deal where the Lemieux draft choice would be traded away for some player help and a significant infusion of cash. After all, Pittsburgh had two more high picks that June.

"No," said E.J.

Ken Schinkel, an Original Pen and the team's Director of Player Personnel, favored Kirk Muller, the superb two-way center with Guelph in the Ontario junior league.

"No," said E.J.

It was *"No"* to Quebec, Toronto, Montreal, Minnesota and all suitors.

On Saturday, June 9, shortly after one o'clock, Johnston stood at the podium on the temporary stage at the Forum and, in his fractured French and not-so fractured English, announced to the world that Mario Lemieux was a Pittsburgh Penguin.

"No," said Mario Lemieux, refusing to join the team at their draft table and shaking his head when a Penguins shirt with 66-Lemieux on the back was proffered. Contract negotiations had broken down a day earlier over a signing bonus and his agents suggested a statement had to be made.

"I'm not going to their table because the Penguins don't want me badly enough," he said then.

Some 3,000 fans were watching the draft on closed circuit TV at the Civic Arena, and the shock was palpable. Several were quoted as saying they wouldn't purchase season tickets until the name Mario Lemieux was entered on an NHL contract. All rancor was forgotten several days later when the deal was done.

Looking back, Mario Lemieux regrets embarrassing one of his best friends that way.

"I was advised to do things that way, and I was a young guy listening to advice from people who were in charge of my career path," he said.

"I wish I had done things differently, to spare Eddie the embarrassment. Still, things turned out pretty good for the both of us and we're the best of friends today."

Several days later, he kept a promise to himself that he had made at five years of age, penning "Mario Lemieux" on the dotted line of an NHL contract.

Mario Lemieux had been a professional, in reality, for four years and in spirit, since he was a pre-schooler.

Now it was official.

MONTREAL 1   **PITTSBURGH** 3

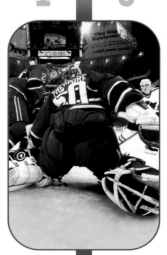

The Penguins get revenge for their first loss since the return of 66, and MARIO LEMIEUX is front and center, scoring all of his team's goals in a 3-1 win over the Habs.

75

MARIO LEMIEUX WAS SUPER-SIZED AND SUPER CONFIDENT WHEN HE ARRIVED AT HIS

first NHL training camp in September 1984. Still, he was a shy, shivering

rookie on spindly Bambi legs compared with what he would become. Few

in attendance that last day of summer could comprehend the depths of

the total package he brought to western Pennsylvania. How could they?

Watching the first tottering steps of one of the best five players in history

to ever lace on skates is something that happens only once in a lifetime and

can only be deciphered contextually many years later.

THE DEBUT

I'VE **NEVER SEEN** ANYONE OF **JUNIOR**

The newly appointed Penguins' coach was Bob Berry who, until the previous mid-season, had filled the same role with the Canadiens during most of Lemieux's junior career in that city.

"I've never seen anyone coming out of junior with as much potential as Mario Lemieux." said the man who just recently had been Guy Lafleur's coach and a teammate of Marcel Dionne, two of the league's bigger luminaries.

"He's going to be a very special hockey player."

What was so special about Mario Lemieux in Pittsburgh? Simple question, simpler answer: He was heralded as a superstar before he arrived on the scene, and he began demonstrating his otherworldly chops from the get-go. Penguins' fans were never given the opportunity to doubt his talent.

Roberto Clemente had been hidden in plain sight in Montreal by Branch Rickey, one of a dozen or so future Hall-of-Fame players who would move up to the Dodgers. When Rickey moved to the Pirates in the 1950s, he knew where several budding superstars were "buried" and Clemente was Pittsburgh-bound. Willie "Pops" Stargell was another sports icon in the city of Three Rivers, who had endeared himself to Pirates fans one season at a time.

The only other Pittsburgh athlete who could compare was Terry Bradshaw, a hotshot quarterback at Louisiana Tech and No. 1 in the NFL draft.

PIERRE LAROUCHE   TOM ROONEY   THE MATTHEWS   DOUG SHEDDEN   GARY LUPUL

COMING OUT
WITH AS **MUCH POTENTIAL**
AS MARIO LEMIEUX |Bob Berry|

However, he struggled for his first several seasons and would suffer the slings and arrows of disgruntled fans in the Steel City until he began to deliver.

Mario Lemieux was, as his name said, expected to be "*the best,*" and he would not disappoint. This would put some very special pressure on him, however.

1 5

ATLANTA PITTSBURGH

Five different Penguins score as the team outclasses the visiting Thrashers. JAN HRDINA starts the ball rolling seven minutes into the game, with Alexei Kovalev, Kevin Stevens, Robert Lang and Jaromir Jagr rounding out the scoring. Super 66 has two assists.

79

JANUARY 27, 2001

14

GAME 50

SEPTEMBER 16, 1966, LONDON, ONTARIO

Goaltender Eddie Johnston is one of several veteran Boston Bruins taking part in the team's first training session and trying not to go cross-eyed. While players generally take care of their own business in camp, this one is special. Circling the diminutive ice surface, similar to the Boston Garden bandbox and wearing No. 27 (it soon will be changed to 4), is the much-heralded Robert Gordon Orr, six months past his 18th birthday.

They call him The Franchise, and he is being scrutinized out of the corner of every eye on the ice, as well as by the larger-than-average crowd of onlookers in the stands. The pitiful Bruins have finished out of the playoffs for the last seven years, dead last in five of them, and anyone or anything that holds out hope for the future is welcome indeed.

"We'd heard about this 18-year-old kid, Orr, who was going to save the franchise," E.J. recalled two decades later. *"After years of adversity, we wondered if this kid was the real thing, and what he would do against NHL competition.*

"After Orr's second practice, it was: 'Whoa! Look what we found!'"

Veteran Bruins blue-liner Ted Green took in the New Kid's performance during that first workout, and skated over to him by the boards.

"Whatever it is they're paying you, kid, it ain't enough!" Green said.

The Bruins would finish last again that season, and then would win the Stanley Cup in 1970 and 1972, losing a hard-fought semi-final to the Canadiens in 1969. They would never again miss the playoffs on Orr's watch.

Bobby Orr was in the thick of it from the moment he arrived in Boston.

SEPTEMBER 20, 1984, MOUNT LEBANON, PENNSYLVANIA

Mario Lemieux skates out onto the ice and for Eddie Johnston, leaning against the boards and beaming like a proud *Papa*, it is *"déjà vu all over again."* The Penguins have missed the playoffs for the previous two seasons, finishing dead last in the Patrick Division each time. Everywhere on the ice, on the benches and in the stands, all eyes are focused on the lanky center with 66 on the back of his sweater.

Early in an intrasquad scrimmage, the Montreal-born supertanker takes a pass and peripherally perceives the imminent arrival of an onrushing defenseman. As veteran teammates cringe in anticipation of a veteran-on-rookie —How-do-you-do!— collision, Lemieux waits until the last nanosecond, nimbly sidesteps the defender while, insult of insults, tipping the puck through his skates. In the same motion, he picks up the puck on the other side and sweeps it toward the net, where it eludes fellow Montrealer Michel Dion, a goalie who once had toiled as a catcher in minor leagues for the Expos (and should have handled a high, hard one).

Hel-l-l-lo Rookie! For the rest of the workout Lemieux, who will turn 19 in 15 days, puts on a clinic, easily eluding checkers and

Scrambling against the New Jersey Devils

defensemen with his reach and stick-handling, holding onto the puck forever until a winger finds open ice and the puck on his stick simultaneously.

"Yeah, I remember what Teddy Green told Bobby Orr after that first practice in Boston," E.J. recalls after the practice.

"But since I'm the guy paying him. I think we're paying him enough. Well, maybe deep down... "

E.J. has a positively moony look on his face.

Mario Lemieux entered the National Hockey League with the impact of a Bobby Orr, and he would spend his NHL days challenging Wayne Gretzky for individual supremacy in the league.

This is the company this golden rookie would keep during his entire career.

81

Another pressure-builder was the special relationship Pittsburgh enjoyed, if not demanded, of its superstars. Clemente who had been seen by many as aloof over most of his career, would finally earn the everlasting respect and admiration of Pirates fans. Willie Stargell and his "We are fam-a-lee" Bucs of 1979 were loved to distraction by the throngs at Three Rivers.

Bradshaw, Jack Lambert, Franco Harris, *Mean* Joe Greene and a stellar cast of Steel Curtain NFL stars made the Steelers the pride of the National Football League for the 1970s and into the 1980s, and the team sank deep roots into the community.

"The Pirates and Steelers had both come down to earth by the mid-'80s and left room for the Penguins to fill the void, if they could," said Paul Steigerwald, Director of Marketing for the Penguins at the time.

MY HOMETOWN

Somewhere, some time, long before Mario Lemieux sank millions of dollars into the Pittsburgh Penguins in September, 1999, he acknowledged to himself that he had sunk even deeper roots into western Pennsylvania.

In other words, home is where the heart is and where the memories are, and home for Ville Emard's finest was Pittsburgh. It was that deep-rooted feeling of belonging that made it so easy for him to invest his entire future in a hockey club he had already left as a player.

Much water had flowed in the Three Rivers since that fateful date in 1984 when Paul Steigerwald drove Mario, his father and his agent into town and cautioned them to prepare for "the view coming out of the tunnel."

IN 1997, MARIO LEMIEUX PLACE, ON THE EAST SIDE OF MELLON ARENA WAS INAUGURATED.

In mid-career, Mario occasionally was asked: When did you stop being another former Montrealer and start being a Pittsburgher? For a time, it was a question he couldn't answer.

"In my mind, that transition happened in the early '90s. It really takes a while to get used to another city, but I came to the realization around Stanley Cup time, by that I mean when we won the Cup. Something like a Stanley Cup win is so emotional that it galvanizes not only the city and the team, but everybody. Holding up the Cup over your head before almost 50,000 fans at Point State Park is a shared memory par excellence.

"It ties you to the city forever. You've done something special together, and the recognition we got as the players and organization, and the recognition the city got, is pretty powerful stuff."

The first Cup win was a catalyst, because it made all concerned realize what existed already. It was all about shared goals, setbacks and triumphs, on an emotional level, as well as any other.

It is not uncommon for professional athletes to adopt, or be adopted, by the city where they will spend the majority of their careers. This is especially true for stars and team leaders who, by their contributions to team success, are able to build business careers or lives away from the arena or stadium.

"You make many relationships and deep friendships away from your sport, people who become important in your life 365 days a year, not just during the season," Mario added. *"The list of close friends and contacts in this category is as long as that of my current and former teammates."*

MARIO, NATHALIE AND THE CHILDREN ARE SNUG AS BUGS IN A RUG IN THEIR PITTSBURGH-AREA HOME.

After a while, too, you realize that your life has been woven into the fabric of a city. Mario's recollections of his Ville Emard neighborhood and growing up in Greater Montreal were the memories of childhood and his adolescence.

His memories of adulthood began the day Eddie Johnston, another former Montrealer, stood up at The Forum and announced that Mario Lemieux was moving to Pittsburgh.

"Although I didn't or couldn't realize it at first, I was a citizen of Pittsburgh. And what became evident after several years is that all of my adult memories – career, friendships, professional relationships, family (my own kids) revolved about this town."

After that, it's all about putting in the years. As he nears his 36th birthday, he realizes that he has lived half his life in each city.

"But Pittsburgh is where I call home, the place most familiar to Nathalie, the kids and me.

"It will always be home."

"That made Lemieux's arrival even more important in that he wouldn't have to compete with championship teams in the other sports. About the biggest star in Pittsburgh at the time was wide receiver Louis Lipps with the Steelers, and the Barry Bonds-Bobby Bonilla Pirates tandem was right around the corner."

Now it was hockey's turn to connect.

Steigerwald, the man who picked up Mario Lemieux at the airport on his first trip to Pittsburgh, is now a broadcaster with the team. In 1984, however, he was charged with flogging the team's newest asset all over western Pennsylvania.

Paul Steigerwald chauffeured Mario Lemieux on his first visit to Pittsburgh.

Mario arriving at the Pittsburgh airport with his father Jean-Guy

"Mario was accompanied by his agent and his Dad when I met them at the airport. I distinctly remember him being kind of regal; he had a princely quality to him right from the start. He was quiet but very attentive.

"I would turn and tell him something about Pittsburgh, and he'd listen and nod and smile. I told him about the tunnel, and how you come out onto a spectacular view of the city. I warned him: 'Get ready for this.' His eyes lit up when we came out of the tunnel, as you would expect, and we went down into the middle of the city and I showed him PPG Place which had just been built—it's a pretty spectacular glass building—and took him to the hotel.

"What stands out about that trip was his Dad didn't say a word and Bob Perno and I conversed because he was the guy I had contacted in advance of meeting Mario.

"Looking back, he seemed like a Prince at the time, and now he's sort of like the King," Steigerwald recalled.

PITTSBURGH **6** | **3** ATLANTA

The Penguins overcome a 2-0 deficit with MARIO LEMIEUX scoring the game winner with an unassisted power-play goal with 25 seconds remaining in the second period, to go along with two assists. Pittsburgh's record against Atlanta since the Thrashers joined the league is an unblemished 7-0-0.

15

JANUARY 30, 2001

GAME 51

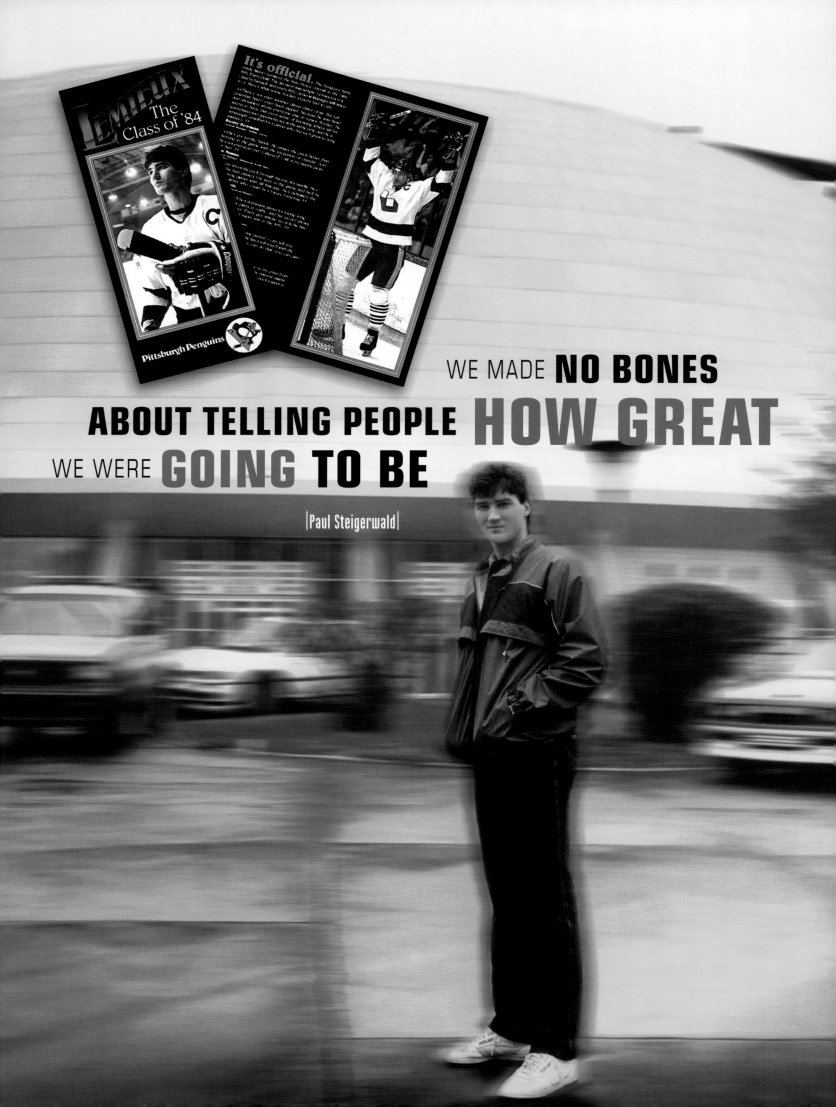

WE MADE **NO BONES**
ABOUT TELLING PEOPLE **HOW GREAT**
WE WERE **GOING** **TO BE**

|Paul Steigerwald|

The cellar-dwelling 1983-84 Penguins had a season-ticket base of 2,170, and averaged 6,800 fans per game in the 16,033-seat Civic Arena. More embarrassing was the fact that the indoor soccer team outdrew the NHL team by more than a thousand fans per game that year.

"We made no bones about telling people how great we were going to be," Steigerwald said. *"I remember the first brochure we passed out in his first press conference the day after I picked him up at the airport. I think it says a lot about how far the Penguins needed to go at that point that we held the big luncheon at the Allegheny Club in Three Rivers Stadium, because there wasn't a place in the Arena that was really worthy of this announcement."*

The brochure had "The Class of '84" on the cover with a picture of Lemieux standing at the team bench during the anthem before a game in

A cold shower at Mellon Arena for Penguins fans as the cross-state rival Flyers dominate in all facets of the game, led by former Pen MARK RECCHI'S two goals. Mario Lemieux scores the only Pittsburgh tally.

PHILADELPHIA 5   PITTSBURGH 1

his Laval uniform, his head held high. There was another picture on the inside of him in full flight, surrounded by laudatory quotes from hockey luminaries Scotty Bowman, Emile Francis, Glen Sather, Wayne Gretzky and others. All predicted a fabulous career.

Three Penguins: Mario is the one in the middle.

Several years earlier, Pierre Larouche also had emerged from the Quebec league as a record-setting offensive machine, but there the comparisons ended. *"The expectations were there for Pierre too, but not even close to Mario,"* Steigerwald added. *"Pierre was a first-round draft choice; Mario was the guy we said would be the savior of the franchise."*

Pierre Larouche was a record holder in the Quebec junior league when he was drafted by the Penguins in 1974.

Seventeen years later, journalists fondly reminisce about Lemieux's rookie year, and how the team "shamelessly dragged him all over western Pennsylvania" to sell Penguins hockey. Steigerwald corrects some faulty memories.

"It wasn't a barnstorming tour," he said. *"I think people get the impression we were carting Mario all over the city, all the time and it really wasn't the case. He did a couple of appearances early. He did one at Gimbel's department store, on his birthday (October 5) and very few people showed up. You have to understand that we were telling people he was a great hockey player, but hockey in the city was at its all-time low in terms of interest, so people weren't buying it right away.*

PHILADELPHIA **4**   **9** PITTSBURGH

ALEXEI KOVALEV, still basking in the afterglow of a defenseless All-Star Game, scores three goals and two assists to propel the Pens to a runaway over the visiting Flyers. Jaromir Jagr adds a pair of goals and assists and Mario Lemieux enjoys a three-point night for the home team.

17

FEBRUARY 7, 2001

GAME 53

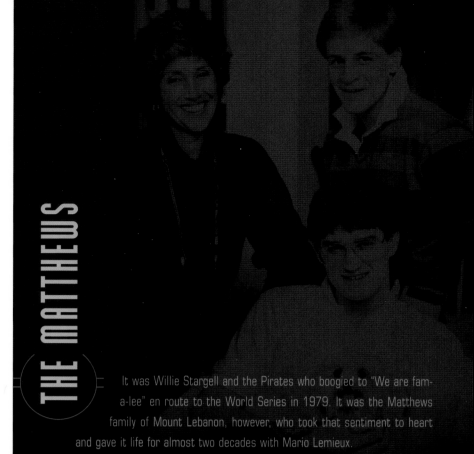

"He did a few appearances, but he wasn't the Pied Piper in the first year. A couple years later he did an appearance at the Century 3 mall, which was owned by Edward DeBartolo, and they were lined up all the way down the Mall to get his autograph. After he had a couple good years, people realized we weren't fooling around. Then you started to see reaction to him."

"They never gave the kid a moment's rest. Everybody conveniently forgot that this was still a teenager" were some media criticisms of the marketing efforts. He was an adolescent who proved the stress was getting to him with occasional acne breakouts, something that forced a hyper-shy player to withdraw even more into the shadows whenever he could.

Tom Rooney, the team's current COO who was lured back to the Penguins by Lemieux in his takeover of the club, was in the Pittsburgh front office in 1984. Rooney said the rookie center was "opening phone booths for us" because the team desperately needed to promote the product.

"This was still a team in jeopardy," he said. *"We needed people in the seats, people at the concession stands, and kids buying Pittsburgh sweaters with the number 66 on the back."*

THE MATTHEWS

It was Willie Stargell and the Pirates who boogied to "We are fam-a-lee" en route to the World Series in 1979. It was the Matthews family of Mount Lebanon, however, who took that sentiment to heart and gave it life for almost two decades with Mario Lemieux.

In the summer of 1984, Pittsburgh GM Eddie Johnston approached Tom Matthews Sr. and his wife Nancy with an unusual request. The Matthews had met Johnston at a Christmas party a couple years before and a friendly relationship blossomed.

"E.J. told us that he had pretty much looked after Bobby Orr in his first years in Boston (Orr shared a house in Nahant with Johnston, defenseman Gary Doak and Bruins' trainer John (Frosty) Foristall) *and felt it would be a good experience for a young player in a new city,"* Nancy Matthews recalled. *"E.J. wanted Mario with a family if he could arrange it."*

In retrospect, it was as much for Nancy Matthews' benefit as it was for the Penguins that the Matthews family decided to try the lodging experiment with the Montreal native: She was suffering from empty nest syndrome with all three of the Matthews boys, Tom Jr., David and Mike, away most of the year.

"My three sons were all away at school and I was eager to have someone around the house. After we met Mario, we knew that we would enjoy having him with us."

Mario agreed with his GM's lodging strategy.

"It was a lot easier living with a family because I was 19 years old and didn't speak the language very well," he said. *"It was a great experience to live with them and to discover Pittsburgh. Nancy was my second mother, cooking all of my meals and taking care of laundry and stuff like that."*

Did a 19-year-old, league-wide celebrity, earning hundreds of thousands of dollars a year, have a curfew?

FOLLOWING PAGE 90 ▶

"Absolutely; the team had an 11 o'clock curfew and he never missed it," Nancy said.

As the family and their star boarder got used to each other, a warm relationship grew.

"Mario was very quiet and cool at first. As he got used to us, we discovered that he was a jokester, easy going. When you have someone living under your roof, you eventually watch their personality unfold. He wasn't the superstar to us, he was just Mario."

The long-term relationship grew to include Nathalie Asselin, Mario's girlfriend, when she moved to Pittsburgh in his sophomore season and the young couple set up house in a condo a short walk from the Matthews residence.

GRANDMAMAN PIERRETTE LEMIEUX, FAMILY FRIEND NANCY MATTHEWS, AND BABY LAUREN SAY CHEESE.

"Those two kids couldn't be more perfect for each other, and we became very close to both of them, and I was there to teach her."

One important subject was English as a second language.

"They were both so eager to learn the language that they wanted us to teach them the right way; they wanted to know how to enunciate. They had lots of questions, they never felt that you were criticizing them; they were always very happy if you corrected them and helped them to do it better. Now, they speak English beautifully."

Eighteen years have elapsed, and the Matthews-Lemieux relationship is an extended family that includes Mario's parents and siblings, as well as the Asselins, Nathalie's family. When the Lemieux's fourth child was born, daughter Alexa, Tom and Nancy Matthews were proud godparents. They are also proud grandparents five times over, with all three sons established in southern California.

"Those lovely young people we met 18 years ago have a beautiful family and we're proud to call them our friends," Nancy Matthews said.

Coach Bob Berry felt differently as he fought to protect his franchise player. *"It bothered me that they had him doing too many things away from the rink. Remember, this was a teenager, in a new town far from home. There were days his head was swimming, but to his credit, he never once complained."*

Berry was also worried about another, more immediate problem. Some veterans in the dressing room had their noses out of joint because *"the show was very obviously Mario, and some of them felt neglected or even disrespected by the front office."*

Steigerwald and Rooney discounted that concern, although acknowledging that the coach was right to worry about team harmony with some veterans unable to accept that the team's icon was a kid who had yet to lace them up in an NHL game.

"We weren't concerned in the least, because it was obvious that those veterans would be long gone by the time Mario got this thing turned around," said Steigerwald. *"We were thinking five-year plan, some of them were thinking five minutes from now; we knew we were right."*

Pierrette Lemieux and husband
Jean-Guy, in background

Another concern, Lemieux's this time, was language. A perfectionist from his earliest childhood, Mario was the kind of person who would not demonstrate an ability or talent until he had mastered it.

"You would never see Mario do anything new until he could do it perfectly," Pierrette Lemieux explained. *"He would go off by himself and work on whatever it was until he was confident that he could do it without a mistake."*

So it was with the English language. Montreal sportswriters who had routinely interviewed Mario for half a decade, would be amazed at his comfort and command of English as early as his third season in Pittsburgh. Berlitz lessons had helped, but the first year was a struggle for the French-speaking teen.

For Lemieux, selling the Penguins *wasn't* difficult when he did his talking on the ice, but acting as a team ambassador off the ice was problematic because it was difficult linguistically.

"It was hard because I didn't speak English very well. The fans would talk to me but I couldn't respond like I wanted, and that was the toughest thing. It wasn't tough to go out and promote the game, which I was willing to do. The language barrier was difficult for the first two or three years."

Afternoon soaps substituted for Conversational English 101 for the shy young Montrealer.

"I took language courses for about three weeks to a month when I got drafted, just to get a base of the English language, and then I just started watching soaps. It was pretty much all by myself—Days of Our Lives is the one I remember the most—just trying to get a feel for the language."

NEW JERSEY 4 PITTSBURGH 5 | OT

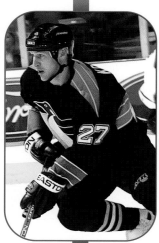

ALEXEI KOVALEV'S second consecutive hat trick, including the deciding goal in overtime, helps Pittsburgh overcome a 3-0 first-period Devils' lead and keys a dramatic Pengins victory. Mario Lemieux contributes one assist in the contest.

MARIO LEMIEUX, **MEET**
THE **NATIONAL HOCKEY LEAGUE;**
PITTSBURGH,
MEET **MARIO LEMIEUX**

The daily conversations and situations in the afternoon soaps helped him the most.

"Every day's episode was closely related to something that had happened the day before, there was continuity, so it was easier to follow. It was almost a recipe for a great conversational language course."

What really helped was that Eddie Johnston arranged to have the rookie live with Tom and Nancy Matthews, and their three sons, where he could relax in an ordered family environment.

As the homesick teenager learned English off the TV screen, Pittsburgh's hoi polloi became dedicated Francophiles. *"Do you know that Lemieux means 'the best' in French?"* fans said breathlessly, as others reached for their French-English dictionaries. *"Isn't that a great coincidence? All he has to do is live up to his name!"*

Mario was in town, the exhibition season was over. The town was agog with the impending Lemieux debut and now it was time for the real thing: Mario Lemieux, meet the National Hockey League. Pittsburgh, meet Mario Lemieux.

Penguins' fans were encouraged when Super Mario scored on his first shot on his first shift in the season opener in Boston, especially after stealing the puck from All-Star Raymond Bourque. The very average Vancouver Canucks would be the visitors for that first game at home, and Pittsburgh was pumped.

Doug Shedden was one of the few veteran Penguins with a scoring touch, having netted 56 goals in 185 games in the previous two-and-a-half seasons. He started the season on Mario's right wing.

Doug Shedden scored the goal on the first point Mario Lemieux registered in Pittsburgh.

The expansion Wild have built a stifling defensive system under veteran coach Jacques Lemaire, and shut out Mario Lemieux in the first meeting between the clubs. Goalie JAMIE McLENNAN stops 25 of 27 shots to backstop the victory.

PITTSBURGH 2   MINNESOTA 4

"What really stood out was the confidence of a kid who had just turned 19 a week before," Shedden recalled. "He was all-world in talent and everyone knew it, which made it easier for everybody to accept him within the team. Early on in training camp, he came to me and told me to go to the net and the puck would find me."

In Boston, Lemieux had scored at 2:59 of the first period, or 1:18 into his first shift. In Pittsburgh where he had put close to an extra 10,000 fans in the stands, he took the opening face-off.

Shedden picks up the narrative of Super Mario's first shift in his new hometown.

"We carried the puck into Vancouver's end and I did what Mario told me to do," Shedden said. "I went to the net and, suddenly, the puck was on my tape. 1-0. It was an easy goal, really."

It was an easy goal, really, only 18 seconds into Mario Lemieux's career in Pittsburgh. So much for building suspense.

Doug, what was the local response to this blitzkrieg?

"Everything you would expect. The players realized we finally had something special. The bench went crazy—we knew we had Gretzky. The crowd went nuts because there had been so much hype about this guy, and there he was delivering the goods, right on schedule."

Mario accepted the praise with customary aplomb.

"I just focused on trying to be successful. I was able to do it early in my career, in my first shift on the ice in Boston and scoring on my first opportunity, it really gave me a lot of confidence right from the start. As the first few years elapsed, things would not always come easy. There were too many superb players in the league. But I learned, too."

I'D SOONER
AGITATE **A LOCOMOTIVE;**
IT'D BE **SAFER** |Gary Lupul|

Later that game, Mario dropped the gloves against that notorious non-pugilist Gary Lupul and proceeded to pummel him to the delight of the crowd.

"He was agitating me," Lemieux told reporters in the post-game scrum.

"You've got to be kidding," Lupul was saying in the visitors' dressing room. *"I'd sooner agitate a locomotive; it'd be safer."* That message spread throughout the league.

Whatever the reasons for the non-characteristic outburst by both centers, the paying customers adored it and there was something special in the air as the fans were discharged into the Pittsburgh night.

Buzz.

The excited crowd conversation where everyone talks at once in superlatives. Sentences that start: *"Did you see... ?"*

In that first season, Mario scored 43 goals and added 57 assists for an even 100 points, capturing the Calder Trophy as the league's top rookie, becoming only the third rookie in league history to hit the century mark.

More importantly, the team's average home attendance rose to 10,018, just short of a 50-per-cent improvement over the previous season. This was still under two-thirds capacity for The Igloo, but for the first time in almost a decade, optimism reigned in the front office.

The future had finally arrived for Pittsburgh hockey.

THE FIRST SEASONS OF MARIO LEMIEUX'S CAREER WERE ALL ABOUT THE INEVITABLE

comparisons with Wayne Gretzky. There has always been a Quebec-Ontario

or Quebec-English Canada subtext to hockey greatness in Canada: Howe vs.

Richard, Orr vs. Harvey, and inevitably, Lemieux vs. Gretzky. Hockey fans in

Pittsburgh, who saw Mario Lemieux play every day and believed that he was

the best player in the National Hockey League, would find themselves in the

middle of that Made-in-the-North buzz saw. English Canadians, especially

those in the populous heartland of Ontario, saw the arrival of Lemieux as

that of a usurper, The Pretender who would dare to wrest the crown from

The Great Gretzky, a hockey icon in Canada since his ninth birthday.

TWO FOR

THE AGES

5

There was a large problem for this contingent; it was patently obvious that Lemieux was Gretzky, only bigger. Everything Gretzky could do, Lemieux could do as well, or even better. One-on-one with a goaltender, it was conceded, Lemieux was probably the best there ever was.

When those in the Lemieux camp would insist that Mario had every song in the Great One's repertoire, but played them on a much bigger piano, the Edmonton supporters retorted that Gretzky possessed several Stanley Cup rings, the true measuring stick of greatness.

That was easily countered; compare their supporting casts. Gretzky's teammates would have their own future wing in the Hockey Hall of Fame: Glenn Anderson, Jari Kurri, Mark Messier, Kevin Lowe, Paul Coffey and Grant Fuhr.

Mario's teammates would come from the Lunch Pail Athletic Club: Terry Ruskowski, Doug Shedden, Rob Brown, Warren Young and others.

How iffy was the Pittsburgh roster when Mario joined the team? Two of the players listed were Minnesotans Jack and Steve Carlson. Steve, other brother Jeff and Dave Hanson played the legendary bespectacled Hanson Brothers in the 1977 hockey cult classic *Slap Shot*, starring Paul Newman.

WE WERE GETTING
BETTER
EVERY YEAR,

The best defense being an unrelenting offense, the Lemieux detractors spent a lot of energy at poking holes in Mario's game. The Oilers were winning Stanley Cups while the Penguins languished in the NHL nether regions. Conclusion: Lemieux had a poor work ethic or was deficient in leadership.

Mario's wingers included Ruskowski (a tremendous leader and cerebral hockey man, but not a natural scorer the likes of Kurri), Bob Errey, and Brown (a man with golden hands and platinum hockey brains, but slow feet). Mario racked up huge point harvests with Errey and Brown on his flanks, but they were not Anderson and Kurri, and neither were the Penguins a force in the league.

So it was all about growth for the Penguins and Mario Lemieux, and triumph for Wayne Gretzky and the Alberta juggernaut.

BUT NEEDED **SOME MORE BIG GUNS**

|Mario Lemieux|

Neither player resented the comparisons — who could? — but distinctions or qualifications were commonly inserted into the equations.

Mario Lemieux had two missions in his first four seasons with Pittsburgh. The first priority task was to build his personal career and develop into the dominating player who could challenge Wayne Gretzky. The second was to build the Penguins into a legitimate playoff contender.

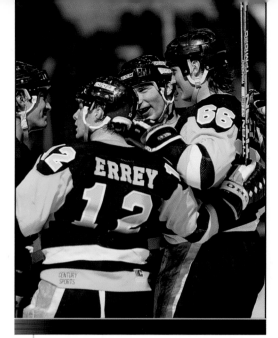

Bob Errey was one of Mario's early wingers with the Penguins.

In his second season, Lemieux finished second in the scoring race with 141 points, a whopping 71 behind Gretzky's record 215. Nevertheless, Mario was selected best player in the league by the players, receiving the Lester B. Pearson award from the NHL Players' Association. The Penguins missed the playoffs by two points.

That development inspired team owner Edward DeBartolo to negotiate a significant reduction in rent at the arena, as well as to elicit a promise from city and county administrations that $11 million in building improvements would be forthcoming. DeBartolo's part of the bargain was a signed commitment to keeping the team in Pittsburgh at least until 1991. Several months before, he had seriously entertained a very rich offer to move the team to Hamilton, Ontario, near Toronto, where a capacious new rink had been built (where Mario Lemieux would score the winning goal in the 1987 Canada Cup).

20

Minnesota's stifling defense continues in the home half of the back-to-back games, allowing only two goals once again, but that's where the similarities end. MARIO LEMIEUX scores both goals, the Pens allow only one, and Pittsburgh avenges the three-day-old loss.

MINNESOTA **1** PITTSBURGH **2**

A year later, in 1986, the team began the season with a seven-game win streak, but missed the playoffs at season's end, primarily because a knee injury and bronchitis combined to fell Lemieux for 17 games. While he was out of action, the team could only amass 11 of a possible 34 points, and they would fall short of post-season play by four points to the Rangers.

Lemieux's third season was significant in several ways. He received 35,000 more votes than Wayne Gretzky as top center in the annual All-Star Game, and Pittsburgh's average attendance climbed to 13,000, a team record.

He was also coming out of his self-imposed hermit-like existence, as he finally felt his English was serviceable enough for more public contacts. As an example of his growing popularity and impact, he received the 1986 Dapper Dan Award, given to the number one sports figure in Pittsburgh.

When Lemieux emerged as the No. 1 draft choice in 1984, he understood fully that the team drafting him was in that position because it was the worst in the entire NHL.

"I made a vow that I would have patience because it would take at least five years for the Penguins to build a contender," he said. The Penguins would need several more significant early draft choices, like Craig Simpson, No. 2 pick overall a year after Mario, and Zarley Zalapski, No. 4 in 1986, to start on the road to success.

"We were still short of players, but you could see it coming," Mario recalled. *"We were getting better every year, adding solid players, but we still needed some more big guns. These kinds of players aren't readily available."*

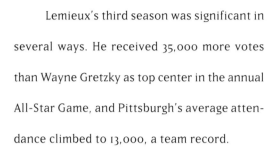

I MADE A VOW THAT I WOULD HAVE

PATIENCE BECAUSE IT WOULD TAKE

AT LEAST FIVE YEARS

FOR THE PENGUINS
TO BUILD A CONTENDER

| Mario Lemieux |

For sure, the draft route can be a slow process. In addition to Simpson and Zalapski, the Penguins also drafted Doug Bodger in 1984 and Rob Brown in 1986 — all eventually became productive NHL players — but Lemieux had to shoulder most of the burden himself during his early years in Pittsburgh.

Midway through Lemieux's rookie season, linemate Warren Young, who aggressively protected the large rookie and still found the time to score 40 goals, was asked about his illustrious teammate.

"Mario seems able to do anything he sets his mind to doing," he said. *"But, he'll be even better when he sets a goal for himself, something to strive for, and then drives towards it with all he has. He can do it because he's truly a great talent."* At season's end, Young signed a three-year deal with Detroit as an unrestricted free agent. He played parts of two seasons with the Red Wings before he was returned to Pittsburgh.

MARIO GOT VERY FRUSTRATED WHEN HE WAS COVERED CLOSELY

|Terry Ruskowski|

Did he notice a change in Lemieux during his hiatus?

"Night and day! That's the difference," came the reply. *"Mario always had all the tools, but now he has a little experience, he has the confidence to get the most out of them. For instance, he's learned to use his skating to get in the clear much more. He never looks as if he's going fast because his stride is so long and easy, and I don't think he looks on himself as having great speed. Now, when a little opening is there, he gets there in one stride and is clear."*

Ruskowski, a worker drone in NHL terms, was a plugger with an eye and ear for the game, whose leadership qualities were recognized at almost every league stop he made with the C on his shirt. He was a player-coach, and he attempted to pass on some valuable lessons to Mario.

The right-winger was made captain of the Penguins when they traded away Mike Bullard in November 1986. He already was on Lemieux's line, and one of his first tasks was to encourage his linemate not to be lethargic or soft in the heavy checking traffic.

Growing up in Montreal, Mario Lemieux's childhood hero put the O in offense and the delirious Forum crowds would fill the air with joyous choruses of *"Guy! Guy! Guy!"*

Later, playing in the National Hockey League against the vaunted Canadiens, another Hab put the D in Defense, and the Forum crowds once again would fill the air with joyous choruses of *"Guy! Guy! Guy!"*

The first was Lafleur, the second, Carbonneau, and the latter would become recognized throughout the NHL as one of the top defensive forwards of his generation. And the fact that he would never resort to clutch-and-grab hockey had Mario Lemieux tipping his hat to the Montreal forward.

Asked to name some of the top defenders he faced in his career, the first name Lemieux mentioned was Carbonneau, a standout with Montreal, St. Louis and Dallas in an 18-year NHL career.

BOB GAINEY, PERHAPS THE BEST DEFENSIVE FORWARD IN NHL HISTORY, TAUGHT A ROOKIE LEMIEUX MANY THINGS IN HIS EARLY DAYS AS A PRO.

"Everybody was different," Lemieux explained. *"Guy was a very, very smart player and he was good offensively as well. If you look at his career in junior, he was a top offensive player. He knew how to play the game, but he became a defensive specialist in the NHL.*

"He was a very good skater, always in good position, not taking too many chances – all part of being a good checker – and on the right side of the puck all the time. He was everything you wanted in a good checker and obviously one of the best ever."

Carbonneau concurred.

"The biggest danger playing stars like Wayne Gretzky and Mario Lemieux was to overplay them," he said.

"Both of them were so good with the puck, they could suck two or three guys in, which would leave two or three of their teammates open, and that's how they would kill you. Wayne was a bit better with his ice vision and passes; Mario was much better with the physical side of the game and absolutely deadly on one-on-ones.

"When I was out there against them, I played my own game, and I made sure I knew where they were at all times."

A polar opposite from Carbonneau was the ubiquitous Esa Tikkanen, an agitator who would try *"to climb into your pants,"* Mario said.

"Esa drove me nuts, sometimes. He was all over you and always giving you a little slash and chattering at you in some language that nobody understood. But, he did his job, because he was supposed to drive me nuts."

MIKE PECA, RIGHT, IS ONE OF TODAY'S BEST DEFENSIVE FORWARDS, IN MARIO LEMIEUX'S ESTIMATION.

Other top defenders included a Hall-of-Fame forward renowned for his game on the opposite side of the puck, Bob Gainey, Carbonneau's linemate in the mid-1980s.

"Bob Gainey was one of the best defensive players of all time," Lemieux recalled. *"I remember my first couple years playing against him; it was very, very difficult for a young kid who didn't know the game that much at that level to play against guys who had won Cups, and were in their 30s."*

One of the best defenders today is recently acquired New York Islander, Mike Peca, a Carbonneau clone. *"Peca is like Guy Carbonneau with the speed and the strength, and he's always in a good position to get to you,"* said Lemieux. *"As soon as you get the puck, he's right on you. He takes your time and space away from you and that's the key to being a good defensive player."*

"Mario got very frustrated when he was covered closely," said Ruskowski. "He didn't move the way he can and that made him easier to cover. It's not the pounding he took that did it. He wanted the puck all the time and was accustomed to having it, and when he was shut off from it, he wasn't heading for the openings where he might get it back."

The diminutive team captain tried to pass on the tricks and feints he had seen used by previous all-stars, who were "shadowed" all the time and forced to elude tight coverage.

"I knew about their dodges. For example, when Stan Mikita was covered closely by an opponent, he would position himself near another opposing forward, which meant that he had two guys close to him and that the Blackhawks had a man uncovered somewhere else on the ice."

Terry Ruskowski was a valued teammate in Mario's early years.

Lemieux's reluctance to fight through to open ice was more mental than physical: He was insulted by the attention, especially the borderline illegal tactics used by checkers.

PITTSBURGH 4   NEW JERSEY 4 OT

The Chorus is heard from on this night, as Jeff Norton and BILLY TIBBETTS score their first goals of the season, and Darius Kasparaitis his second, in the tie with the defending Stanley Cup champions. Mario Lemieux is the only scoring star on the Pens to find the net with a third-period tally.

105

FEBRUARY 16, 2001

21

GAME 51

WE ALWAYS
THINK A STEP AHEAD,

"It's to the point where it's not hockey any more," he would say later. "It's like football on skates. They grab you whether you have the puck or not. It's very, very aggravating."

Ruskowski gave Mario pointers; his roommate returned the favor with a unique hockey experience.

"With Mario, you were always being forced up to the next level, and you never really knew where that would be. I loved the challenge of playing with him; every game was a new experience."

PITTSBURGH **3** COLUMBUS **2** | OT

ROBERT LANG scores twice and Alexei Kovalev's overtime goal is the difference as the Pens edge another defensively oriented expansion team. Jean-Sebastien Aubin turns aside 32 of 34 Bluejackets shots, and Mario Lemieux is blanked by former Pen Ron Tugnutt.

22

FEBRUARY 17, 2001

GAME 58

It took a major hockey tournament, the 1987 Canada Cup, for all of the hockey world to see what Canada, and the National Hockey League had, two priceless pearls, two players for the ages, Béliveau-Howe, Hull-Mahovlich, Morenz-Boucher, Schmidt-Apps—name your comparison of previous eras!

Those Hall-of-Fame players never had the opportunity to team up in a real competition and show how they could play together. Damn R. Alan Eagleson if you will for his sins against the players and their association, but praise him to the skies for putting Mario and Wayne in the same uniform for a month.

AND THAT'S WHY WE MAKE BETTER DECISIONS THAN OTHER PLAYERS

|Mario Lemieux|

The result was hockey on a higher plane. The beauty of it all was the fact that they were on the same team, and that Lemieux finally had a supporting cast worthy of his game. Finally, each protagonist could closely scrutinize the other in the hothouse that was the Team Canada training camp and the Canada Cup tournament.

Lemieux was asked if he saw his game in Gretzky's. Watching from the bench, did he say to himself after another Gretzky gem, "that's the play I would have done?" For once he was anxious to answer.

"We always think a step ahead and that's why we make better decisions than other players, because we always know what we are going to do before we get the puck.

"At times, I could see what he could see and nobody else could. We could anticipate that play, and at the Canada Cup when we played together, we knew pretty much what the other guy was thinking."

A modern hockey legend emerged from Team Canada's camp that Wayne Gretzky sat Lemieux down and gave him advice on the life of the NHL superstar and issues of comportment.

It didn't happen. *"There wasn't a lot of conversation,"* Mario explained. *"We spent a little bit of time together, but it was for lunches and team dinners and stuff. As far as on the ice, we didn't have to say much because we knew exactly what the other guy wanted to do. We were always in good position."*

I WAS GENUINELY **EXCITED** TO PLAY **WITH** AND **AGAINST** SOME OF THE **BEST** PLAYERS **IN THE WORLD**

|Mario Lemieux|

Which is not to say that he couldn't and didn't learn from the Edmonton superstar.

"There were common issues, but it was more than words. It was by watching him through the practices and games, how he was dedicated to the game, and how hard he worked. That's really what he taught me; not so much with words and sitting me down and saying 'you've got to do this and that'—but by watching him practice and his dedication to the sport, and how to be a winner."

"People would end up saying that I taught Mario how to score, but that's ridiculous," Gretzky would say. *"It's funny, people love to dream up feuds. But Mario and I hit it off during that month. We found out we weren't just friends, we were icemates."*

One Oilers center who impressed Lemieux throughout was Mark Messier, known as Moose to teammates and adversaries alike.

PETER FORSBERG scores a goal and two assists in the first period, en route to a four-point night, and the Penguins are swamped by an offensive Avalanche. Mario Lemieux is held scoreless for a second consecutive game.

COLORADO 5   PITTSBURGH 1

"Mark is probably the most complete center in the NHL," Mario said. *"He can play any kind of game, finesse, defensive, physical, you name it. And one thing I noticed at the Canada Cup, was how easily he accepted the role of leader."*

Soviet defenseman Vyacheslav Fetisov, who two years hence would finally be freed to ply his trade in the National Hockey League, played against Gretzky and Lemieux twice that year, at the Rendez-vous 87 All-Star Weekend, two-game set in Quebec City in February, and again in September in the Canada Cup.

"Gretzky is still No. 1," he said, *"but some day it will be Lemieux".*

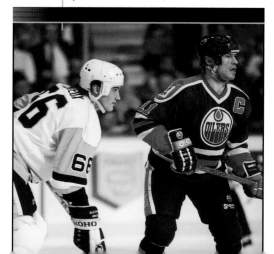

Mario Lemieux had immense respect for the Oilers' Mark Messier.

In 1985, Mario had experienced his second international tournament when he joined the Canadian team at the World Championships in April, after the Penguins had been eliminated from the playoff race. He scored twice and added an assist in a 3-1 win over the Soviets, leading Canada to a bronze medal, but some of the top Canadians, Americans and Swedes were still playing with their NHL teams in the playoffs so that competition was watered down, as it is every spring.

FLORIDA 2 3 PITTSBURGH | OT

Once again, the Usual Suspects weigh in, as Jaromir Jagr and Alexei Kovalev offset goals by Florida's Pavel Bure and Viktor Kozlov, before SUPER MARIO wins the game in overtime.

The Canada Cup was recognized as the true world championship, with all of the participating countries sending their best players.

Although the stream of European players flowing to the NHL was becoming a torrent, the East European pipeline still was blocked, and there was a genuine mystery to the make-up of the Soviets and Czechs.

"I was genuinely excited for the opportunity to play with and against some of the best players in the world, and have a chance to answer the critics who doubted that I could play under pressure," Lemieux said.

As the tournament advanced, it was obvious that the Canadians, Czechs and Soviets had a step up on the improving Americans, Swedes and Finns, especially when the host team came up against the aroused Czechs and their rookie goalie Dominik Hasek in the semi-final. Lemieux scored in Canada's win, setting up a best-of-three final against the Soviets, who had eliminated Team Sweden.

The Soviets prevailed, 6-5, in the series opener in Montreal, and the teams traveled west to Hamilton's Copps Coliseum for the crucial second game.

Until then, Team Canada coach Mike Keenan enjoyed the best of both worlds, with Lemieux and Gretzky pivoting separate trios and he resisted all suggestions of putting the two superstars on the same line.

Canada trailed in the second period of the second game when 66 and 99 skated out together for the first time. The upshot was a hat trick for Mario, including the game-winner scored in double overtime, forcing a decisive third contest.

Game Three has been described by many veteran observers as one of the greatest hockey games ever played, with both teams trading the lead on several occasions. Canada led 5-4 late in the third period until Alexander Semak knotted the score on a determined individual effort.

Coach Mike Keenan resisted putting Mario and Wayne together until late in the Canada Cup competition.

PAUL COFFEY

Paul Coffey was a hockey paradox. He was the foremost practitioner of the full-ice hockey style that Bobby Orr introduced to National Hockey League blue-liners in the late 1960s.

Conversely, the native of Weston, Ontario, wasn't a defenseman at all; he was a throwback to seven-man hockey and a Rover in the style of the Fred (Cyclone) Taylor and Fabulous Frank McGee at the turn of the century. It was pointed out by some that he rarely was bothered with events in his own zone, preferring instead to join, or lead, his team's forwards in attacks up ice.

One of the fastest, most fluid skaters in NHL history, Coffey joined the Pens from the Edmonton Oilers in a trade early in the 1987-88 season.

"It cost us two good prospects, Craig Simpson and Chris Joseph, but Coffey was the dynamic offensive defenseman we'd always needed," said Mario Lemieux.

"We weren't really a slow team, but when Coffey arrived, it seemed that we instantly became a fast team. It really helped me to have somebody back there who was thinking the same way I was on the ice. We'd played together at the Canada Cup and I knew his game... we just clicked and had good chemistry together."

Coffey quarterbacked the Penguins with seasons of 113 points, 103 points and 93 points between 1989 and 1991, and Pittsburgh's offense was third, fourth and second over-all in those years, despite Lemieux's absence in 90 games over that period.

The Penguins didn't make the playoffs in Coffey's first three seasons with the team, but they were on the way. He won three Stanley Cups with Edmonton, and would win a fourth with Pittsburgh in 1990-91.

Coffey logged time with seven teams before being released by the Boston Bruins in the 2000-01 season. He had counted 396 goals and 1,531 points, second only to Raymond Bourque in both categories.

TOM BARRASSO

Tom Barrasso was selected by Buffalo fifth overall in the 1983 entry draft, the highest selection ever for a goalie. He surprised everyone, including Buffalo GM Scotty Bowman, by earning the number one job in training camp and turned in one of the best rookie seasons in NHL history, winning the Vezina Trophy as top goalie, the Calder Trophy as best rookie and earning selection to the first All-Star team.

The Boston native was acquired by the Penguins on November 12, 1988, and played in 44 games, leading the Penguins into their first playoff action in seven seasons. His second Pittsburgh season was limited to 24 games when he missed 23 with a broken wrist and took a 22-game leave-of-absence when his young daughter Ashley was diagnosed with cancer.

Both Tom and Ashley inspired Mario Lemieux in different ways. Lemieux spent six weeks in Los Angeles that summer with Dr. Robert Watkins and physiotherapists working on his back.

"I certainly wasn't going to feel sorry for myself; it was only a back condition. Ashley Barrasso was also flown into Los Angeles to undergo treatments for cancer. That put things into context for me, and my teammates. Fortunately, young Ashley beat the dreaded disease."

Ashley's Dad beat all comers in Stanley Cup playoffs. In 41 appearances in 1990-91, and 1991-92, he had 28 wins and 12 losses, goals against averages of 2.60 and 2.82. In the two final series, Barrasso had a 7-2 won-lost record with a 2.47 average; he put together 11 consecutive wins in the '92 playoffs, and added three more in 1993 for a record 14 in a row.

Mario Lemieux was awarded the Conn Smythe Trophy as top playoff performer in both Cup seasons, yet he would have voted for his netminding teammate in 1992.

"The award should have gone to Tommy; I thought it was his all the way," Lemieux said. *"He was just superb. When we won in '91, I said that we couldn't have done it without the caliber of goaltending he gave us and I said it again a year later. He was the real key to us winning those Cups, the guy who was always there with the big save when we needed it."*

With 90 seconds remaining in the game, Wayne Gretzky was poised to take the face-off in the Canadian end when the Soviets sent out their best face-off center. Keenan countered with Canada's best, Dale Hawerchuk, of the Winnipeg Jets, and the Canadians lined up in a single wing, to counter the Soviets' three-two alignment inside the zone: Gretzky stationed on the far right, Coffey on the far left, with Hawerchuk, Larry Murphy and Lemieux.

Dale Hawerchuk won the face-off that led to the winning goal in the final game of the Canada Cup.

Hawerchuk won the draw and Lemieux picked it up and slapped it up the left boards without looking. Gretzky had raced into full stride on the diagonal with the drop of the puck and he picked up the disk in full flight, with Murphy joining him on the right on a two-on-one against a lone Soviet defender.

It appeared for a moment that the Canadians had skated in too deep, and the Soviet defenseman gambled that Murphy was too close to the net to be dangerous, so he dove to his right at Gretzky.

The Great One had never looked back on the rush, but he dropped the puck to a spot of open ice where Lemieux, who had given him the puck originally, picked it up without breaking stride, and loomed before Sergei Mylnikov in the Soviet goal. The "book" on Mylnikov said he was weak on high shots, and Lemieux adjusted his angle to the net before drilling a laser beam to the top corner, over the goalie's left shoulder.

From face-off to goal took 150 feet and four seconds. Canada went crazy, and for five seconds, the 99 vs. 66 debate was in remission. Lemieux led the tournament in goals, Gretzky in points, and the world of Canadian hockey was at peace.

And nobody was questioning Mario Lemieux's ability to play the Big Game any more.

"The Canada Cup showed me how good I could be, and I was thankful of the opportunity to play with players who elevated my game," Lemieux said at series' end.

RANGERS 4   6 PITTSBURGH

ALEXEI KOVALEV turns in his third hat trick of the month (and will be selected NHL Player of the month of February) and adds two assists as the Pens feast on the visiting Rangers. Mario Lemieux contributes a power-play goal in the second period.

113

25

FEBRUARY 23, 2001

GAME 61

Pittsburgh General Manager Tony Esposito, who had experienced the highs-and-lows of Canada-Soviet hockey in the fabled 1972 Hockey Summit, acknowledged the benefits of this level of competition for his star.

"No question that he changed from a boy to a man playing in the Canada Cup," he concluded. *"He became a leader and a take-charge guy."* He was also a few days short of his 22nd birthday.

Lemieux never skipped a beat when he returned to regular league play for the 1987-88 season. He scored 70 goals and added 98 assists for a 168-point season, beat Gretzky for his first league scoring championship, and liberated the Hart Memorial Trophy as NHL MVP from his Canada Cup teammate, who had held it for eight years.

Mats Naslund of the Montreal Canadiens teamed up with Mario in a record-setting All-Star Game performance.

He gave the hockey world another video clip of his greatness on February 9 in St. Louis at the league's annual All-Star game.

Mike Keenan, coaching the Wales (Eastern) Conference team had the fortuitous idea of teaming Lemieux with Montreal's skilled and deceptive winger, Mats Naslund. The duo was dynamite, with Lemieux scoring three goals and three assists, including the overtime (6-5) winner against Wayne Gretzky and the Clarence Campbell (Western) Conference. Naslund had a pair of goals and three assists, and Lemieux was the game's Most Valuable Player.

Edmonton coach Glen Sather, Keenan's counterpart with the Campbell team, spoke for the hockey world when he said: *"We couldn't have covered Mario with six guys tonight. We could have put a tent around him and he still would have scored."*

On that night, Le Magnifique eclipsed The Great One.

The debate resumed anew.

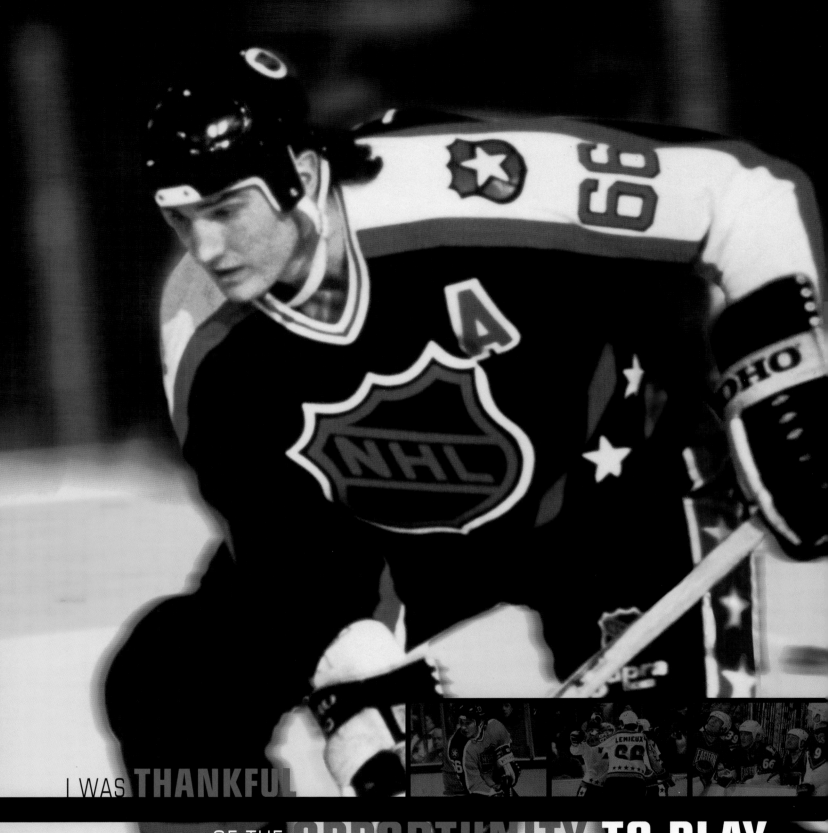

I WAS **THANKFUL** OF THE **OPPORTUNITY TO PLAY** **WITH PLAYERS WHO** **ELEVATED MY GAME**

|Mario Lemieux|

CECIL B. DE MILLE PERFECTED THE FILM EPIC, AMONG THEM SUCH SMOLDERING MELODRAMAS

as The Greatest Show on Earth. Genius that he was, he left nothing to

chance, producing action-packed previews that would entice millions of

filmgoers into the theaters to see his pictures. Hockey's ultimate showman,

Mario Lemieux, learned early on in his career that selling the sizzle with

incandescent previews would leave the paying public hungry for more.

Starting with the 1988-89 and 1989-90 seasons, epic performances by

Super Mario seemed to become the rule, rather than the exception.

GREATEST SHOW

CHAPTER 6   CRAIG PATRICK   BOB JOHNSON   BACK PAINS   DR. ROBERT

ON ICE

Three such performances within eight months spoke volumes for his epic talent. The first came on October 15 in the team's fourth game, and second home contest of the season, when he produced two goals and six assists for eight points in a 9-2 victory over St. Louis.

When the 1988-89 Pens finished second to Washington in the Patrick Division, sixth overall, after missing the playoffs in six consecutive seasons, it appeared that years of unfulfilled promises were at an end. Lemieux won his second consecutive scoring championship with 199 points on 85 goals and 114 assists—all career highs—and marks only surpassed in NHL history by Wayne Gretzky. He also became only the second NHL player (Gretzky) to score 70 goals in a season twice, and established a league record with 13 shorthanded goals.

His output meant he had scored or assisted on 199 of Pittsburgh's total 347 goals, or 57.3 per cent, surpassing Gretzky's 51.8 per cent four years earlier.

Mario's linemates were Bob Errey and young winger Rob Brown, who also had career marks with 49 goals and 115 points. Defenseman Paul Coffey was sixth in scoring with 113 points as the Penguins set NHL records for 119 power-play goals, and penalty minutes—2,670.

Never a sentimentalist, Mario still found a special way to usher out the Old Year, and usher in the new, with a special performance at the Civic Arena that had the Pittsburgh faithful singing Auld Lang Syne late into the night. That night he scored five goals against the visiting New Jersey Devils, and set a record in the process by scoring each in a different manner: even strength, power play, shorthanded, penalty shot and empty net!

THE FIRST SHIFT,

Paul Coffey gave the Pens the quarterback that Mario needed.

His third epic performance — against Philadelphia on April 25, 1989 — was a post-season preview non-pareil, and spoke volumes for future Stanley Cup success in Pittsburgh.

The Penguins swept the Rangers in the Patrick Division semi-final, and then lined up against the Flyers in a tough seven-game division final. The series was tied at two wins apiece and, as the teams prepared for the swing match in Pittsburgh, Lemieux's participation was doubtful. He had suffered a neck injury in the fourth game, a 4-1 loss at Philadelphia, and hadn't appeared at practice between games.

"Injuries seemed to inspire him," linemate Bob Errey said after the game, a 10-7 win for the Pens. *"The first shift, he had extra jump in him and you knew he was going to have a good game."*

A good game?

By the 4:40 mark of the first period, Lemieux already had a natural hat trick. He would go on to score eight points on five goals and three assists, tying an NHL playoff record. Philadelphia rallied to win 6-2 and 4-1 and capture the series in seven games, but a galvanized Penguins team was prepared for a serious challenge in 1989-90.

There is an axiom in sports that rising young teams will often take a step backwards before they make the final successful move forward, and that proved true of the Pens.

When the team opened the new campaign with 10 wins, 14 losses and two ties in their first 26 games, including a crowd-killing .500 at home, general manager Tony Esposito and coach Gene Ubriaco were let go.

HE HAD **EXTRA JUMP IN HIM** AND YOU KNEW HE WAS GOING TO HAVE **A GOOD GAME**

|Bob Errey|

Robert Lang scores twice and rookie blue-liner ANDREW FERENCE scores his first NHL goal as the Pens swamp New York and rookie goaltender Rick DiPietro. Mario Lemieux's contribution is a pair of goals.

ISLANDERS 1   PITTSBURGH 6

Craig Patrick was hired as GM and made selecting a coach simple by taking the job himself, claiming he needed time to assess the team's talent and find the right man to handle it. The view was that he would keep the dual GM-coach post for the remainder of the season because the talent pool of available candidates for the coaching post was deeper in June than December.

From the start, Patrick wanted the Penguins to master team defense to maximize their strong offense; Pittsburgh led in the NHL goals with 318, but only the last-place overall Quebec Nordiques (407 goals against) surrendered more scores than the Penguins' 359.

The downward spiral accelerated on Valentine's Day when back pains forced Lemieux to pull himself from a game at Madison Square Garden, ending a streak of games with at least one point at 46. It would take a lot to keep him off the ice because he was a week away from Wayne Gretzky's league scoring record of 51 consecutive games.

Those who had criticized his character and desire had been silenced as they witnessed his struggle to play over the previous weeks, barely lifting his legs over the boards, one at a time, during line changes. Lemieux led the league in scoring by 12 points when his back problems became too limiting and painful for him to continue and he pulled himself from the line-up.

A Stanley Cup Triumvirate: Mario, Craig Patrick and Paul Coffey

After he withdrew from the Rangers game, Mario went to Los Angeles to consult with back specialist, Dr. Robert Watkins, who prescribed a special program of exercise and stretching in an attempt to circumvent surgery. The hockey world was stunned when he announced he would return for the season finale against Buffalo, after missing almost six weeks.

There was a festive atmosphere at Civic Arena, and Mario produced a goal and an assist in a 3-2 overtime loss, which eliminated the Penguins from post-season play by a margin of two points. Despite missing a quarter of the schedule, Lemieux was fourth in points behind Wayne Gretzky, Mark Messier and Steve Yzerman.

At season's end, Lemieux returned to Los Angeles and Dr. Watkins outlined a program of therapy that helped relieve the pain through April and May. Team doctors cleared him to play golf, but by mid-June, when the pain crept back into his back, legs and buttocks, he made a huge decision: back surgery, with its career-ending potential.

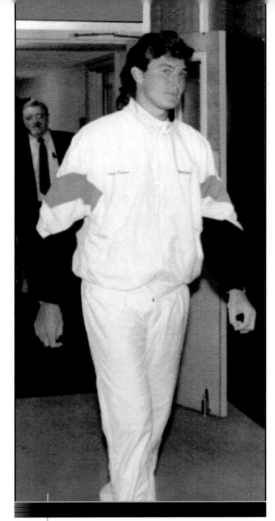

Mario leaves hospital two days after his initial back surgery on July 11, 1990.

On July 11, Dr. Peter Sheptak, a neurosurgeon at Montefiore Hospital in Pittsburgh, performed the 90-minute operation, which involved removing the herniated portion of a disc and freeing a trapped nerve in Lemieux's spine. The medical term for the procedure is a micro lumbar diskectomy with bone decompression. In two days, Lemieux was out of the hospital and talking of readiness for training camp in September. The surgeon predicted a *"pretty fast"* healing process, but cautioned that a mild fracture in the supporting structure of the bone, not treated during the surgery, could cause future discomfort and backache.

BRYAN TROTTIER

Very few National Hockey League superstars have been able to make the transition from team MVP to role player. Fortunately for the Pittsburgh Penguins, Bryan Trottier was a Hall-of-Fame candidate who could sublimate his ego to the team concept.

A large part of the New York Islanders' four consecutive Cup triumphs to open the 1980s, the gritty, skilled and tough Trottier was signed by the Penguins as a free agent in July 1990. At 34, he brought a winner's experience to the dressing room and a veteran's thoroughness to spot duty.

He would score a total of 20 goals in two seasons, 1990-91 and 1991-92, retire, and then return to the Pens for a final season in 1993-94. He added another seven goals and seven assists in 44 playoff games in the two Cup years —impressive totals on the third and fourth lines mucking in the corners with plumbers like Jock Callander, Dave Michayluk, Gordie Roberts, Bob Errey, Phil Bourque, Randy Gilhen and Jay Caufield. Those two Cups ran his impressive personal total to six.

Mario Lemieux recalled Trottier's impact on his new team.

"There were some very big games in the playoffs, and it was comforting to all of us to be able to look over at Bryan in the dressing room, and the four Stanley Cups he represented," he said.

"We all looked up to him, and he didn't disappoint."

Conversely, Trottier had a front-row seat for the post-season Magic Show that was Mario Lemieux.

"If I had to describe him in two words, they would be these: only perfect," 'Trots' said. *"Right now we're living in Mario's world."*

I NEVER MET **A MAN**

While the travails of his superstar certainly preoccupied him, Craig Patrick had a team to manage and undertook several significant moves during the off-season.

The first was the most important. In the summer of 1990, Patrick hired Bob Johnson, a winner in high school and later, college hockey at Colorado and University of Wisconsin, as well as in the NHL with the Calgary Flames. He had left the Flames after losing the Stanley Cup final to Montreal, to become executive director of USA Hockey, the top position in amateur hockey in the country.

With the arrival of Lemieux in 1984, the Penguins had slowly built up a talented young team through the draft, but Patrick knew the team needed post-season experience if it was to advance. That summer Patrick added veteran Joe Mullen in a draft-day deal with Calgary, and Islanders' captain Bryan Trottier in a free-agent signing in July. More trades loomed.

Meanwhile, Lemieux's optimism was boosted by the progress in his strict rehabilitation program.

WHO LOVED
THE GAME OF HOCKEY THE WAY HE DID

|Mario Lemieux|

Badger Bob Johnson was the animated bench general of the Penguins.

"I had not worked as hard at off-ice training as I might have when I was younger," Lemieux said. "But after the operation, the rehab program made me stronger in the legs and lower body than I had been, and other exercises improved my upper body strength.

"I just didn't pay much attention to that earlier. I suppose I was a bit like the players in the NHL many years ago, doing little work on conditioning all summer and skating themselves into playing shape at camp."

Lemieux's agent, Tom Reich, noticed a major change in his star client's attitude.

PITTSBURGH 2   4 MONTREAL

The pre-game hype for Mario's return to Montreal lasted a month, and the Canadiens are waiting for the Ville Emard native and his teammates when they come to visit. Montreal shuts down the Pens while team captain SAKU KOIVU participates in all of his team's scoring with a pair of goals and assists.

27
FEBRUARY 28, 2001
GAME 63

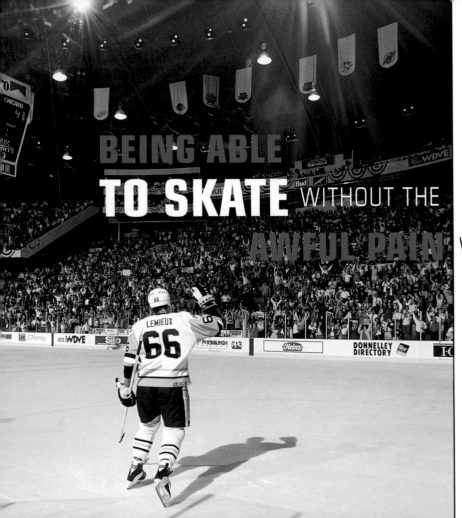

BEING ABLE TO SKATE WITHOUT THE AWFUL PAIN WAS ONE OF THE **BEST FEELINGS I'VE EVER HAD**

|Mario Lemieux|

Watched by a few teammates involved in voluntary summer scrimmages at Civic Arena, Lemieux skated for 15 minutes.

"A serious injury is a big jolt for a professional athlete, often a big wake-up call," Reich said. *"The hard part of what they must deal with is the uncertainty because they take risks with their bodies. The back problem and surgery could have ended Mario's career, and now conditioning became a big part of his game and his life. He was also much more aware of what he had to do if he wanted to continue to play and to excel."*

September 1 was the surgeon's target date for Lemieux to skate again, but excellent progress in a program of therapy — walking and, gradually exercising in his swimming pool — advanced that date by more than a week.

"Being able to skate, even for a few minutes, without the awful pain was one of the best feelings I've ever had," Lemieux said.

"I had to pull back from doing too much, sticking to the program of stretching for up to 20 minutes before I went on the ice. My skating came back fairly quickly and I was even able to join in some scrimmages with the guys."

Super Mario's recuperation, the enthusiastic Johnson, who immediately launched an effort to improve the Penguins defensively, and Patrick's off-season additions of veterans Trottier and Mullen, sent the team to camp with high hopes.

Lemieux, who stayed out of heavy camp scrimmages and exhibition games, planned his return for the season opener against the Capitals in Washington on October 5, his 25th birthday. But halfway through camp, lightning struck again when Lemieux's intense back pain suddenly returned. *"I was feeling fine, making really good progress, and zap! I couldn't bend enough to tie my own shoes,"* Lemieux said.

Tests revealed an infection in his back and while doctors declared the inflammation was very treatable, they predicted at least an eight-week recuperation period. *"It was one heckuva jolt, a terrible down time for me, because I had made such good progress after the surgery and was hungry to get back to work,"* Lemieux said. *"I was in hospital a week on antibiotics and painkillers, then when I went home, I couldn't do anything for almost a month. I was stretched out in bed most of the time because I could barely get out of bed on my hands and knees.*

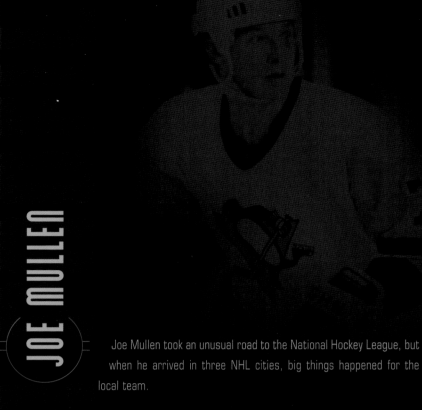

JOE MULLEN

Joe Mullen took an unusual road to the National Hockey League, but when he arrived in three NHL cities, big things happened for the local team.

Mullen was born and raised in New York's Hell's Kitchen, the west-side area near the old Madison Square Garden where his father was employed as a maintenance worker. While he and brother Brian played baseball and basketball, the big games in the neighborhood, their first sports love was hockey, and they spent many hours playing roller-skate hockey in a paved schoolyard.

Joey's prolific scoring in the New York junior league led to a hockey scholarship at Boston College, where he earned All-Conference and All-American honors before signing as a free agent with the St. Louis Blues. After seasons of 40 and 59 goals in the Central Hockey League, Mullen was promoted to the NHL. The Blues had finished out of the playoffs two seasons in a row, and the team was on the verge of being moved when Mullen arrived. His scoring was a key part of a major rebuilding job that turned the franchise around on the ice and at the box office.

Traded to the Calgary Flames during the '85-86 season, Mullen turned in seasons of 47, 40 and 51 goals, then scored 16 times as the Flames won the 1989 Cup. In 1990, the Flames traded Mullen to the Pittsburgh Penguins, the first of 13 players added to the roster by GM Craig Patrick to produce the '91 and '92 Stanley Cup champs.

"It was a stroke of good fortune to land on a team that was building for something good and have the chance to play for coaches like Bob Johnson and Scotty Bowman," Mullen said.

Although injured in the 1992 post-season, he still managed to score 11 goals and add 10 assists in 31 games of the two Stanley Cup series, and had his name inscribed on the coveted trophy for the second and third times. Mullen retired as a player in 1997 as the top-scoring U.S. player with 502 goals and was elected to The Hockey Hall Of Fame in 2000, the year he joined the Penguins as an assistant coach.

MARIO LEMIEUX has the answer for those observers who feared that his comeback had lost steam; he scores twice and adds a pair of assists as the Pens outlast the Rangers at Madison Square Garden.

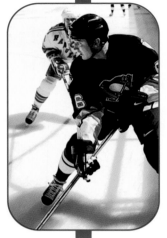

PITTSBURGH 7   RANGERS 5

"Nathalie was strong for both of us during those three months, working at my bedside every day and making sure that I was physically and mentally improving. It had to be hard on her, because deep down she must have felt doubts and worry for me, but she never showed it. Her support and love was amazing."

Even when unable to stand up, Lemieux generated controversy. A report in Pittsburgh claimed his doctors said he had vertebral osteo-myelitis, a debilitating and chronic condition. The medical team denied the story and called his condition diskitis, a less serious problem. Blood tests in early December showed that the infection was gone and he was allowed to resume training, with stretching and light lifting, on December 19.

Ten days later, he skated for the first time in three months and, on January 9, he had his first full-dress practice with the team.

"I was in very good condition during training camp, then I lost most of that by doing nothing for so long," Lemieux said. "On the ice after Christmas, my back was fine but my conditioning was lousy. I worked harder than I ever had to get it back. I think I dragged Badger Bob (coach Johnson's nickname from his Wisconsin days) a few hundred miles, me on one end of two hockey sticks, him on the other, with his skates dug into the ice."

Even without Lemieux, the Penguins were the highest-scoring NHL team with 200 goals in their first 47 games. Leading the attack were John Cullen, Mark Recchi, Kevin Stevens and Coffey plus a big, free-wheeling rookie drafted from the Czech Republic and tagged as a certain major star, Jaromir Jagr.

"We lost the best offensive player in the game and still remained competitive, which was amazing," Johnson said. But despite Johnson's efforts, the Penguins lacked the personnel for the team defense that is the backbone of serious contenders, although the club sported a 26-21–3 record without Lemieux.

WE LOST **THE BEST OFFENSIVE PLAYER** IN THE GAME, **AND STILL REMAINED COMPETITIVE**

Bob Johnson

Pittsburgh's success in 1990-91 was a tribute to Patrick's trading ability and Johnson's coaching. Aided in recruitment by Scotty Bowman, his new director of player development, Patrick made numerous personnel changes during the season, signing Trottier as a free agent and trading for Joe Mullen, Ron Francis, Peter Taglianetti, Ulf Samuelsson, Larry Murphy, Jiri Hrdina, Grant Jennings and Scott Young.

CRAIG CAREFULLY
MADE DEALS

Johnson's deft coaching touch also allowed the club to develop young defensemen Paul Stanton and Jim Paek.

In reality, Patrick used the team's best players as the foundation, and built an entire new structure on that base. His captain was impressed with the results.

"Guys who have been around the NHL for a long time told me that they couldn't remember a GM making as many good deals in one season as Craig Patrick did in 1990-91," said Lemieux. *"We had much talent on the team, but we didn't have the right combination of players to take a serious run at the championship. Craig carefully made deals that season until we had depth and toughness and were a much better defensive team.*

"A really great trade was the one that brought in Ron Francis. Look at Stanley Cup teams over the years. All the strength-down-center talk is right.

PITTSBURGH 3   **WASHINGTON 4**

A pair of third-period goals by RICHARD ZEDNIK overcomes a Pittsburgh lead and propels the Capitals to victory. Overshadowing the game is the fact that Mario Lemieux skips the contest to rest his back.

29

(From left) Ron Francis, Ulf Samuelsson, Peter Taglianetti and Jiri Hrdina all contributed to the 1991 Stanley Cup victory.

THAT SEASON,
UNTIL WE HAD DEPTH
AND TOUGHNESS

|Mario Lemieux|

"Edmonton had Wayne Gretzky and Mark Messier when they were on top and the New York Islanders made their big run (four Cups in a row) when they got Butch Goring to go with Bryan (Trottier) in the middle. Go back to the great Montreal Canadiens teams and they had Jean Béliveau and Henri Richard, a pair of centers that were the heart of many great teams. I think Ron and I gave us that high caliber one-two you must have in the middle."

As the deals gave Johnson more sound defensive players, his patient, repetitive insistence on a team approach to goal prevention slowly paid off. The Penguins cut their goals against by 54 over the previous season while scoring 24 more themselves.

LARRY MURPHY

If Paul Coffey was a jet on skates, the other impact defenseman acquired by Pittsburgh on its Road to the Stanley Cup was anything but.

Larry Murphy, as slow and deliberate as Coffey was fast and mercurial, was an 11-year NHL veteran when Penguins general manager Craig Patrick brought him and another defenseman, Peter Taglianetti, to Pittsburgh in a trade with the Minnesota North Stars in December 1990.

"Murphy showed us that experience, smarts and good hands are as important as great speed in the game," Lemieux said. *"He didn't get caught out of position defensively very often and he never did careless or dumb things with the puck. With Murph on the point, our power play suddenly was more effective."*

Larry Murphy was close to Mario in a historic situation; he was the player who broke away with 66 on the winning goal in the 1987 Canada Cup. When Lemieux chose to shoot and score in the top corner with 96 seconds remaining, Murphy was perched on the right corner of the crease, awaiting a pass.

Was there ever any question of passing to Murphy?

"Are you kidding me?" Mario retorted, and then laughed.

Murphy's value to the Pens was evident when Coffey missed a dozen games in the 1991 playoffs with a broken jaw. Murphy produced 23 points in 23 playoff games, turning the power play into an important weapon.

Murphy's offensive skill from the back line became even more of an asset to the Penguins when Coffey was traded to the Los Angeles Kings in 1992. After a 21-goal, 77-point schedule, Murphy excelled in the playoffs with 16 points.

Murphy remained a Penguin until 1995 when he was traded to Toronto, then was a 1996-97 trade deadline addition by the Detroit Red Wings, coached by Scotty Bowman, the Pens' coach in 1991-92 after the death of Bob Johnson. Murphy was a regular on the Wings' Stanley Cup championship teams in 1997 and '98.

The puck stops here... Tom Barrasso backstopped the Penguins to a brace of Cups.

When a former No. 1 with Hartford joined the Penguins in March 1991 and found himself quickly demoted to No. 2, he "took it out on" the incumbent No. 1.

The parties in question were Mario Lemieux and Ron Francis, the latter acquired in a Craig Patrick blockbuster that saw John Cullen, Zarley Zalapski and Jeff Parker move to Connecticut in exchange for Francis, Ulf Samuelsson and Grant Jennings. The engine that drove the Hartford attack for a decade, Francis became the perfect No. 2 center for the Penguins, a two-way workhorse to team with Mario Lemieux in the strength-down-center serious Cup challengers must have. During Lemieux's absences with injuries and illness, Francis became the main man in the middle, a role he filled with distinction.

"In Hartford, there was a lot of pressure because only one line really scored much while with the Penguins, I could play an all-round game," Francis said. *"I was much more comfortable doing that."*

Another role he played was team instigator and facilitator, and his first "victim" was the man on the pedestal, Mario Lemieux himself.

"Ulf and I noticed that while Mario was a huge presence in the team, he was sort of on the sidelines when the locker room stuff was happening, and we took it upon ourselves to 'integrate' him into the ebb and flow of locker room life. One day after practice, everybody was fooling around and I gave Mario a jab, just like Ulf and I had agreed, and there was total silence in the room. I'm saying to myself, 'Ulfie, time to pitch in, don't leave me dying out here,' while Mario was saying something like 'you don't like Pittsburgh very much, do you?'

"To his credit Ulfie came through, and Mario got it and started to laugh, and the place lightened up real fast. He seemed to enjoy it, and took part in the give-and-take of the room from then on."

Francis was a huge addition to the team, Lemieux conceded, both on the ice and off.

"When we landed Ron Francis, it was the last piece in our Stanley Cup puzzle. Our power play improved, our penalty-killing was much better and he taught us all how to be ready to give all you had every night." Francis contributed 43 points in 45 games in the two Cup post-seasons, tallying 15 goals along the way.

Francis spent seven-plus seasons with the Penguins before joining the Carolina Hurricanes as a free agent in 1998.

For all of that preparation, the Penguins managed to trail in all four playoff series. They started with a seven-game ouster of the New Jersey Devils, losing the opener and down, 3-2, after five games. Their jaunt to the Stanley Cup final was in jeopardy in New Jersey in Game Six: Mario was a shadow of himself, suffering from anemia, and Tom Barrasso was out of the series with an injury. In stepped back-up netminder Frank Pietrangelo.

"Frankie literally saved us in New Jersey with a stop on Petr Stastny that fans in Pittsburgh would call 'The Save,'" Mario said. *"And then he shut out the Devils in Game Seven while Jiri Hrdina scored twice, and we moved on. That's the usual story in Stanley Cup play: contributions come from all levels of the team totem pole."*

The Pens dropped the opening game of the division final to the Washington Capitals, and then rebounded with four consecutive victories, Kevin Stevens scoring the winning goal in the first three.

Power-play goals by Alexei Kovalev and Mario Lemieux tie the game at 3 in the third, but come to nought as the Caps' JEFF HALPERN wins the game with just over three minutes remaining.

WASHINGTON 4 — 3 PITTSBURGH | OT

The Boston Bruins scored 11 goals in winning the first two games of the conference final when the Penguins played loose defense. But they held the Bruins to seven goals in the next four matches as rehabilitated goalie Tom Barrasso excelled, scoring 20 goals themselves. An emotional Mario Lemieux put a cap on the series, scoring into the empty net to ice a 5-3 win in Game Six. He sank to his knees, his fragile back arched and arms raised to the skies: he was never so close to his destiny.

That sent the Pens to the Stanley Cup final against the Minnesota North Stars, a team 12 points below .500 during the schedule. But with two distinguished former players, GM Bob Clarke and head coach Bob Gainey, at their controls, the Stars had parlayed scoring balance, team defense and the strong goaltending of Jon Casey into playoff upsets of the Blackhawks, St. Louis Blues and Edmonton Oilers, teams that had been well in front of the Minnesota club during the season.

Mario broke the spirit of the North Stars when he skated through the whole team and scored a highlight goal in game two.

The Stars won the opener in Pittsburgh, 5-4, and the Pens were holding on, 2-1, in the second game on May 17 when Super Mario scored the kind of goal that breaks the opponent's back. Picking up the puck near the top of the circle in his own end, he charged straight up the middle of the ice and into the North Stars zone, where defensemen Shawn Chambers and Neil Wilkinson converged on him. Lemieux blew by both of them like their skates were lodged in concrete, dropped Casey to the ice with a shoulder dip and, casually, flipped the puck into the net. The Pens evened the series with a 4-1 victory.

Casey had one more miracle left, leading the North Stars to a 3-1 win when the series resumed in Minnesota — a game Lemieux sat out with back spasms. Thereafter, the Pens attack kicked into gear, producing 19 goals in the final three contests, including a record 8-0 victory, the biggest Cup-winning margin ever, to claim the crown.

TO WIN THE

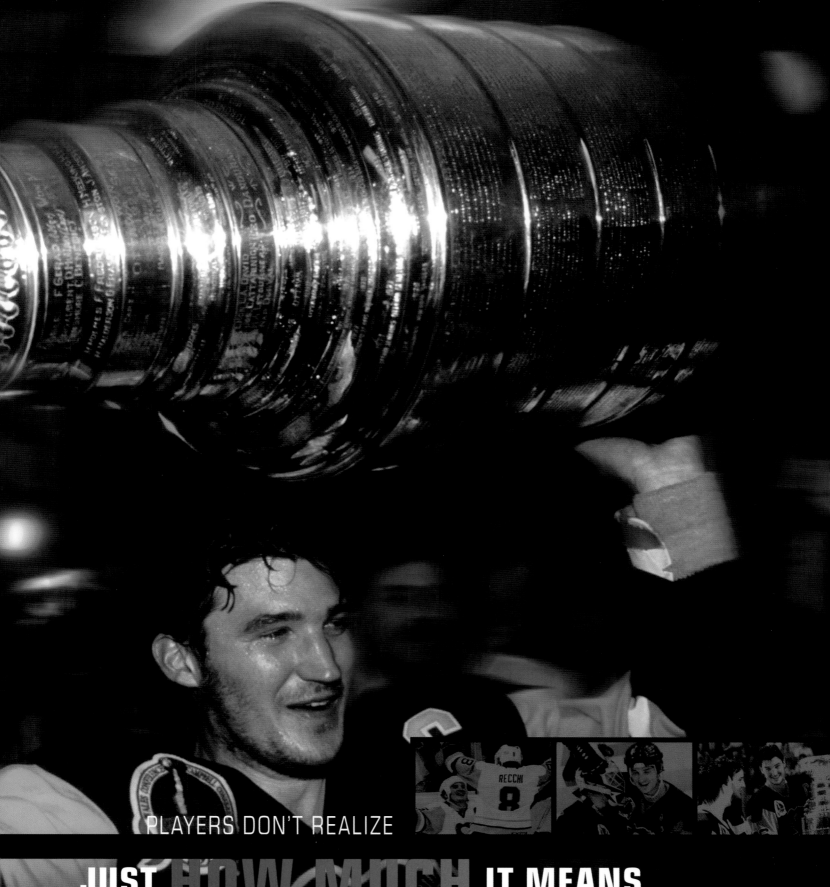

PLAYERS DON'T REALIZE

JUST HOW MUCH IT MEANS

STANLEY CUP UNTIL IT ACTUALLY HAPPENS

|Mario Lemieux|

Lemieux was magnificent in post-season, producing 16 goals and 44 points to win the Smythe Trophy as most valuable playoff performer. Other major contributors included Recchi (10-24-34), Stevens, who led playoff scorers with 17 goals, and defenseman Murphy, who averaged a point per game. Goalie Barrasso had a 2.60 average and a .919 save percentage.

What Patrick had built was a roster that was deep enough in competent NHL players to survive the ultra-heavy playoff schedule (24 games in 52 days). Backup goalie Pietrangelo won four of five playoff starts. When defensemen Samuelsson, Coffey and Taglianetti were injured, rookie Paek, who had spent the season with the Canadian national team, filled the hole capably.

The Cup triumph ended 24 years of "keeping the faith" for the core of devoted Penguins fans, a group that had dwindled badly in the pre-Lemieux mediocrity. After his long run of health problems, Lemieux actually improved as the playoffs progressed. He had eight points in seven games against the Devils, nine in five games against Washington, 15 in six games against the Bruins and 12 in the five games he played in the final against the North Stars.

"Players don't realize just how much it means to win the Stanley Cup until it actually happens," Lemieux said. *"There were times during that season when I wondered if I would ever be back to the game or able to play well again, yet alone win the Cup. Many times I wondered if I would be ever be part of a team strong enough to win it."*

During the team's victory celebrations, the Cup wound up in the swimming pool at the Lemieux home, maintaining the traditions of champions taking the Cup to unusual places, i.e. a strip club in Edmonton, Red Square in Moscow. Over 50,000 fans jammed into downtown Point State Park for the official congratulatory party.

"We gave the Stanley Cup to the fans because no one deserved it more. They had hung in with the franchise for 24 years without much reward," Mario exulted.

From a historical standpoint, it would be easy to say that the powerful Penguins had enough to win a second straight Cup the following year, but nothing comes simply, or pain-free in Pittsburgh hockey. Bad news that made Lemieux's previous back woes pale to insignificance emerged that August from the camp of Team USA, preparing for the 1991 Canada Cup tournament. "Badger Bob" had been felled by a massive brain tumor; exploratory surgery performed on August 29 only confirmed that the mass was inoperable and Johnson died at his home in Colorado Springs on November 26.

"He was an amazing person who taught us how to be winners," Lemieux said. *"I never met a man who was as optimistic or who loved the game of hockey the way he did.*

"He was very positive, even when things were going bad. The way he battled against an extremely serious disease was a big example in my own life when I became ill a few years later.

"His illness, which was obviously so serious when it was discovered, and death was devastating for us all. Our whole team flew to Denver during his last days and spent an hour with him. Even though he couldn't speak and was paralyzed on one side, you could tell when he saw the whole team there, it really meant a lot to him."

Fortunately for the Penguins, the "winningest" coach in NHL history, Scotty Bowman, was in the fold and Patrick asked him to fill in behind the bench.

BOB TAUGHT US HOW TO BE WINNERS

|Mario Lemieux|

Scotty Bowman joined Pittsburgh as the director of player development and later took over as coach after Bob Johnson passed away.

IN MY ESTIMATION, GENIUS IS THE ONLY WORD FOR BOWMAN

|Mario Lemieux|

Bowman as coach stressed strong play when the other team had the puck even more devotedly than Johnson. He locked horns with several players during the schedule but, gradually, a jittery peace was established as the workers realized that teams coached by Bowman had not won five Stanley Cups and all those games because he did not know what he was doing.

The defending champs struggled along near the .500 mark through much of the unusual and challenging season. At one point, Patrick met with the players and told them to quietly *"just play the game"* and not to worry about Bowman's aloof approach.

"From the start, the relationship between Bowman and the players was a bomb that was on the verge of blowing up at any time," said winger Mark Recchi, after he was traded to the Philadelphia Flyers late in the season.

"We needed time to get over Bob Johnson, who was so open, so big on communication. Bowman was the opposite because he never said anything to the players. You never knew where you stood unless he scowled at you. Craig cleared the air with the players."

"Bowman has been an extraordinary coach over his career and an amazing man in that he can deal with all the different personalities and get the most out of his players and teams," Lemieux said. *"In my estimation, genius is the only word for him. During his first season as coach, some practices were very long and there was much standing around. The players talked about it and I mentioned it to Craig* (Patrick). *Scotty decided to leave it up to his assistants to run most of the workouts."*

Lemieux played in 64 games and won his third scoring title with 131 points. On March 24 at Detroit, he counted the 1,000th point of his career in his 513th game. Stevens scored 54 goals and was second to Lemieux in points with 123.

On February 19, trader Patrick struck again. First, he dispatched defenseman Coffey to the Los Angeles Kings in exchange for defensemen Jeff Chychrun and Brian Benning plus a first-round draft pick. The same day, Benning, Recchi and that first-round pick were traded to the Philadelphia Flyers for winger Rick Tocchet, defenseman Kjell Samuelsson and goalie Ken Wregget.

Again, the Pens made things hard for themselves early in the playoffs, only to pick up steam as the post-season continued. They rallied from a 3-1 deficit to beat the Capitals in seven games, and then held off the belligerent Rangers in a six-game set that was heavy on acrimony. New York won the opener, and then

Rick Tocchet added grit and a deft scoring touch to the 1992 Stanley Cup winners.

took out two Pittsburgh stars in the second contest. First, Mullen's season ended when he suffered head injuries from a hard hit by Kris King, then Adam Graves of the Rangers slashed Lemieux, breaking a bone in his hand.

During the season, Lemieux had complained about the assortment of cheap shots he was forced to absorb and called the NHL "*a garage league,*" because it did not crack down on the fouls and restraining tactics that good players were forced to endure. He even hinted of retirement at 26. Later in the playoffs, Lemieux was quoted as saying the injury was inflicted deliberately and that the Rangers had "*taken out a contract*" on him.

JAROMIR JAGR's second goal of the game into the empty net finally ices a win over the tenacious Thrashers, who have never beaten the Pens in eight tries. Super Mario's two assists put him over the 50-point mark (25-26–51).

PITTSBURGH 5   ATLANTA 3

The Penguins continued their romp to the crown with a sweep of the Chicago Blackhawks in the final, but it wasn't that simple.

Led by the defensive tandem of Chris Chelios and Steve Smith, the Hawks swaggered into the Civic Arena and put three goals on the board by the 13:43 mark of the first period of the series opener. The Pens rebounded with a power-play goal before the period ended, but trailed 4-1 midway through the second period before goals by Tocchet and Lemieux drew them to within one. Ed Belfour and the Chicago defense seemed impregnable until Jagr tied the contest with a miraculous goal with less than four minutes remaining. Lemieux then scored a dramatic game-winning goal in the final seconds, and the Penguins were off and running.

Graves was suspended for four games, which drew a strong reaction from Penguins' owner Howard Baldwin because it appeared that his team's star was finished for the playoffs, effectively dashing dreams of a second Cup. But with Barrasso playing superbly in goal, Francis, Stevens and young Jagr (two game-winners) took up the scoring slack as the Pens again won three consecutive games to oust the Rangers, 4-2.

Jagr scored his third consecutive winner as the Pens opened the conference final with a 4-3 victory over the Boston Bruins and Lemieux returned for the second game, leading the club to a sweep of the series with eight points in three games.

Leader vs. Leader: Mario Lemieux moves in on Chris Chelios. leader of the Chicago defense in the 1992 final.

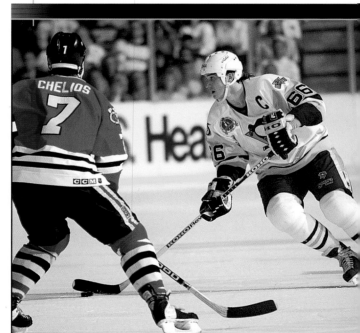

COULD BEAT YOU IN ANY NUMBER OF WAYS,
USING ANY NUMBER OF STYLES

|Mario Lemieux|

Chicago never again led in the series, and Lemieux added the game winner in the second game on his way to a second consecutive Smythe Trophy selection.

"Our 1991-92 team could beat you in any number of ways, using any number of styles, and we proved it in the series against the Blackhawks," Mario recounted. *"We won, 3-1, in the second game, 1-0, in the third game and then, 6-5, to clinch. Tighten it up. Run and gun. It didn't matter."*

Lemieux felt that goalie Barrasso should have been the playoff MVP, but the voters figured that a 34-point total and five game-winning goals in 15 games earned him the award. *"I was able to come back and finish pretty strong, and maybe that's why they gave it to me. If there was another guy that deserved it as well it would have to be Tommy. He played a major part in us winning two Cups."*

Mario Lemieux delivered on the promise that he brought with him to Pittsburgh in 1984 with two championships. But, as was the case with the NHL's star-crossed superstar, with ultimate success came an inordinate amount of misfortune.

And more of the same loomed on the horizon.

139

On January 7, 1993, Dr. Charles Burke, the Pittsburgh Penguins team surgeon,

attended a game against the Minnesota North Stars, accompanied by

Dr. Steve Jones, the team's ear, nose and throat specialist. They visited the

Penguins locker room after the game, and Burke checked the condition

of Mario Lemieux's back because discomfort had flared in the area of the

1991 surgery and infection. The doctor suggested rest, and it was agreed

that Lemieux would stay off skates for two weeks. Immediate speculation

centered on how the layoff would affect the potential challenge of Wayne

Gretzky's single-season points record of 215.

DOCTORS IN

## CHAPTER 7

DR. CHARLES BURKE   DR. STEVE JONES   HODGKIN'S DISEASE

THE HOUSE

When his "rest" was announced, Lemieux had played in 40 of 41 games and led in all scoring categories with 39 goals, 65 assists and 104 points.

The previous week, Lemieux had shown Burke a lump on his neck he had noticed months earlier that seemed to be growing, and Jones said he would deal with it during the back treatment. The lump was a swollen lymph node that Jones removed under local anesthetic and sent to a lab to be analyzed. The results three days later were chilling: Lemieux had Hodgkin's disease, a form of cancer that attacks the lymphatic system.

The news was devastating.

"Nothing is more scary than that word, cancer," Lemieux said. "I couldn't help it: I cried when I heard it. I guess you could say I broke down.

I managed to drive home and my fiancée (Nathalie Asselin) and I had a rough day. I'm not ashamed of it, but I cried a lot that day. Telling my family was very difficult."

Lemieux had the nodular lymphocytic form of Hodgkin's that was identified in Stage One of the four-stage disease. That causes a swelling of the lymph nodes, the small structures in the blood vessels that produce antibodies to fight infection, and inflammation of such organs as the spleen and liver.

NOTHING IS MORE SCARY THAN THAT WORD, CANCER

[Mario Lemieux]

The encouraging news was the 95 per cent success rate in treatment when the disease is found in a single lymph node, as in Lemieux's case.

"What really helped Mario was his force of character," said Tom Reich. *"He reverted to self, the same drive, approach, courage and mind-set that had made him successful in everything else he had done, and which, in the future, would propel him into ownership of the team."* As always, Mario attacked the problem head-on, matter-of-factly. Investigation, process, strategies and dignity were his stock in trade.

"After a really bad first day when I heard about it, I found out as much as I could about my disease and the treatment (radiation) *in talks with the doctors, and my family was very supportive,"* Lemieux said. *"There had been cancer in my family — one cousin had died of Hodgkin's — so it wasn't a completely foreign subject.*

"I'd fought a few battles for good health in my life and I just decided that I was going to win this one. I was always positive right from the start. The first day was a very difficult one, but the next day I talked to a lot of doctors and learned that the cure rate was over 90 per cent, I felt a lot more positive."

Two days later, Lemieux visited the team and told his teammates about his illness.

"Our room was noisy much of the time, plenty of needling and guys chattering away," Lemieux said. *"But when I walked in, everything went silent and it was rather strange. People don't know what to say to a person who has cancer."*

A somber Mario Lemieux at the press conference announcing his cancer.

Lemieux was scheduled for five-minute radiation treatments five-days-a-week for three-plus weeks, but that course of treatment was delayed for two weeks while a respiratory ailment was treated.

On January 15, a press conference in Pittsburgh was attended by more than 100 media members from both the U.S. and Canada, a somber occasion during which Lemieux was surprisingly optimistic.

Several reporters remarked afterward that they were surprised at Mario Lemieux's positive approach to his disease.

"I was determined to be upbeat about it," Lemieux recalled. *"Dr. Burke was certain I would play again because I felt quite good, and there were no indications that anything else was wrong. He assured me that I would be able to have a normal life and a long one, too. I told the media that I was confident that the treatment would be successful and I would be back with the team. I just couldn't predict when, two months or next season, but I would be back."*

Lemieux talked of the radiation treatment as a paranormal experience.

"My head was strapped to a table and a machine zapped me with something that I couldn't feel. I didn't have much energy for the rest of the day after the radiation, but the worst part was wondering if it was doing the job it was supposed to do."

CALGARY 3 | PITTSBURGH 6

The Pens spot the visiting Flames a 2-0 first-period lead before JAROMIR JAGR and Mario Lemieux go to work. The strapping Czech scores three goals and adds two assists, while Super Mario chips in a goal and three helpers, to key the victory.

144

The Penguins players were concerned that the career of their great teammate was finished, although they had seen Lemieux fight through debilitating injuries that had turned hockey into a physical hell for him.

"I knew he had battled serious health problems, but until I saw it firsthand I had no idea that playing often was sheer torture for him," said winger Rick Tocchet. *"I'll never forget the first time I saw him putting on his hockey pants and wincing in pain or how getting his sweater on could be such agony. There were nights when it was like the medical guys and the training staff were putting him together, then he would go out there and be in complete control of the game."*

After the press conference, Pittsburgh's most celebrated outpatient dropped from public sight for three weeks while on radiation therapy. He rejoined the team for practice on February 12, and his mates were amazed that he could play at such a high level. Lemieux told them that he hoped to play before the radiation was completed, but the doctors' plan was to keep him out until the treatment was finished.

MARIO LEMIEUX FOUNDATION

Personal misfortune is often the inspiration and guiding force for positive actions, and that was especially true of the formation of The Mario Lemieux Foundation.

"My battle with Hodgkin's disease in 1993 made me realize how fragile life can be," Mario stated. *"It also helped me to realize how fortunate I'd been to live the life of a professional hockey player and win a pair of Stanley Cups."*

When Lemieux underwent radiation treatments for his disease, he was acutely aware of the suffering of others around him, especially those who had difficulty making ends meet.

"That's why the Mario Lemieux Foundation was founded; I wanted to be able to raise funds that could be used for research into Hodgkin's and other diseases," Mario added.

The Penguins superstar has been cancer-free for eight years. Four years after his remission, the Lemieux family once again benefited from the excellent medical facilities in greater Pittsburgh when Austin Lemieux was born prematurely after a difficult pregnancy.

Tom Grealish is executive director of the Foundation, and is ably assisted by Nancy Angus, associate director. Grealish, a Pittsburgh insurance executive, met Lemieux on the golf course and they became friends. When Jack Kelley retired as Penguins' president and executive director of the Foundation, he recommended Grealish as his successor.

"Mario had helped the cancer association in fund-raising before he had the disease and after his treatment was successful, decided he wanted to do something to help and formed the Foundation. The main thrust is to contribute money to medical research," said Grealish.

Since its inception, The Mario Lemieux Foundation has awarded several grants.

FOLLOWING PAGE 146

"This year, the Foundation made a gift of $5 million to establish the multi-disciplinary Mario Lemieux Centers for Patient Care and Research at UPMC Health System," said Grealish. *"The bulk of it went to the University of Pittsburgh Cancer Institute for both patient care and research. Other recipients were Magee-Womens Hospital for neonatal research because Austin had arrived so early that only specialized medical expertise allowed him to survive, and the McGowan Center for Artificial Organ Development (early stage research).*

THE LEMIEUX FAMILY IS FRONT-AND-CENTER AS THE MARIO LEMIEUX FOUNDATION DONATES $5 MILLION TO THE UPMC HEALTH SYSTEM.

"The Foundation also from time to time makes one-time donations when worthy requests are received. A sub-committee —myself, Steve Reich, and Chuck Greenberg—checks out all requests and makes recommendations to the Foundation Board." Additionally, The Mario Lemieux Foundation supports other organizations, such as the Leukemia Society, Lupus Foundation, and Children's Hospital of Pittsburgh.

"The Mario Lemieux Celebrity Invitational Golf Tournament has served as our major fundraising event for the Foundation since its inception," said Lemieux.

"The 2001 event brought together celebrities from the worlds of sports and entertainment for four days, and raised over $1 million for the Foundation. Everyone with the Foundation is very thankful for the public's participation in the tournament and the various galas that were part of our special week."

The "miracle" was 18 days away. On March 2, Lemieux had his last radiation treatment in the morning, and tried to fly to Philadelphia in mid-afternoon to meet his teammates, but his plane was fogged in, in Chicago. He called the front office and requested a private plane for the trip, and motored from Pittsburgh International to Allegheny County Airport while the replacement apparatus was being fueled. Although his teammates weren't aware that he was coming until they bumped into him at the team's hotel late that afternoon, the Spectrum switchboard was suddenly deluged with callers seeking tickets, and what had seemed an uneventful regular-season contest was a sellout.

A REMARKABLE RETURN

When the starting line-ups were announced just prior to game time, the mention of Lemieux drew uncharacteristic cheers from the notoriously surly Flyer faithful. As he appeared on the ice for the national anthem, Philadelphia's finest temporarily postponed their collective animus for anything in a visitor's sweater and let out with a 90-second standing ovation that drew a raised stick and a wave from Lemieux.

"It's an unusual experience to hear the fans in Philadelphia actually applauding a visiting player," Lemieux said. *"It's not that they're particularly hard on visitors, just that they're so strong for the Flyers."*

That night, he scored a goal and an assist in a 5-4 loss to the Flyers, and although he rated his performance as "mediocre," he impressed the opposition.

"You can't give him enough credit for the way he played," said Philadelphia coach Bill Dineen. *"You can't give him enough credit just for showing up."*

Third-period goals by Mario Lemieux (shorthanded), Jaromir Jagr and Robert Lang erase a 2-0 New York lead, and the Pens are headed for a third straight win over the Rangers in a month until BRIAN LEETCH ties the contest with 68 seconds on the clock.

PITTSBURGH 3
RANGERS 3 | OT

A litany of back problems and two outstanding performances in Stanley Cup victories had rendered Le Magnifique a more popular figure throughout the National Hockey League. The aloof, cold superstar stories had long disappeared. The cancer blockbuster now made him one of the most sympathetic athletes in sports, and he would be greeted with respect and reverence at arenas around the circuit.

Super Mario had more mundane issues on his mind, like winning another scoring championship and leading his team to a third-straight Stanley Cup. When Lemieux returned in the Penguins' 65th game of the season, he trailed Pat LaFontaine in the scoring race, 116 to 104.

Out from under the shadow of Martin Brodeur after a trade from the Devils to the Islanders, CHRIS TERRERI struts his stuff in Pittsburgh, turning aside 33 of 34 shots to lead the Isles to a second win over the Pens. Mario Lemieux scores the only goal for the home team on a long breakaway, the 28ᵗʰ goal of his comeback.

ISLANDERS 3   PITTSBURGH 1

Then Lemieux exploded with back-to-back four-goal games against the Capitals and the Flyers, adding a five-goal game against the Rangers later in the schedule.

With three points against the Caps at Washington on March 28, the 12ᵗʰ game of his return, giving him an astounding output of 27 points in seven games, Lemieux assumed the points lead, 139-138, over LaFontaine. At season's end, Lemieux's totals were 69-91—160 in 60 games to LaFontaine's 53-95—148 in 84 contests. That pace, if maintained over a full 84-game season, would have given Lemieux a record 224 points. In addition, Lemieux led the NHL with a plus-55.

"I thought about the scoring title when I was having radiation because it took my mind off what was happening. My first goal was to get back to help the team, but regaining the points lead wasn't far behind."

Three days later on March 5, Lemieux was blanked as the Penguins lost, 3-1, to the Rangers at New York. The team then embarked on an astonishing streak of success, an NHL record 17-game win streak that still stands, wiping from the books the New York Islanders' mark of 15, set in the 1981-82 season. LaFontaine made a valiant attempt at holding the scoring lead. Although Lemieux had two goals and six assists in his first five games back, LaFontaine boosted his lead to 14 points over that stretch.

Mario's career paralleled that of Buffalo's classy Pat LaFontaine

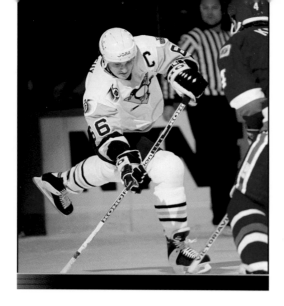

The word "dynasty" was heard often as the Stanley Cup playoffs opened with the Penguins heavily favored to win their third consecutive crown and join the few other elite teams who had accomplished that feat. They opened the playoffs impressively, ousting the Devils in a five-game series, Lemieux's nine points the key to a 23-13 edge in goals. That sent the Penguins against the New York Islanders in the second round, a team that had finished 32 points back of the Pens in the season. But Lemieux's back pain became unbearable again.

"The back pain sometimes was as bad as it had ever been and don't forget, I was taking time off to give it a rest when the cancer was discovered," Lemieux said. *"When I came back, it steadily got worse and I was really hurting in the series against the Devils. We had six days off before the second series and I was hoping the rest might help a little. But it didn't."*

Lemieux's ice-time was reduced; his play hampered by pain and exhaustion as the teams split the first six games. Then, early in the seventh game at Pittsburgh, 55-goal scorer, Kevin Stevens met with disaster. Stevens slammed into Islanders defenseman Richard Pilon's visor. The unconscious Stevens fell face first to the ice and suffered serious facial injuries, including a broken sinus bone, a broken nose and a concussion. The Penguins fought back from a two-goal deficit in the last four minutes to send the game to overtime where little-used winger David Volek ended any notions of a Penguins' dynasty with a goal in the sixth minute.

"Losing to the Islanders was tough, especially with the high hopes we had for the playoffs," Lemieux recalled. *"Very few teams over the years — the Canadiens a few times, the Leafs, the Islanders and the Oilers — won it all several times in a row, and we felt we could do it. Saying 'what if?' was easy and tempting, in 1993 — what if Kevin hadn't been hurt or what if I could have played full out in that series. But every team that ever lost a game or a series has a bout of that. What was sad was we had a feeling the team would be broken up because our payroll was stretched beyond the limit for a small-market club. And it came about that some key players were traded away that summer."*

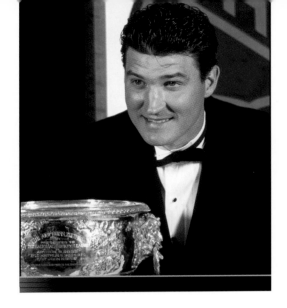

Lemieux collected the Hart Trophy as the league's most valuable player, the Art Ross Trophy as scoring champ and was named center on the first All-Star team. In addition, he won the Bill Masterton Trophy as the player who best exemplifies the qualities of perseverance, sportsmanship and dedication to hockey, and the Lester B. Pearson Award as the best NHL player, selected in a vote of the players.

Mario graduated to a much higher league that summer as he and Nathalie were married in Montreal on June 26, at a carefully guarded location and secret date and time to avoid a media circus. By mid-summer, however, it was obvious that the off-season repose and the Lemieux nuptials were not improving his finicky back. Another consultation with Dr. Watkins ensued, and everyone agreed on more surgery in late July to repair a herniated muscle and clean out scar tissue and a bone chip.

"Some discomfort went away for a while but the pain and stiffness returned. I found out, too, that radiation takes strength and stamina and replaces them with fatigue. The 1993-94 season was frustrating for me. I missed the pre-season, thinking I'd be ready for the season but I wasn't. I'd feel pretty good, set a target date to play again, that day would come and I just couldn't go. I worried about making a fool of myself if I did play."

Lemieux returned for a game at Quebec on October 28, picked up two assists, but two days later he missed another game. On November 12, after playing four games (one goal, seven assists), it was announced he would be out indefinitely.

"I wasn't helping the team and was hurting myself," Lemieux said. *"The doctors figured two months off would at least give me a chance to get my game back. I guess when you have surgery and work hard to come back, you always figure the problem will be solved. That made the early part of that season very frustrating, and the late stages of it were no better."*

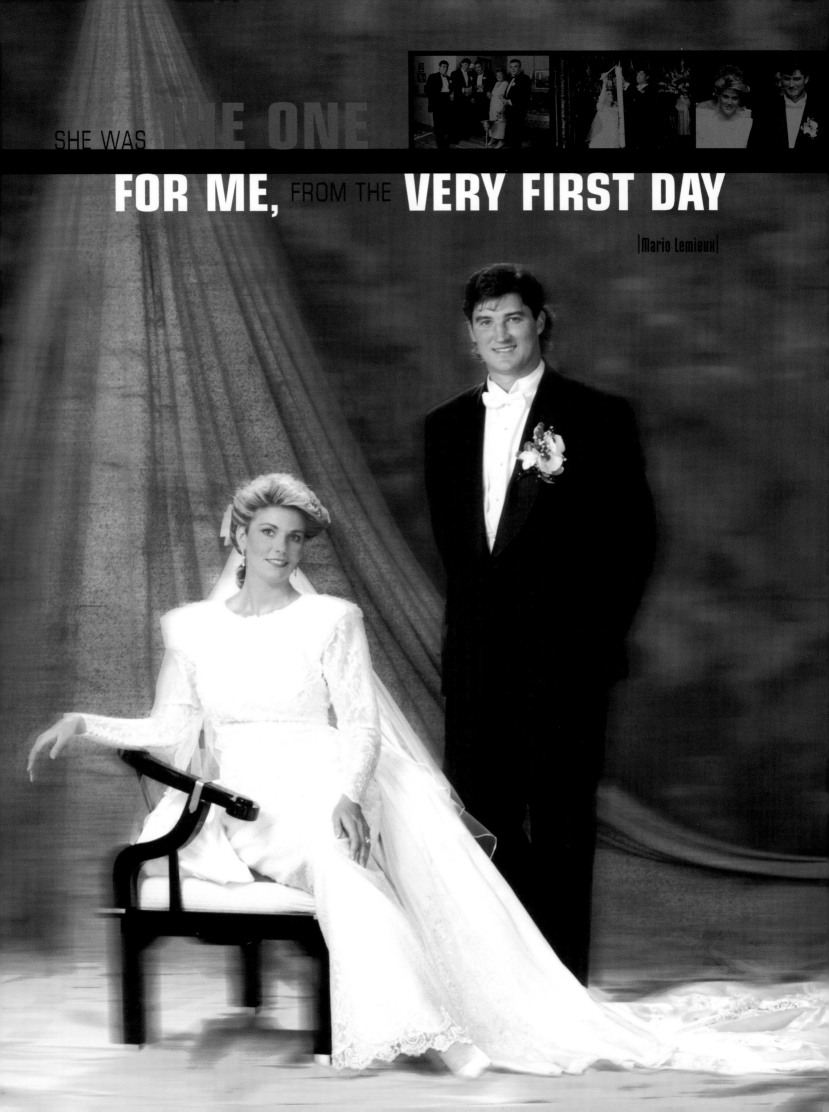

SHE WAS **THE ONE** **FOR ME,** FROM THE **VERY FIRST DAY**

|Mario Lemieux|

THE DOCTORS FIGURED
TWO MONTHS OFF
GIVE ME A
MY GAME BACK

|Mario Lemieux|

Lemieux logged time in Florida for what the club called "a complete rest." A February 1 game against the Florida Panthers was the target for a return, but his back was too stiff and sore. He tried again three days later in Detroit, but left the morning skate early. He had two cortisone shots in eight days and, while he felt more comfortable, the pain and stiffness didn't stay away.

Lemieux did return for a game at Montreal on February 19 and played in 17 more games before the schedule ended. He had 37 points in the 22 games he played, seven more in a losing six-game opening playoff round against the Washington Capitals.

Late in the schedule, he again hinted at retirement, how playing in 15 or so games and hoping for the playoffs was not the way he wanted to conduct a career. The increased use of the neutral zone trap and what Lemieux saw as the NHL's failure to crack down on restraining fouls, especially against the top stars, continued to eat at him. In an April game against Tampa Bay, the Pittsburgh center was hauled down by a blatant hooking foul, but referee Kerry Fraser did not call a penalty. What Fraser did see was a retaliatory Lemieux elbow against a Lightning player, penalizing him, and tacking on a 10-minute misconduct when Lemieux stormed after the official.

After the game, Lemieux opened his guns on the league, saying he would no longer participate in any NHL promotions.

152

WOULD **AT LEAST** CHANCE TO GET

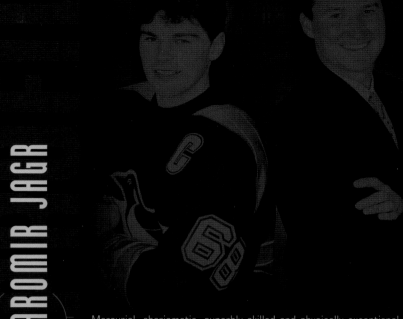

"They can promote the marginal players, who seem to get all the preferential treatment these days," Lemieux steamed.

"The clutching and grabbing and the restraining fouls especially in the neutral zone, have gotten worse the past two or three seasons. Many players neutralize the best players by hanging on to them and it's got to a point where skill is not much of an advantage. That's not right. If a player has offensive skill, then it should take defensive skill to stop him, not riding on his back."

JAROMIR JAGR

Mercurial, charismatic, superbly skilled and physically exceptional, Jaromir Jagr was the total package for the Penguins; a dazzling star many experts claimed was the best hockey player of his time.

Jagr arrived in Pittsburgh at 18 as first-round choice of the team in 1990 entry draft and helped the Penguins to Stanley Cup titles in 1991 (13 points in 24 games) and '92 (24 points in 21 games).

Throughout his 11 seasons as a Penguin, Jagr produced many dazzling efforts – 62 goals and 149 points in 1995-96, and four consecutive NHL scoring titles from 1997-98 through 2000-01. In 806 games with Pittsburgh, Jagr had a 439-640-1079 points total, as well 65 goals and 147 points in 140 playoff games. He earned six nominations to the league's first All-Star team.

Jagr also was a member of the Czech Republic team that won the gold medal in the 1998 Olympics in Japan; the first time NHL players competed in the Games.

Few players his size (six-foot-two, 230 pounds) can match Jagr's agility on skates. Add prodigious strength and puck-control skills, and he produced many of the NHL's greatest highlight moments of the 1990s, especially in the attacking zone corners, holding off opponents with one arm, controlling the puck with the other arm on his stick, and pivoting in a surprisingly small circle to move to the front of the net.

Plagued by a separated shoulder from a hit in a late-season game, Jagr was below form in the 2001 playoffs. Without full use of his upper-body strength to hold off defenders, he was held well in check by the New Jersey Devils in the third round of the playoffs.

After three separate requests for a trade, both during the season and after, the Penguins honored Jagr's wishes and moved the super-sized Czech winger to the Washington Capitals for three young prospects, Kris Beech, Michal Sivek, Ross Lupaschuk, and cash.

After a spring and summer of speculation, Lemieux announced on August 29 that he would sit out the 1994-95 season because of a variety of health problems, notably the sore back and fatigue. He wondered aloud if his career were finished.

"The back was a big problem and I was still so tired from the radiation that sometimes it was tough to get up in the morning. I'll admit now that there were times when I thought my career was over. There was speculation that all my health problems had taken away my determination to play the game, but that just wasn't right. I still loved hockey, but my stamina for the past couple of years wasn't the same as it had been and I felt run down.

"The doctors said that feeling run down was from several factors, especially the dozen cortisone shots I had for my back and the long-term fallout from the radiation. The good news was that the Hodgkin's was gone and so was the anemic condition from the radiation. I had several medical tests before I made the decision to take a year off, and the results showed that I needed time off to try and get my stamina back."

I NEVER HAD
LIFTED WEIGHTS BEFORE,
AND MAYBE I SHOULD HAVE

THERE WAS **SOME DEFINITION** TO **MARIO'S BODY**

The 1994-95 schedule was reduced to 48 games by labor conflict, called a work stoppage by the NHL and a lockout by the players' association. The season did not start until January 20 and stretched to the last game of the Stanley Cup final on June 24 when the New Jersey Devils won their first Stanley Cup since entering the NHL in 1974 as the Kansas City Scouts.

Lemieux disappeared from sight in Pittsburgh, his only appearance at a February charity game when he said that he had not decided on a return and he would be back only if healthy.

In the early spring of 1995, Lemieux began workouts under the guidance of sports-massage therapist Tom Plasko, a program that included stretching exercises, time on both a stationary bike and treadmill plus lifting weights. He appeared at camp in excellent condition.

"There was some definition to Mario's body which I never had noticed before," said GM Craig Patrick. *"I don't think I ever saw him look so good."*

"I never had lifted weights before, and maybe I should have," Lemieux said at the time. *"My hopes are high about my back. I hope it's good enough that I can be one of the best again. Maybe in my early years I wanted to do it just on talent and not work as hard as other players. I eventually came to realize that I had to work harder to get the most out of that talent."*

Lemieux picked up a fifth scoring title (69-92—161 points), even though his season was reduced to 70 games. A bruised back and the 'flu each cost him a game and he missed 10 more for precautionary rest. A small lump under his chin proved benign, and his tiredness was the result of an under-active thyroid, a condition that often is the product of radiation.

There was external stress, too, the worst kind of tension for someone who was used to controlling his environment.

156

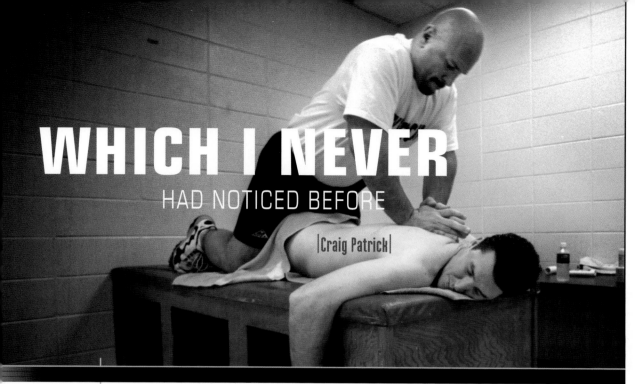

WHICH I NEVER
HAD NOTICED BEFORE

|Craig Patrick|

Tom Plasko works on Mario so Mario can work in the NHL.

When the various afflictions had beset him, he could control his actions and reactions, as well as reassuring friends and loved ones that things would get better.

When Nathalie experienced serious health problems during her third pregnancy, essentially bed-ridden late in her second trimester, Mario was reduced to a bedside spectator. Thus, when son Austin Nicholas—who arrived three months early (two pounds, five ounces) to join sisters Lauren and Stephanie—was pronounced healthy, a gargantuan weight was lifted from the shoulders of a father and husband. Two nights later, Proud Papa celebrated the special event with five goals and seven points against Wayne Gretzky and the St. Louis Blues.

The Penguins were the top scoring team in the NHL when they finished fourth overall, second in the Eastern Conference. Jagr emerged as a major star with 62 goals and 149 points, runner-up as top scorer, and the reliable Francis was fourth (27-92—119).

PITTSBURGH 6   3 FLORIDA

Mario Lemieux's two goals and an assist edge out PAVEL BURE'S two tallies in the "personal battle" and the Pens double the Panthers in goalie Johan Hedberg's NHL debut. Bure's first score is his 50th and he is the first player to reach that plateau in the 2000-01 NHL season.

MARCH 16, 2001
GAME 11
35

Player	Number of Assists
JAROMIR JAGR	92
Paul Coffey	72
Kevin Stevens	70
Ron Francis	60
Bob Errey	40
Rob Brown	39
Doug Bodger	31
Rick Tocchet	30
Moe Mantha	27
Terry Ruskowski	25
Larry Murphy	23
Dan Quinn	23
Randy Cunneyworth	22
Tomas Sandstrom	22
Zarley Zalapski	18
Craig Simpson	17
Warren Young	17
Mike Bullard	14
John Cullen	14
Joe Mullen	14
Randy Hillier	13
Mark Recchi	13
Phil Bourque	12
Rod Buskas	12
Markus Naslund	12
Doug Shedden	12
Petr Nedved	11
Ville Siren	11
Sergei Zubov	11
Wayne Babych	10
Kevin Hatcher	10
Jim Johnson	10
Martin Straka	9
Troy Loney	8
Dmitri Mironov	8
Ulf Samuelsson	8
Jason Woolley	8
Ron Duguay	7
Tom Barrasso	6
Jock Callander	6
Chris Dahlquist	6
Alexei Kovalev	6
Norm Maciver	6
Dan Frawley	5
Dave Hannan	5
Dave Hunter	5
Darius Kasparaitis	5
Kevin LaVallee	5
Francois Leroux	5
Fredrik Olausson	5
Gord Roberts	5
Bryan Smolinski	5
Peter Taglianetti	5
Randy Gilhen	4
Hans Jonsson	4
Joe McDonnell	4
Kjell Samuelsson	4
Charlie Simmer	4
Chris Tamer	4
Jan Hrdina	3

Player	Number of Assists
Robert Lang	3
Bryan Maxwell	3
Kevin McCarthy	3
Mike Blaisdell	2
J.J. Daigneault	2
Joe Dziedzic	2
Gord Dineen	2
Andrew Ference	2
Corey Foster	2
Jiri Hrdina	2
Grant Jennings	2
Chris Joseph	2
Chris Kontos	2
Willy Lindstrom	2
Andrew McBain	2
Shawn McEachern	2
Jim McGeough	2
Dave McLlwain	2
Glen Murray	2
Wilf Paiement	2
Norm Schmidt	2
Paul Stanton	2
Tony Tanti	2
Dave Tippett	2
Stu Barnes	1
Roger Belanger	1
Neil Belland	1
Josef Beranek	1
Marc Bergevin	1
Doug Brown	1
Greg Brown	1
Jay Caufield	1
John Chabot	1
Todd Charlesworth	1
Rene Corbet	1
Steve Dykstra	1
Bryan Erickson	1
Bryan Fogarty	1
Greg Fox	1
Steve Gatzos	1
Lee Giffin	1
Steve Guenette	1
Andreas Johansson	1
Greg Johnson	1
Petr Klima	1
Janne Laukkanen	1
Kevin Miller	1
Ian Moran	1
Eddie Olczyk	1
Jim Paek	1
Barry Pederson	1
Frank Pietrangelo	1
Mike Ramsey	1
Gary Rissling	1
Dave Roche	1
Dwight Schofield	1
Wally Weir	1
Chris Wells	1
Neil Wilkinson	1
Scott Young	1

Jaromir Jagr is the player who has the mosts assists on Mario Lemieux's goals.

In the playoffs, the Penguins eliminated the Washington Capitals in six games, one decided near the end of the fourth overtime period on Petr Nedved's goal. The Pens then ousted the New York Rangers in five games to meet the surprising Florida Panthers in the conference final. In only their third NHL season and first playoffs, the Panthers played a dull defensive style, specializing in the neutral zone trap. Lemieux seemed to have a Panther or two on his back through the entire series, which the Penguins led after five games before dropping the final two.

The restraining defensive style used by Florida was what Lemieux wanted the league to ban.

"That style was frustrating for players with skill and killer-dull for the fans." Lemieux said.

"Give the Panthers credit for strong execution of that system to make a big splash in their third season, but it was the style of hockey I'd campaigned against for many years."

Lemieux won his third Hart Trophy as the NHL's most valuable player to go with his scoring crown. With 11 goals and 27 points in 18 playoff games, he finished second in post-season scoring to Joe Sakic of the Cup champion Colorado Avalanche.

During the summer of 1996, Lemieux met with NHL Commissioner Gary Bettman and executive vice-president Brian Burke to discuss the game and the league officials told him that a crackdown on restraining fouls was planned.

"They promised to do some things to make the game better," Lemieux said. *"I told them that the top players had to be able to play their games, but they couldn't."*

That assurance, plus the knowledge that his presence would make things easier for owner Howard Baldwin, brought Lemieux back for the 1996-97 season after much retirement speculation. Lemieux told only Baldwin that it would be his last season.

It's not always clear sailing in the NHL, as Florida defender Robert Svehla proves.

IT'S LIKE **FOOTBALL;** SOMEBODY IS ALWAYS **GRABBING YOU** WHETHER OR NOT **YOU HAVE THE PUCK**

|Mario Lemieux|

Mario Lemieux was doubleteamed by the opposition for his entire career.

"I had a little dream that my career would end carrying the Stanley Cup around the ice," Lemieux said.

His "final" season was one of the most difficult and frustrating of Lemieux's career. From the start, he felt *"sluggish"* and had *"no jump in my legs."*

"For some reason, even though he worked hard off the ice, Mario just never re-energized that summer," said agent Steve Reich. *"He just never had that Lemieux burst that enabled him to beat players one-on-one."*

"I played the worst hockey of my life at the start of that season," Lemieux concurred. He scored only eight goals in the first 19 games, and then had a stretch from mid-December to mid-January when he had 14 goals and 37 points in 14 games. Early on, however, he saw no change in how the rules were enforced.

"The same old boring hockey!" Lemieux raged. *"The league must enforce the rules. It's like football; somebody is always grabbing you whether or not you have the puck."*

On April 5, Lemieux spoke at the Dapper Dan Charity Dinner in Pittsburgh, and announced he was retiring at the end of the playoffs. Lemieux won his sixth scoring crown and was a runner-up for the Hart Trophy, but the Penguins barely made it above the .500 mark with a 38-36-8 record.

The Pittsburgh fans gave Lemieux a loud farewell in his concluding regular season game when he had 11 shots on goal, but managed only an assist in a 3-1 win over the Boston Bruins. The Penguins lost the first three games in the opening playoff round to the Philadelphia Flyers, then prolonged the series with a 4-1 home-ice win in the fourth game.

Mario had lost none of his flair for the dramatic, in what was a rink overflowing with emotion. All 17,355 in attendance knew that the Flyers would soon close out the series, and that this would be Le Magnifique's last curtain call at home.

Late in the third period, with Pittsburgh nursing a 3-1 lead, Lemieux corralled a lead pass from Ian Moran and broke in on Garth Snow, burying a shot between his legs at 18:56. The ovation swelled and rose and threatened the arena roof.

"That moment is engraved in my mind forever, something that doesn't happen very often to an athlete. It was the most emotional I've ever been."

VINCENT LECAVALIER wins the Battle of the Quebec-born giant centers as the Lightning surprise the Pens at the Ice Palace. Another, much shorter Quebec product, Martin St. Louis, leads the Bolts with a pair of goals, one short-handed, and Super Mario has the only Pittsburgh score.

PITTSBURGH 1   TAMPA BAY 5

The Flyers eliminated the Penguins with a 6-3 win at Philly, and Lemieux had a post-game farewell press conference. As he left the media room, he was asked how many pain-free games he had played in his 12 seasons. *"Less than half, I would say,"* Lemieux replied.

Lemieux was asked if he would stage a post-career crusade to turn the game away from restraining fouls and back towards the skilled players. *"When I'm done playing, I won't give a damn,"* he said. *"I tried for 10 years to change the game and it hasn't changed. When I'm done, I'm done."*

For once, Mario Lemieux was wrong.

THAT **MOMENT** IS **ENGRAVED** IN MY MIND **FOREVER**

|Mario Lemieux|

DOUG CAMPBELL WAS NOT AT A DINNER WITH MARIO LEMIEUX IN A PITTSBURGH

steak house in October 1998, but when he heard of the idea born at that

table, he was the one with indigestion. That night, the Pittsburgh superstar

dined with an inner group of advisors and friends, including agents Tom

and Steve Reich, and his personal attorney Chuck Greenberg. Somewhere

between entrée and dessert, they decided to buy the Pittsburgh Penguins.

"When the men at that dinner told me what they wanted to do, I suggested

they were a bunch of Looney Tunes," recalled lawyer Campbell, a noted

Pennsylvania bankruptcy specialist.

PINSTRIPES: A

## CHAPTER 8

DOUG CAMPBELL   TOM & STEVE REICH   HOWARD BALDWIN

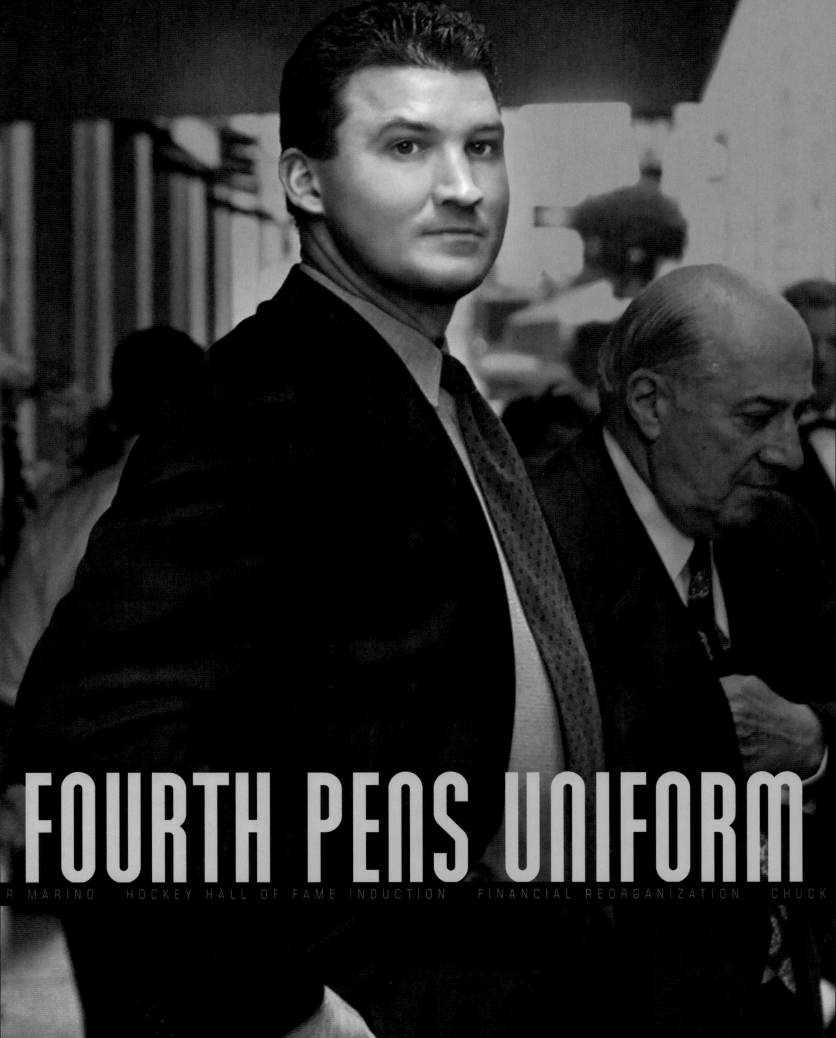

FOURTH PENS UNIFORM

8

A few days earlier, Penguins' co-owners Howard Baldwin and Roger Marino had filed for Chapter 11 bankruptcy protection after several seasons of being tossed around on stormy fiscal seas.

Mario Lemieux was the primary creditor. When he had retired at the end of the 1996-97 season, he was owed more than $26 million in deferred payments, as well as another $7 million in unpaid salary from the guaranteed $42 million, seven-year deal he had signed with the team after the Penguins' second consecutive Stanley Cup win in 1992. He had agreed to several deferments in an attempt to help Baldwin keep the team alive and competitive in Pittsburgh, but when the Penguins defaulted on scheduled payments in February 1998, Lemieux hired Campbell to help him collect.

"Mario had renegotiated his contract several times to give the team more favorable terms," Campbell said. *"But in the end, they couldn't afford to pay him. Eventually, he did recover some money from Roger Marino."*

The NHL's plan to cover teams that go broke has two main options if a local buyer cannot be found; sell to interests who will move the team, lock, stock and barrel to another city; or stage a special draft to disperse the players to other NHL teams, and fold the franchise.

"None of us wanted to see the team die or moved out of Pittsburgh," Lemieux said. *"The answer, which we agreed on quickly, was for me to buy the team with some other investors and keep it in Pittsburgh.*

NONE OF US
WANTED TO SEE
THE TEAM DIE

GREENBERG   BERNARD MARKOVITZ   RONALD BURKLE   TOM ROONEY   CRAIG PATRICK

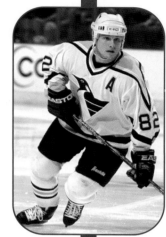
MARTIN STRAKA's two helpers key a comeback from a 2-0 deficit as the Pens salvage a point against a Boston team that is fighting for its playoff life. Rookie Johan Hedberg turns aside 27 of 29 shots, and the Bruins' Byron Dafoe stops 22 shots.

BOSTON 2   PITTSBURGH 2 | OT

"The city was home for our family, the only place where I had played in the NHL and where I had gone with the team from last overall to Stanley Cup champions. The fans had been loyal to all of us over the years and the support I received during my cancer and back problems was incredible. To lose hockey in a good hockey town would have been a big blow to a great city.

"If this had happened immediately after I retired, I might not have wanted to be involved in the ownership. I needed a couple of years away from hockey to build my interest again. The first season I was away, I really got away. I went to Florida to live for the winter and didn't watch a lot of hockey or go to many games. Then I came back to Pittsburgh the next winter, I started watching again and missing it."

OR MOVED OUT OF PITTSBURGH

|Mario Lemieux|

Campbell had good reasons for his doubts about the purchase of the team by a Lemieux-led group: the lack of precedence for such a move.

"It's a very rare occurrence when the reorganization of a company is done by a creditor because it is usually done by a principal, and I never had heard of it being done by an unsecured creditor, as Mario was in this case," Campbell explained.

"But in reality, it was the only possible solution to Mario's difficulties with the team. I remember walking with Mario on a Pittsburgh street at twilight, a dark and damp February night, and it was quite depressing. We knew we had to do something to the process for him to recoup a big part of his career earnings."

FAMILY VALUES

Mario Lemieux's favorite word has only three letters, and he hears it a lot from four special persons in his life – Dad.

Daughters Lauren, 8, Stephanie, 6, and Alexa, 4, and son Austin, 5, are the overwhelming pride of Mario's existence as he and Nathalie Lemieux have embraced parenthood with the same zest he has brought to his many successful careers.

"Our kids have been a huge part of our lives the last eight years, and we can't remember or ever imagine life without them," he says, misting slightly.

"It is pretty incredible to be there when your first child (Lauren) is born. It is something that stays with you forever and was the happiest time of my life."

There are Lemieux traits shared among the quartet. Lauren and Austin are shy and demure, like Dad and *Grand-papa*. Stephanie and Alexa have *Grand-maman's* outgoing personality.

How do the four, Pittsburghers born and bred, relate to the Quebec side of the family?

"They relate very well," Mario replies. *"My parents visit quite a bit and so does Nathalie's Mom, brother and sister, so they get to see them a lot. The kids are struggling a little bit with their French for the fact that they're not in that environment day-to-day. We speak to them in French, they answer in English, and we're trying to coax them a little. Lauren is probably the best because she's been at it longer."*

Alexa's Godmother Nancy Matthews has no qualms about the Lemieux brood maintaining contact with their mother tongue.

"Mario and Nathalie showed a lot of character in how they picked up English, and I know they are just the parents to ensure that these beautiful kids will be as bilingual as they are."

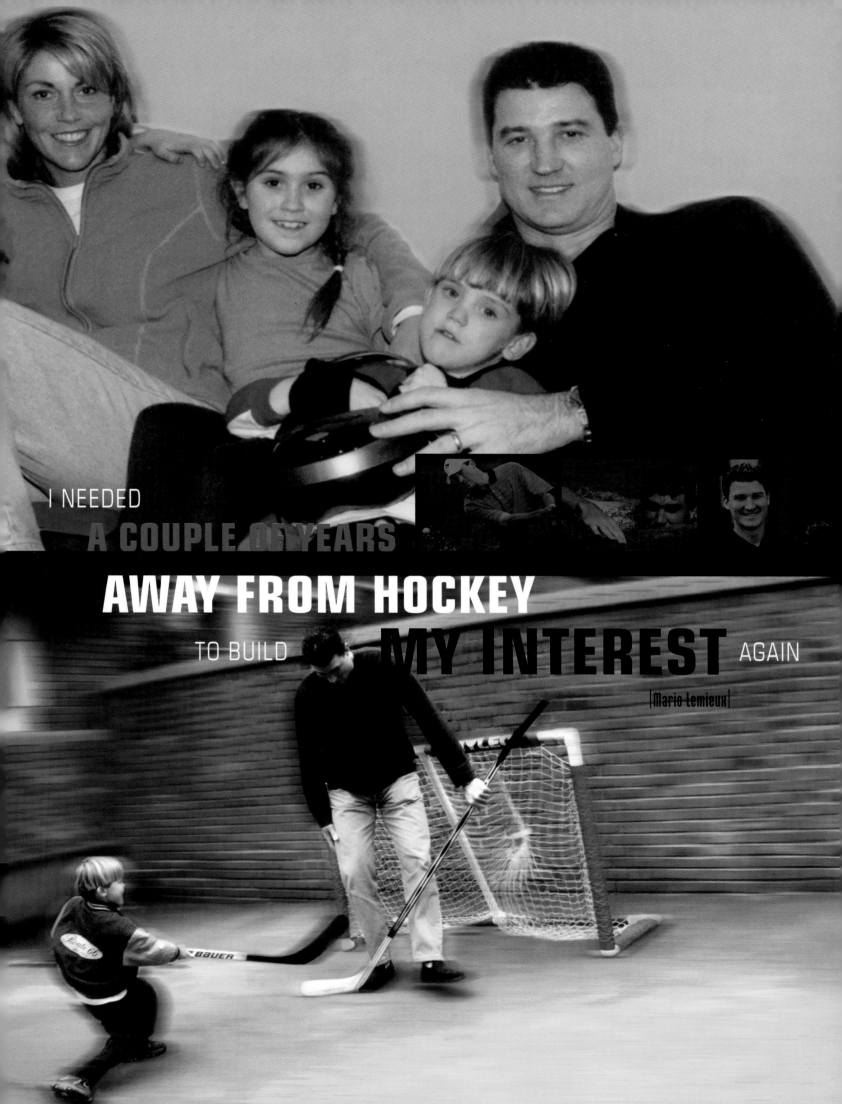

I NEEDED A COUPLE OF YEARS AWAY FROM HOCKEY TO BUILD MY INTEREST AGAIN

[Mario Lemieux]

Edward J. DeBartolo

The Penguins had entered the NHL in the original 1967 expansion, and the franchise struggled to exist from the start. Several ownership groups tried unsuccessfully to make the game pay its way in the western Pennsylvania city, and bankruptcy was not new to the Penguins, having visited the club in 1975. Three years later, Edward J. DeBartolo and his family, who ran the country's leading shopping center development and management firm, purchased the team and controlled the Civic Arena.

After considerable losses, and despite a Stanley Cup victory in 1990-1991, DeBartolo sold the team to Howard Baldwin and his partners, Thomas Ruta and Morris Belzberg in November 1991.

Baldwin had raised enough money to purchase the Penguins, but not enough to take over the arena rights. Those rights were sold for $24 million through to 2012 to SMG of Philadelphia.

Many, including Marino who later invested in the team, claimed the SMG deal was the contributor to the team's fiscal woes, primarily because of a steep annual rent of $6.8 million, far above what the majority of NHL teams pay. SMG's deal also included a large percentage of revenues from parking, concessions, luxury suites and arena advertising rights, important revenue streams for major league sports teams. Baldwin asserted, however, that the cash from SMG had allowed the Pens to remain in Pittsburgh. Ticket prices were raised after the two Stanley Cup wins and attendance was strong, but costs increased as the team's top players, including Lemieux, signed big contracts.

When the lockout/strike reduced the 1994-95 schedule to 48 games, the Penguins lost close to $25 million and the franchise sank deeper into debt.

The Pens overcome a 3-0 deficit in Carolina, only to fall short on Finnish sniper SAMI KAPANEN's second goal of the game. Arturs Irbe stars in goal with 20 tough saves.

PITTSBURGH **3**   CAROLINA **5**

A Boston businessman whose worth was placed in the $300 million range, Marino joined Baldwin as an equal owner of the team in 1997.

But the team was on a slide with Lemieux's retirement at the end of the 1996-97 playoffs, as season ticket sales dropped significantly the next season. By December 1997, the team needed an infusion of $2 million every couple of weeks to meet payroll.

Marino had earned some minor concessions from SMG in a reworking of the deal, but when he sought further changes a year later, SMG refused. Marino also failed to rework deals with Fox Sports Television and Lemieux.

Baldwin and Marino seemed to wage an endless argument with occasional name-calling about who was in control. Without his "partner" knowing, Marino went to Kansas City, where an NHL expansion team had lasted only two seasons in the 1970s, to check out a possible move to that city. The ownership matter seesawed back and forth through the summer of 1998.

Early in the summer, Baldwin hinted that he had the resources to buy Marino's share of the team and in September, rumbles were that Marino would take control when he appointed a corporate turnaround specialist as interim CEO.

In the middle of the Baldwin-Marino upheaval, Lemieux launched a $33 million lawsuit against the Penguins, who had defaulted on contract payments.

Howard Baldwin

111

The hastily assembled trio of Martin Straka, Robert Lang and ALEXEI MOROZOV, put together when Alexei Kovalev was handed a three-game suspension, combines for all four goals and 10 points overall as the Pens double the Devils, abruptly ending their league-leading 13-game winning streak.

PITTSBURGH 4   NEW JERSEY 2

On October 13, 1998, the situation changed dramatically when the team filed for bankruptcy protection. Court documents showed team debt at $137.45 million with Lemieux as the biggest unsecured creditor, at $28.7 million. Lemieux was named co-chairman of a court-appointed, seven-member panel, mostly team creditors, to participate in devising a plan to pay the creditors.

Lemieux immediately hired bankruptcy experts. Later that month, Marino made a second $2.5 million loan to the team to meet the payroll and in November, the owners revealed that they were seeking a $20-million bank loan to carry them through the season. A November 25 trade that sent center Petr Nedved to the Rangers for winger Alexei Kovalev and $2.5 million in cash, helped meet another payroll.

In December, the team reached an agreement with a French bank for a loan to provide working capital through August 1999, but the deal hit snags in bankruptcy court. It finally was approved in January, but in smaller amounts.

Early in 1999, reports surfaced in Pittsburgh that Lemieux was attempting to assemble a group to buy the team.

The 1998-99 Pittsburgh Penguins

A few days later, Chuck Greenberg, Tom Reich and Mike Lee, an employee of the Reich's athletes' agency, wrote the basics of a plan that would pay off the team's debt and raise more than $50 million from outside investors.

"The easiest thing for me was for the team to be sold and moved to Portland where there seemed to be big interest in an NHL franchise, and then to try to collect what I was owed from the new owner," Lemieux countered.

"But when your whole life is invested in something, you're going to try to save it. I didn't spend 12 years of my career playing for the Penguins only to have the team disappear two years after I retired."

"The idea of Mario buying the Penguin franchise was extremely bold," Campbell said. *"But, in reality, there was no alternative.*

"Mario's challenge was finding investors for a business that, in that season, would have revenues of $40 million and expenses of $60 million. I think daunting was the correct word for the situation. The big problems were the arena lease with SMG and the broadcast deal."

HOCKEY HALL OF FAMER

Mario Lemieux resides in many elite groupings of hockey's greatest players, and one select circle of much distinction involves the Hockey Hall of Fame. He is one of 10 players for whom the three-year, post-retirement waiting period was waived and one of seven of who went directly from the ice to the Hall.

The seven who took the direct route are Bobby Orr, Gordie Howe, Dit Clapper, Jean Béliveau, Maurice (Rocket) Richard, Lemieux and Wayne Gretzky. Terry Sawchuk and Ted Lindsay entered the Hall after a one-year wait, Red Kelly two years after he retired.

It comes as no surprise that Lemieux was on the golf course when the Hall's selection committee voted him in on September 9, 1997. He had retired from the Penguins after the team was eliminated in the '97 playoffs, his injuries and illnesses taking a toll, and publicly unhappy with what he felt was the NHL's failure to eliminate the action-killing restraining tactics from the game.

"There had been talk that the three-year waiting period might be waived in my case, but when I heard I had been elected to the Hockey Hall of Fame, it was a surprise, a bit of a jolt," he said. *"It's not something you think about in your career, although when you have accomplished some good things, the thought crosses your mind that you might be considered. Winning the Stanley Cup is the ultimate, but being named to the Hall is right up there.*

"It added to the thrill that Bryan Trottier was named that year, too. He was such a great player when he won four Cups with the New York Islanders. And then he came to Pittsburgh to finish his career and he taught us all a great deal about winning. Bryan was a valuable contributor to our two championships."

Admitted to the Hall in 1997 along with Trottier and Lemieux were Glen Sather in the builders' category, founder of *The Hockey News*, Ken McKenzie, and broadcaster Gene Hart in the media categories.

When he made his comeback to the Penguins in 2000, Lemieux was one of only three NHL stars to return as active players after being inducted. Howe and Guy Lafleur were the others.

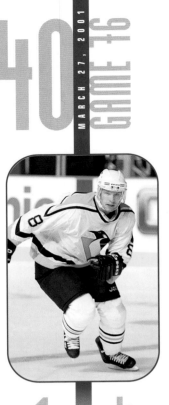

A quick strike 47 seconds into the game leaves the visitors reeling and Pittsburgh cruises to a three-goal margin over Buffalo. Defenseman HANS JONSSON gets things going less than a minute into the contest, and Pittsburgh leads 3-0 before the Sabres manage a goal of their own against Johan Hedberg.

BUFFALO 1   PITTSBURGH 4

The Penguin owners, however, had exclusive rights to submit a financial reorganization for the franchise, but when they withdrew that request on February 9, Lemieux went public for the first time with his plan to lead an ownership group that would buy the franchise.

"I had met with Gary Bettman (NHL commissioner) and he was very encouraging about our plan," Lemieux said.

Asked if he would consider a return as a player, Lemieux said: "I have had no thoughts whatsoever about playing again. I'll be an owner and if I'm an owner, I can't be a player."

In early March, Lemieux met with Pennsylvania Governor Tom Ridge and asked about state support for the construction of a new building to replace the Civic Arena.

He had additional discussions with the NHL and also squelched rumbles of a partnership with Marino in the ownership of the team.

On March 18, the Lemieux group submitted its financial reorganization plan to the bankruptcy court and said they were close to raising $40 million, although no investors were identified. A week later, Lemieux said that he had $50 million.

Bankruptcy judge Bernard Markovitz ordered the team to play in Pittsburgh until 2007, no matter which ownership group had control. In April, the judge turned down a Marino request to shop the team in other cities.

By April, the NHL had a plan in place to revoke the franchise and either move it to another city or disband the team and stage a draft of the players by the other clubs. The Fox Sports Net and SMG also submitted a plan to the bankruptcy court. SMG was allowed to continue its operation of the Civic Arena for a fee by the Public Auditorium Authority of Pittsburgh, which owned the building.

Almost from the birth of his idea to buy the franchise, Lemieux and his advisors realized that the SMG "revenue streams problem" had to be solved before investors would consider joining the ownership group.

I DIDN'T SPEND 12 YEARS OF MY CAREER WITH THE PENGUINS ONLY TO HAVE THE TEAM DISAPPEAR TWO YEARS AFTER I RETIRED

|Mario Lemieux|

While the NHL kept pushing back the deadline on its revocation scenario, Pittsburgh mayor Tom Murphy accused SMG of "stonewalling" the bid to keep the team in Pittsburgh and threatened to invalidate the Philadelphia firm's deal on the arena.

"When I decided on a serious bid to take over the team, I knew there were many problems to overcome," Lemieux said. "But I had been a hockey player all my life, not a lawyer or a businessman or a judge, so I really had no idea of what I was getting into.

"It was incredibly complex, and being so deeply involved in it and trying to keep informed on what had happened, was happening or was about to happen was like studying for a degree in business and law at the same time. Fortunately for me, I had such great people around me to help, men who are tops in their fields, but who had the patience to help me learn about what was going on, detail the problem of the day and offer solutions."

As a bankruptcy specialist, Campbell was pivotal to the project, guiding the Lemieux group through the labyrinth of dysfunctional finance. He produced a pinwheel diagram, Lemieux in the middle as the hub and each spoke representing a problem to solve.

"That drilled home just how much there was to be done and how large some of the problems were," Lemieux said. "In simple terms, we had to buy out the previous owners of the team.

"We had to gain approval from the league for our plan, which was a big part of winning the okay from the bankruptcy court.

"We had to bring in new investors and get a restructuring of the debt at the arena. There would be negotiation on something one day, a re-doing of it the next day and a renegotiation of that on the third day. Our guys started calling it Groundhog Day after that movie when Bill Murray lived the same day over and over again. Doug Campbell, Tom Reich and Chuck Greenberg worked tirelessly to solve each problem that came up."

"There were at least 13 different spokes outlining problems to be solved, including SMG, broadcasting, the auditorium commission, the NHL and NHL Players' Association. It was time-intensive and we were working with a very tight deadline," Campbell said.

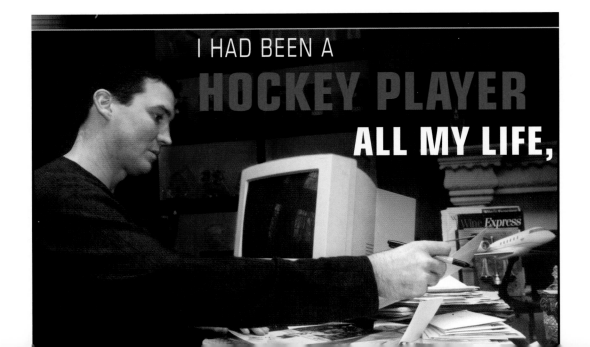

I HAD BEEN A HOCKEY PLAYER ALL MY LIFE,

The spokes on the wheel disappeared slowly as the previous owners' contracts were reworked. Then, in a move Campbell calls critical to the entire process, the terms of the SMG deal to control the Civic Arena were changed.

"SMG and Fox were making a heavy bid for the Penguins and SMG was very difficult to deal with for us," Campbell said. *"The key for us was a complex legal piece that turned out to rule that what SMG had was not a lease, but a financial arrangement and not a real estate deal, but a financial one, an incredibly complex arrangement.*

"The day the SMG-Fox plan was turned down by the court we said: 'The Titanic just hit an iceberg.' It stopped them and left the field to us, even though it was still loaded with mines. What it accomplished was to bring SMG to the table for some truly miserable negotiations. It was a gain-an-inch, lose-two type of dealing with them. Thank heavens for Judge McCullough."

SO I REALLY HAD **NO IDEA** OF WHAT **I WAS** GETTING INTO

|Mario Lemieux|

The accolades have poured down unabated from all quarters, celebrating the individual brilliance of a hockey career in two parts, to say nothing of an astonishing coup that brought about Mario Lemieux's ownership of the Pittsburgh Penguins.

It took a while for the hockey world to realize the pearl of great price that was this super-gifted athlete from Ville Emard. Perhaps in mild apology for coming to acknowledge his greatness late, the hyperbole had reached new heights. There has been only one dissenting voice, as the adjectives and superlatives have collided in a pile-up of epic proportions: Mario Lemieux's.

"I thank everyone for the kind words and thoughts," he says shyly. *"But, this has always been a team thing, a family thing, ever since my earliest childhood. Hockey is a team sport, hockey management even more so, and I could never have done any of it without my family and my teammates, at all levels, on and off the ice."*

"And that," says Steve Reich, *"is exactly why Mario Lemieux has a coterie of family, teammates, friends and acquaintances second to none."*

"Mario inspires loyalty and dedication in everything he does," says the man who shares the title of sports agent with his uncle, Tom Reich. For those sports fans who think HBO's Arli$$ is state-of-the-sports-agency art, nothing could be farther from the truth with Reich, Lemieux and friends.

"Our relationship with Mario has been much more than a player-client and agent thing. There is honest friendship there, a deep-rooted relationship, because that is the way Mario is."

The Reich player agency and Lemieux came together in the spring of 1988, as the hockey player cast about for an agency with deeper Pittsburgh and U.S. roots.

"Tom (Reich) was friendly with the Matthews family and we had the great fortune of getting an opportunity to interview for that position," Steve Reich recalled. *"The interview took place in the sunroom at Tom Matthews' house. I can remember that day vividly; it was the first time we had ever met Mario. We were in baseball and not in hockey at that time, but we were huge sports fans and Mario was one of the most exciting things to happen in Pittsburgh sports."*

FOLLOWING PAGE 178 ➜

Shortly thereafter, a business relationship developed.

"Things developed because we learned to listen. Mario is a very quiet, very intuitive kind of guy and he listens a lot before he talks. He's very methodical. Our relationship gradually evolved as Tom and I grew closer to him."

Out of adversity came friendship and deep-seated commitment.

"It took a few crises along the way to take it beyond business only," Steve Reich said. *"When Mario's back got real bad the first time, he went out to Los Angeles to see Dr. Watkins and I went with him. Tom was already out there and we had an opportunity to spend a lot of time with him during what was a career crisis. That's when it started to evolve into something more than business."*

Lemieux concurs.

"As our relationship grew, it certainly got a lot closer than just the agent-player relationship. It's a friendship that is very, very close and not only to myself, but to my whole family, and that's the way it has been for many years.

"I feel that once I get close to people I'm very loyal to them and try to keep in touch as much as I can, even though I'm fairly busy owning a team and being a player now. I do keep in touch with pretty much all of my friends."

DOUG CAMPBELL IS AN ACTIVE PART OF THE INNER CIRCLE OF CONTRIBUTORS THAT BRING THEIR SPECIAL EXPERTISE TO TEAM LEMIEUX.

Other contributors, partners and friends came into the Inner Circle, including Tom Grealish and Chuck Greenberg, and later, Tom Rooney, Ken Sawyer and Doug Campbell.

"These people all have their special expertise, and bring unique talents to the mix of what they call in Pittsburgh, Team Lemieux," Mario laughed. *"But the most important title each one carries is friend. I trust them implicitly, just as I do my teammates on the ice. I am blessed to have such friends."*

Judge Bruce McCullough of the bankruptcy court became an important cog, an unpaid mediator in the process. *"Outside of Mario, the most important part of the process was Judge McCullough, a remarkable, imposing man who was a top-drawer lawyer before he became a judge,"* Campbell said. *"He took a big interest in the case and guided us through some very rocky areas."*

SMG concessions proved pivotal in the final agreement. The Philadelphia concern dropped its rent charge to $1.8 million per year, and gave the team more than $3 million annually from suites, advertising, food sales and parking. In addition, SMG signed a deal to turn over management of the arena to the team in 2004, eight years earlier than called for in its lease with the city.

SMG also invested $5 million in the team in return for a seat on the board of directors, while Fox Sports Net gave the Lemieux group a $10 million letter of credit and $9 million annually in a new TV deal.

"Those were very positive things, agreements that gave us an idea that our financial plan could work so that we could have a competitive team and make a profit," Lemieux said. *"The renegotiation of the arena deal gave us a better base, and the TV contract was very, very important to make the franchise viable."*

A key component of the deal was that Lemieux had decided to move his $26 million-plus from debt to an investment in the future ownership of the team, at a value of $20 million, wiping out $6 million of the money he was owed. In addition, he added $5 million of his own money to the new effort.

As a result, Lemieux would become the Penguins' chairman, president and chief executive officer.

"I had kicked the idea around for several days from every angle I could think of," Lemieux said. *"I figured that the best way to start a completely new phase of my life was with a clean slate, no strings attached. I could do that by rolling everything I was owed into equity and, besides, it would improve the chance we had to make the franchise work and pay its way."*

MARIO LEMIEUX scores twice and contributes a pair of assists as the Pens continue their mastery over the floundering Hawks. Jaromir Jagr, with two, and defenseman Hans Jonsson, with a goal in a second straight game, round out the scoring against a beleaguered Jocelyn Thibault.

CHICAGO 2   PITTSBURGH 5

His closest advisors claim that those second-guessing the motivation for Lemieux's efforts to purchase the team obviously had not studied his character in previous situations.

Happy partners all. Craig Patrick, Mario Lemieux and NHL Commissioner Gary Bettman

MARIO WAS **AMAZING**

BECAUSE HE CAME TO **UNDERSTAND** THE WHOLE

BANKRUPTCY PROCESS VERY QUICKLY

|Steve Reich|

"The money Mario was owed was not an issue because he could have played somewhere else and earned it back in two or three years," said agent Steve Reich. *"When Mario made his incredible fight through cancer, he showed that his determination had no boundaries. His taking on the complex issue of the Penguins' future demonstrated it again. Just as he was determined to come back and play at a high level after his illness, no matter what it took, he tackled the task of gaining control of the franchise, which had many roadblocks, with the same grit."*

Campbell has only high praise for Lemieux and his efforts to make the ownership idea work.

"Mario was amazing because the guy came to understand the whole bankruptcy process, an extremely complex deal, very quickly and it was the same for the entire financial picture. He did a better job for the other creditors than anyone else could have done. All the creditors were paid in full with no cut corners like in many bankruptcy settlements.

"That it was such a high-profile case made it even more difficult. The bankruptcy process is a little like making sausage. It's not something you should do in public. But Mario wanted everything out in the open. He went straight in the front door on everything."

Large in the venture's success was the team of top level associates Lemieux attracted to the project, both as direct participants and investors: Tony Liberati had been chief financial officer for the DeBartolo group, the Penguins owner in the 1980s; Tom Grealish was a Pittsburgh businessman who served as executive director of the Mario Lemieux Foundation, which Mario had formed in 1993. They produced lists of potential investors in the franchise.

An important breakthrough came when Lemieux was in Florida talking to potential investors. Ronald Burkle, a grocery store magnate from California, a business associate of Liberati and a friend of Tom Reich, was on his way home from Europe and agreed to meet Lemieux at a private airport.

Mario Lemieux with his personal attorney Chuck Greenberg

CRAIG PATRICK

When Penguins' chairman/CEO Mario Lemieux said that the team's most important move in the 2001 off-season was to sign general manager Craig Patrick to a new contract, he was serious.

Potential turnover in playing personnel and a lengthy list of player contracts to be negotiated were large factors heading into the "new era" of franchise history. But making certain the team's anchor through its decade of accomplishment and upheaval was firmly in place was critical to the team's future in Pittsburgh.

In one June week, Patrick was elected to the Hockey Hall of Fame in the builders' category and signed a new five-year contract to continue as executive vice-president and GM of the team he joined in 1989. He had quickly built the Penguins into an NHL power that won Stanley Cup championships in 1991 and '92 with a series of trades that ranks among the finest accomplishment of any executive in NHL history.

LESTER PATRICK (CENTER) AND SONS LYNN AND MUZZ AFTER THE SILVER FOX'S INDUCTION INTO THE HOCKEY HALL OF FAME IN TORONTO.

NHL history is a Patrick family story in which Craig is the latest – but continuing – chapter. Through much of the twentieth century, a Patrick was in a prominent position in professional hockey and the NHL. Craig joins his grandfather Lester and great uncle Frank – two of hockey's most important founding fathers – and his father Lynn, a player and executive for more than 40 years, in the Hall. His uncle Murray (Muzz) was an NHL player and executive, too.

"For as long as I can remember, talk in our home was about hockey," Patrick said. "There wasn't much of a chance that I would be involved in any other field."

Patrick played junior hockey in Montreal, earned two NCAA titles and a business degree at the University of Denver and spent eight years as an NHL player with four teams.

He was assistant GM and assistant coach of the 1980 "Miracle On Ice" U.S. Olympic team, before joining the Rangers as director of personnel. He later served as New York's GM, a post he held for five years. After two years as athletic director at his alma mater, Patrick joined the Penguins as GM in December 1989.

He hired Bob Johnson as coach, Scotty Bowman as director of personnel, and engineered a series of masterful trades to produce the Stanley Cup championship teams in 1991 and '92.

Notable was the 1998-99 season when the owners sought bankruptcy protection, as rumbles of potential missed paydays were heard and the team lurched from one fiscal crisis to another. Such ownership and front-office upheaval can destroy a team and its performance, but Patrick's calm demeanor and astute handling of the situation produced another solid campaign.

"Craig was truly remarkable through that season, which was one of constant rumors and problems," said Tom McMillan, the Penguins vice-president, communications/marketing. "There were many really anxious times, but he carried on as if everything was normal and that rubbed off on the team and the organization."

CRAIG PATRICK, THE ARCHITECT OF THE PENGUINS' TWO STANLEY CUPS, CELEBRATED ALONGSIDE THE PLAYERS HE ACQUIRED.

Loyalty is another Patrick strength. He acknowledged that he could have earned more money had he made himself available for other offers when his contract with the Penguins expired in 2001.

"I'm paid well enough, but Pittsburgh is the city where my family wants to live and I want to work," Patrick said. "Sure, the challenge is a big one, but when has winning not been that way?"

The one-hour meeting ultimately brought Burkle on board with a $20-million investment in the Penguins, a move inspired by Burkle's admiration for Lemieux as an athlete plus his efforts to keep the Penguins in Pittsburgh.

"Having Ronald Burkle involved was an unbelievable boost to the project's credibility," Lemieux said. *"It helped us attract several investors to the plan. I was starting to find out that business moved in unusual ways."*

The Lemieux group's first "D-Day" was June 24, 1999, when Judge Bernard Markovitz of the bankruptcy court ruled in their favor ahead of the SMG, Fox and the NHL "Doomsday plan" which likely would have moved the team to Portland, Oregon. On September 3, the Lemieux group was granted ownership of the Penguins franchise and the immediate target was to build the strong organization necessary to make their plan function within a tight budget.

Ken Sawyer, who had worked for the NHL for 14 years as the league's chief financial officer, was hired. Pittsburgher Tom Rooney, a former Penguins' executive and a cousin of Dan Rooney, the owner of the NFL Pittsburgh Steelers, joined as chief operating officer.

Mario Lemieux and chief operating officer Tom Rooney

"Ken and Tom were very important in the make-up of our management team," Lemieux said. "From the start, one of the keys, I felt, was to surround myself with some guys who had been successful before and had been there in business and who understood the hockey business as well.

"Ken Sawyer was perfect, spending 14 years with the NHL and it was important to bring him in. Tom Rooney knew the Pittsburgh scene well, had been with the team when I started, and left for another company. I was fortunate to get him to come back and work for the Penguins."

Rooney was director of marketing for the Penguins in the DeBartolo era and for the previous 10 years had operated outdoor concert venues.

Fast forward two years: The Penguins earned a profit of more than $2 million in the 2000-01 season, boosted, of course, by Lemieux's return as a player and a berth in the conference final.

Owner Lemieux is confident—but realistic—about Pittsburgh's future as a small market team trying to compete against big-budget clubs.

"We set a budget and we will stick to it carefully because there's simply no other way we can keep the team viable," Lemieux said.

"I know we have a top-level team in the front office with Tom Rooney and Ken Sawyer in the revenue and financial sides, and Craig Patrick in charge of the hockey side."

There are two Lemieux teams within the Penguins organization, one in the front office and the other on the ice.

Both are very adept at stick-handling.

ST. LOUIS **3**   **5** PITTSBURGH

Everybody joins Mario Lemieux in comeback mode as the Penguins overcome a 3-1 deficit, sparked by their leader's three-point performance (a goal and two assists). After allowing a goal to Keith Tkachuk at 4:11 of the second period, rookie netminder JOHAN HEDBERG slams the door to record his fifth win in seven games.

42 MARCH 31, 2001 GAME 85

Debut Two was in the books, but the buzz continued. The sports world was

in All-Mario, All-the-time mode, and each revelation or factoid was greed-

ily swallowed. One voice previously unheard was that of Nathalie Lemieux,

who laughingly admitted, *"the wife is almost always the last to know"* in

the case of her celebrated spouse's comeback. *"I knew deep down that*

something unusual was going on and I asked him about it many times. He

said he needed the exercise to lose a little weight. Then one night we were

going out for dinner, and we were stuck in traffic on the way downtown.

That's when he told me he was going to play again."

ANOTHER DANCE

## CHAPTER 9

NATHALIE LEMIEUX · COMEBACK · BIOTONIX · 2000-01 SCORING

No one knew better than Nathalie how unsatisfying was her husband's departure from the game in 1997.

"My only worry was that a big reason why he had quit was that he didn't like the way the game was going, the way it was being played with all the restraining fouls, and maybe that hadn't changed," she said. "But I knew he would come back only if he was certain that he could do it at a high level. If he had any doubts, even small ones, about being just another player, he would not have returned."

Interest in Lemieux's return had attracted more than 200 news media representatives to Pittsburgh for the game with Toronto. During a press conference with the horde after the game-day morning skate, Lemieux expressed nervousness about his return and cautioned that he would be nowhere near his peak to start the comeback.

"I'm not at the level, or close to it, that I want to be at and I'm hoping the excitement of being back will help to carry me through it," he said.

"Being patient and not trying to rush things will be the key for me and I hope everyone is patient with me. Three-plus seasons is quite a long time to be away from game action and it will take time for me get used to the pace and speed and contact of the game. But I'm hoping to get back in the groove in two or three weeks."

That night, ticket scalpers, a rare sight in recent years outside The Igloo, were getting $500 a ticket for the game.

IF HE HAD **ANY DOUBTS ABOUT BEING** JUST

Attendance was a standing-room-only crowd of 17,148, the majority rising to give Lemieux a five-minute ovation before the banner-lowering ceremony and the opening face-off.

The ovation swelled when Lemieux notched his first comeback point on Jaromir Jagr's goal 33 seconds into the game. When the final buzzer sounded on Pittsburgh's 5-0 victory, the night's work for the team's CEO included a goal and two assists, 23 shifts, and total ice time of 20 minutes and 46 seconds. Linemate Jagr, who admittedly had been in a funk in recent weeks, chipped in with two goals and two assists once reunited on a forward line with 66.

"I didn't skate flat out all the time I was on the ice, but I had more stamina and was less tired at the end than I thought I would be," Lemieux said. *"There were moments when it* seemed strange to be in a game again, times when I hesitated just a little before I made a move, something that should become automatic as I play more."*

Lemieux quickly established that his first-game-back effort was no fluke. Three nights later in a 5-3 win over the Ottawa Senators, he had a goal and three assists. After eight games in mid-January, he had 19 points (nine goals and 10 assists), above his NHL-leading career average of 2.005 points per game.

Lemieux did not attempt to outskate opponents in the early games of his comeback. Instead, he allowed his incredible skills and instinct to do the job while his legs gained strength and his body adjusted to the grind of the heavy schedule. As Gordie Howe described his play in his concluding season, 1979-80, his 32nd as a pro: *"I'm poetry in slow motion."* Lemieux played a deliberate, brainy game.

"A triumph for velvet hands and a Mensa head," wrote Michael Farber of *Sports Illustrated*.

ANOTHER PLAYER, HE WOULD NOT HAVE RETURNED

|Nathalie Lemieux|

A TRIUMPH FOR VELVET HANDS AND A MENSA HEAD

| Michael Farber, *Sports Illustrated* |

"My first goal was to play better than I had in 1997, when my back was bad and my stamina was low," Lemieux said. *"I will never be as good as I was in the Cup years, but then I was a lot younger with less mileage on my body. I'm confident I can get pretty close to that, but it will depend on my back holding together and getting my legs to where I want them. After a few games, I was able to carry the puck through the neutral zone like old times, a really encouraging advance."*

In mid-January games, after the euphoria of his return had turned into the grind of the schedule, Lemieux discovered that very large opponents left little room for skill guys.

Hal Gill (6-7, 235 pounds) of the Boston Bruins and Zdeno Chara (6-9,255) of the New York Islanders pushed, crowded and leaned on No. 66.

"It seemed that in the time I was away from the game, the players got bigger, much bigger," Lemieux said. *"There are some giants in this league and they don't leave much room to work. Players like Gill and Chara make a good case for the need to enlarge the ice surface."*

To keep pace with other teams as the "grind" part of the schedule and the playoffs approached, the Penguins, a team built on speed and finesse, much of it with a European influence, added some muscle in changes to the roster.

In late December, defenseman Marc Bergevin, a childhood friend and teammate of Lemieux, was acquired from St. Louis and GM Craig Patrick really went to work on bulking up the Pens in January: defenseman Jiri Slegr, the team's top offensive blue-liner, was dealt to the Atlanta Thrashers, while forwards Steve McKenna (6-8, 255), Krzystof Oliwa (6-5, 235) and Wayne Primeau (6-3, 220) were acquired in trades and tough forward Bill Tibbetts (6-2, 215) was recalled from the minors.

Last, but not least, power forward Kevin Stevens, a fan favorite for his excellent work on Lemieux's line in 1991-92 and 1992-93, rejoined the team from the Philadelphia Flyers in exchange for defenseman John Slaney.

Those additions supplied an opening for critics of Lemieux over his previously expressed concerns about goon hockey and restraining fouls.

"A hockey club needs a variety of players because not all our opponents have the same approach," Lemieux said. *"The players we added give us a better chance to handle certain clubs, the ones that with big players who specialize in a physical game."*

INTERNET SOLUTION

After years of suffering in silence, an "eHealth" solution to Mario Lemieux's celebrated back problems was awaiting him as he returned to his hometown for a game in February.

The Penguins would lose to the Canadiens for the second time in three tries since the Comeback, but Mario would emerge a winner from his trip home. Two days before the Penguins met the Habs for the third time in eight weeks, Mario and Tom Plasko quietly slipped into town and visited the headquarters of BioTonix, a Montreal-based company with a leading-edge, Web-based program that would make Plasko's task of maintaining the health of The Back much easier.

"Mario heard about BioTonix through a relative and the two of us, along with his father, visited their offices. They put Mario through the paces," said Plasko.

"The paces" is a Web-based, biomechanical measurement system that focuses on a person's posture. Light-reflective markers are placed at specific reference spots on the patient's body and a series of four pictures in different views – including anterior (front), posterior (back) and lateral (sides). *"The pictures will identify a person's posture deviations or misalignments, and the computer will provide printouts of the deviations. We then recommend a 10-week exercise program with daily charts and instructions that are specifically designed to correct the problems,"* said Sylvain Guimond of BioTonix.

"Our client is the health professional whose patients are usually serious athletes who need the fittest bodies possible to make a living." Among some of the earliest proponents of the system were a quartet of then-Atlanta Braves, pitcher John Smoltz and infielders Walt Weiss, Keith Lockhart and Tony Graffanino. The BioTonix system also was tested with good results at the 1996 Olympic Games in Atlanta. *"The real advantage is that the health professional sends the pictures to us via the Internet, and we return the program he needs by the same medium,"* added Guimond. *"You can work with people anywhere in the world as long as they are on-line."*

Posture deviation is primordial in that rounded shoulders may lead to breathing problems, a tilted pelvis may lead to lower back strain and misalignments of the hips, ankles and feet may lead to an increased incidence of sports injuries.

"Mario had a vertical flexion problem; if you think from the hips, he was always at a forward tilt," said Plasko. "Always leaning forward like this put a lot of pressure on his back, which led to a shortening of the hip flexors.

"On February 26, 2001, he had a forward protrusion, and at his pelvis the right side was a little higher than his left. On March 21, he was already back a little bit," Plasko added. The read-outs identify deviations by degrees, but that can also identify misalignment by weight. "They weighed Mario's head and it actually weighed 19.5 pounds; at one time it weighed 28.7. The actual weight of his head and trunk was 155, but with the forward lean, that reading was 246 pounds. That's his effective weight; or how much forces are exerted on the joint (hip)."

BioTonix and Plasko combined forces and went to work on Mario Lemieux.

"We did deep trigger points, actually getting some muscles to release, and were elongating him, stretching him with the tools that were put together by BioTonix. We did neck strengthening stuff for his cervical deviation (the head).

"On a game day, we had a package that started with the warm-up, and then some abdominal curls, side curls and isometrics in the morning. And then he did three series of stretches, one of which was a figure four stretch, a psoas (lower back) stretch and a hamstring stretch. Pre-game, we did the same thing with the warm-up, and then we did the hip flexor, hamstring stretch and pre-game massage, to let those muscles release."

How has Mario Lemieux responded?

"It has saved my comeback," he admitted.

"About three weeks after I returned to play, I started having some back problems and I kept trying to play through it, but I wasn't able to play very well because of this. After seeing Sylvain and his people in Montreal with Tom, we began the directed exercise and stretching program two weeks later. I was pain-free and I've remained that way until today. I've always had back pain, as far as I can remember, and all of a sudden one day to get up and be pain-free over a long period of time is quite an amazing thing."

Adds Guimond: "Mario underwent the standard 10-week directed exercise and stretching program after his postural deviations were measured, and the results are excellent. But, by no means do we need to stop there.

"We can work with Tom Plasko on an ongoing maintenance program, or especially on designing a program that will put him in optimal shape for next winter's Olympic Games in Salt Lake City, and for the rest of his career."

The first dark cloud on the sunny Lemieux horizon came when he left a February 9 workout early, his back in an old-time lock.

"It was a freak thing," he explained. "Early in the practice, I reached for the puck and my back went out on me. I was all jammed up, just like the old days, where I couldn't tie my skates. I can't deny having a few anxious days."

This time there was a solution, however, as the team's massage therapist Tom Plasko and BioTonix combined to effect a long-term "cure."

The result was a personalized 10-week exercise regimen that went a long way toward alleviating his chronic back pain.

"Two weeks after I started the new exercise program, I had no pain for the first time in 15 years," Lemieux said. "I had no problems or pain for the rest of the season and the playoffs. At one time, I knew if I couldn't put on my own socks in the morning, I was in for a bad day. That's why it amazes me that something so simple has made such a change."

Just like old times, some magnificent Lemieux efforts were scattered throughout the schedule. A brilliant game was one in which he scored all three Penguins' goals in a 3-1 win over the Montreal Canadiens, the 40th three-goal game in his career.

Montreal goalie Jose Theodore, who wasn't in the league when Lemieux had retired, could only shake his head and smile.

PITTSBURGH 1   4 ISLANDERS

Mario Lemieux sits out his second game of the spring, and CHRIS TERRERI, recently acquired from New Jersey, stops 35 shots as Pittsburgh loses the season series to the Islanders. Second-period goals by Dave Scatchard and Claude Lapointe break a 1-1 tie and carry New York to victory.

43

APRIL 2, 2001

GAME 79

LEMIEUX'S RETURN
GAVE THE NHL

Also like old times, there were frustrating days. After a 4-2 loss at Minnesota, Lemieux was critical of the expansion Wild for their dull, non-attack approach. That led to a lively exchange between Lemieux and Wild coach Jacques Lemaire, a passionate proponent of the neutral-zone trap who had coached New Jersey to a Stanley Cup in 1995.

"It would be hard to get fans to pay to see a team playing the trap all the time," Lemieux suggested.

Lemaire, 55, countered quickly, tweaking his fellow veteran.

"I'll make a comeback and play, even at my age, if I can get a guarantee that no one will hit me or back check when I have the puck, which is what Mario seems to want," he said.

Lemieux got his revenge in a rematch only three days later, however, scoring both goals in a 2-1 win over the Wild at Mellon Arena.

Super Mario's appearance also turned the NHL All-Star Weekend at Denver into a special occasion. When the league's elite gathered for the game between teams representing North America and the World, he was the center of attention.

In many ways, the All-Star Weekend turned into a celebration of Lemieux, his return to the game and the surge in interest he injected into the NHL.

"It seems that interest in the NHL had hit a flat spot because a wonderful group of great stars had either retired or were nearing the end of their careers," said Red Kelly, who played on eight Stanley Cup winners with the Detroit Red Wings and the Toronto Maple Leafs.

The voice of the Neutral Zone Trap, Minnesota Wild coach Jacques Lemaire.

192

A BIG LIFT
WHEN IT NEEDED ONE

|Red Kelly|

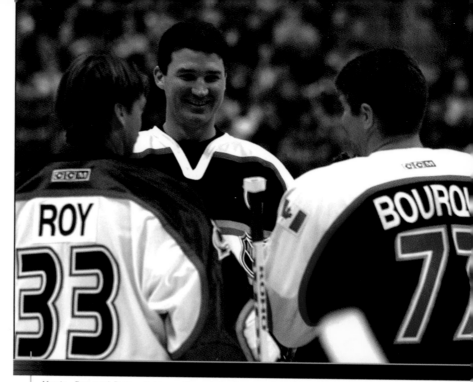

Mario, Pat and Ray... a generation of Quebec-produced, Hall-of-Fame hockey players share a smile at the All-Star Game. Mario and Patrick Roy also share a birthday, October 5, 1965.

"That's happened before when there was a change in the top players. Just as Gordie Howe and Rocket Richard lit up the league in the post-war years, and then Bobby Hull in the late 1950s and early 1960s when interest lagged because the Montreal Canadiens (five consecutive Cup wins from 1956 to 1960) were so dominant. Then Bobby Orr's arrival really helped the 1967 expansion work, and Guy Lafleur took over in the 1970s. Then along came Wayne Gretzky and Mario Lemieux, ruling the 1980s and into the 1990s."

Kelly's analysis was dead on. With injuries, holdouts, playing funks, and other situations, the stars who were supposed to pick up the slack and carry the NHL into the new millennium, among them Eric Lindros, Paul Kariya, Teemu Selanne, Steve Yzerman, Sergei Fedorov, Chris Pronger, Rob Blake, Joe Sakic and Peter Forsberg, were not getting the job done, individually or collectively.

Storied teams with huge followings, the Philadelphia Flyers, Boston Bruins and Montreal Canadiens among them, were decimated by injuries and defections, or both, for several consecutive seasons.

Everywhere in the NHL, team marketing directors and ticket sales departments wrung their hands and prayed for a savior.

And along came Mario.

Red Kelly said it for everyone: *"His return gave the NHL a big lift when it needed one."*

During the All-Star Weekend, Lemieux announced that he wanted to be "a big part" of Team Canada in the 2002 Olympic Games in Salt Lake City. The general manager of the Canadian team, someone named Wayne Gretzky, immediately named 66 to the squad and appointed him team captain.

What had league sales departments turning cartwheels was the new, media-friendly Mario Lemieux. Le Magnifique had played in eight previous All-Star games, injuries and illness keeping him out of five others, scored four goals in one, three in another. He always had been a reluctant participant in the media schmoozefest that is All-Star Weekend, but in Denver he was Mr. Congeniality, front-and-center at all interview sessions, packing the room to overflowing for sit-down interview sessions.

Lemieux won many friends among writers and broadcasters who once had knocked him when he performed his gentle, self-effacing Act of Contrition for his formerly aloof and occasionally abrasive approach. As Paul Hunter wrote in *The Toronto Star*: *"He* (Lemieux) *exhibits a passion for hockey that seemed so absent previously. More than just a joy to watch, now he is also a joy to be around."*

"I really learned a great deal in the two years since I took over as team owner," Lemieux admitted. *"I realize that I did far less than I could have earlier. I know now how important it is for me to try to promote the game and give time to the media and the fans. At this point in my career, I'm willing to do that. When I was younger, I was really uncomfortable doing it because, basically, I'm a somewhat shy, private person and I always felt that the less people knew about me the better."*

When his new pre-game exercise preparation program eased the back problems, Lemieux stepped up his game and his enjoyment of playing hockey. Gone was the almost sour approach of the pain-laden mid-1990s, replaced by a small boy's sheer joy at being on skates.

TAMPA BAY 2 4 PITTSBURGH

JAROMIR JAGR scores twice, to increase his lead in the scoring race to six points, as Pittsburgh doubles the visiting Bolts. Mario Lemieux assists on a pair of goals, increasing his comeback point total to 73, on 34 goals and 39 assists.

44 GAME 80 APRIL 4, 2001

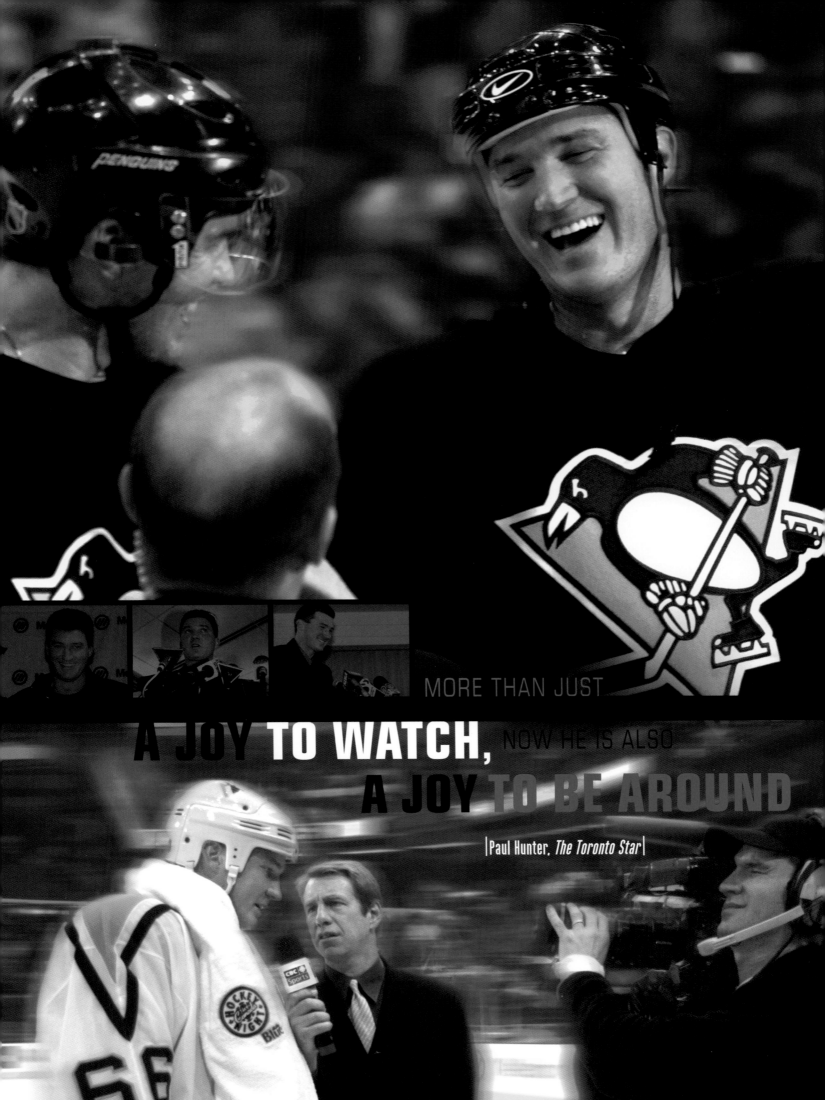

MORE THAN JUST
A JOY TO WATCH, NOW HE IS ALSO
A JOY TO BE AROUND
|Paul Hunter, *The Toronto Star*|

GM Patrick experienced the metamorphosis up close.

"I watched him play when the pain was very intense," Patrick said. *"I remember one night in Madison Square Garden when we really needed the points, and Mario dressed when he should have been in bed. To go on the ice from the bench, he handed his stick to a teammate, sat on the boards, used both hands to lift one leg over, then both hands to lift the other leg over, retrieved his stick and played a shift. To see him play close to pain-free after he came back was a great joy."*

In late February, Lemieux announced that his legs felt stronger than since early in his career and he stepped up his game, carrying the puck more, fore-checking more aggressively and checking deep in his own zone.

"This is maybe the best time in my life," Lemieux said. *"To have the chance to play one more time has been great. I think I didn't really know how much I loved to play hockey until I stopped."*

When the NHL trading deadline approached in March, speculation had the Penguins making a major deal for a serious run at the Stanley Cup.

I THINK **I DIDN'T REALLY KNOW HOW MUCH I LOVED** TO PLAY

Frequent rumbles had the team following the NHL's annual "rent-a-star" routine, picking up an impact player like power forward Keith Tkachuk of the Phoenix Coyotes or defenseman Rob Blake of the L.A. Kings for the end of the season and the playoffs, and then moving them when the season ended. Tkachuk was dealt to St. Louis, however, and Blake ended up in Colorado.

Instead, Patrick made a small trade that would loom large in the team's post-season picture when he sent defenseman Jeff Norton to the San Jose Sharks in exchange for defenseman Bobby Dollas and goalie Johan Hedberg.

HOCKEY,
UNTIL **I STOPPED**

|Mario Lemieux|

Jose Theodore, Montreal	3	4	3
Roman Cechmanek, Philadelphia	3	3	3
Olaf Kolzig, Washington	3	2	4
Jocelyn Thibault, Chicago	2	3	2
Kirk McLean, Rangers	1	2	2
Roberto Luongo, Florida	2	3	1
Mike Vernon, Calgary	1	1	3
Patrick Lalime, Ottawa	1	1	3
John Vanbiesbrouck, Islanders	2	3	0
Kevin Weekes, Tampa Bay	2	1	2
Brent Johnson, St. Louis	1	1	2
Martin Brodeur, New Jersey	3	1	1
Curtis Joseph, Toronto	1	1	2
Damian Rhodes, Atlanta	1	1	2
Manny Fernandez, Minnesota	1	2	0
Byron Dafoe, Boston	2	2	0
Martin Biron, Buffalo	1	0	2
Norm Maracle, Atlanta	1	0	2
Sean Burke, Phoenix	1	0	2
Rick DiPietro, Islanders	1	0	2
Milan Hnilicka, Atlanta	1	0	2
Guy Hebert, Anaheim/Rangers	2	1	0
Ed Belfour, Dallas	1	1	0
Chris Terreri, Islanders	1	1	0
Vitali Yeremeyev, Rangers	1	1	0
Arturs Irbe, Carolina	1	0	1
Jamie McLennan, Minnesota	1	0	0
Ron Tugnutt, Columbus	1	0	0
Patrick Roy, Colorado	1	0	0

GAME NUMBER

TEAM / LEMIEUX	DATE	OPPONENT	RESULT	GOALIE	GAME POINTS		YEAR TOTAL		
					GOAL	ASSISTS	GOAL	ASSISTS	POINTS
37 / 1	Dec.27	Toronto	5-0	Joseph	1	2	1	2	3
38 / 2	Dec.30	Ottawa	5-3	Lalime	1	3	2	5	7
39 / 3	Jan.3	Washington	3-2	Kolzig	1	1	3	6	9
40 / 4	Jan.5	Montreal	3-4	Théodore	1	2	4	8	12
41 / 5	Jan.8	@Washington	5-3	Kolzig	0	2	4	10	14
42 / 6	Jan.9	@Boston	2-5	Dafoe	2	0	6	10	16
43 / 7	Jan.12	Islanders	4-3	Vanbiesbrouck	1	0	7	10	17
44 / 8	Jan.13	@Islanders	5-6	Vanbiesbrouck	2	0	9	10	19
45 / 9	Jan.15	Anaheim	3-2	Hebert	0	0	9	10	19*
46 / 10	Jan.17	@Phoenix	4-5	Burke	0	2	9	12	21
47 / 11	Jan.19	@Dallas	5-6	Belfour	1	0	10	12	22
48 / 12	Jan.21	@Chicago	4-0	Thibault	1	0	11	12	23
49 / 13	Jan.24	Montreal	3-1	Théodore	3	0	14	12	26
50 / 14	Jan.27	@Atlanta	5-1	Hnilicka	0	2	14	14	28
51 / 15	Jan.30	Atlanta	6-3	Rhodes	1	2	15	16	31
52 / 16	Jan.31	Philadelphia	1-5	Cechmanek	1	0	16	16	32
53 / 17	Feb.7	Philadelphia	9-4	Cechmanek	1	1	17	17	34
54 / 18	Feb.10	New Jersey	5-4	Brodeur	0	1	17	18	35
55 / 19	Feb.11	@Minnesota	2-4	McLennan	0	0	17	18	35*
56 / 20	Feb.14	Minnesota	2-1	Fernandez	2	0	19	18	37
57 / 21	Feb.16	@New Jersey	4-4	Brodeur	1	0	20	18	38
58 / 22	Feb.17	Columbus	3-2	Tugnutt	0	0	20	18	38*
59 / 23	Feb.19	Colorado	1-5	Roy	0	0	20	18	38*
60 / 24	Feb.21	Florida	3-2	Luongo	1	0	21	18	39
61 / 25	Feb.23	Rangers	6-4	Yeremeyev	1	0	22	18	40
62 / 26	Feb.25	Islanders	6-1	DiPietro	0	2	22	20	42
63 / 27	Feb.28	@Montreal	2-4	Théodore	0	1	22	21	43
64 / 28	March 2	@Rangers	7-5	McLean	2	2	24	23	47
65 / 29	March 3	@Washington		Did not play					
66 / 30	March 7	Washington	3-4	Kolzig	1	1	25	24	49
67 / 31	March 8	@Atlanta	5-3	Maracle	0	2	25	26	51
68 / 32	March 10	Calgary	6-3	Vernon	1	3	26	29	55
69 / 33	March 12	@Rangers	3-3	Hebert	1	0	27	29	56
70 / 34	March 14	Islanders	1-3	Terreri	1	0	28	29	57
71 / 35	March 16	@Florida	6-3	Luongo	2	1	30	30	60
72 / 36	March 17	@Tampa Bay	1-5	Weekes	1	0	31	30	61
73 / 37	March 20	Boston	2-2	Dafoe	0	0	31	30	61*
74 / 38	March 23	@Carolina	3-5	Irbe	0	1	31	31	62
75 / 39	March 25	@New Jersey	4-2	Brodeur	0	0	31	31	62*
76 / 40	March 27	Buffalo	4-1	Biron	0	2	31	33	64
77 / 41	March 29	Chicago	5-2	Thibault	2	2	33	35	68
78 / 42	March 31	St.Louis	5-3	Johnson	1	2	34	37	71
79 / 43	April 2	@Islanders		Did not play					
80 / 44	April 4	Tampa Bay	4-2	Weekes	0	2	34	39	73
81 / 45	April 7	@Philadelphia	3-4	Cechmanek	1	2	35	41	76
82 / 46	April 8	@Carolina		Did not play					

* Did not score

The Moose is Loose. Johan Hedberg was plucked from the Manitoba Moose to backstop the Pens in the 2001 playoffs.

While Lemieux's return was the year's biggest hockey story in Pittsburgh and the entire NHL, Hedberg's arrival belonged in the Cinderella category. A native of Leksand, Sweden, Hedberg, 27, was in his third season of North American minor pro play with the Manitoba Moose of the International League after five terms in the Swedish Elite Division, when the Pens acquired him.

Pittsburgh's goaltending had been "iffy" all season as Jean-Sebastien Aubin was injured and inconsistent and Garth Snow had missed a large part of the second half with a groin injury. The team's scouts had watched Hedberg closely and felt he had the right stuff to be an NHL goalie. He had a 2.56 average and a 23-12—7 record with the Moose.

Hedberg made his NHL debut against the Florida Panthers—that team's only full house of the season—and faced 44 shots in a 6-3 victory. He lost the next night to the Lightning in Tampa Bay, but finished the season with seven wins and a tie in his nine starts, and a 2.64 average to grab the top goaltending job for the playoffs.

The Penguins finished sixth in the Eastern Conference with 96 points, third in the Atlantic Division behind the New Jersey Devils and Philadelphia Flyers. Owners of a 15-14-6-1 mark for first 36 games of the season, they built a 27-14-3-2 record after Lemieux arrived and upped their offensive production by a goal a game.

Lemieux counted 35 goals, 76 points, in the 43 games he played. That pace over the full 82-game schedule would have given him 66 goals —NHL leader Pavel Bure of the Panthers had 59—and 145 points. Jagr won his fourth consecutive scoring championship with 121 points, and was the only player in the NHL to outscore his linemate from the time after Mario returned, 84 points to Lemieux's 76.

But in the second last game of the schedule at Philadelphia, Jagr injured his shoulder when hit by Dan McGillis of the Flyers, an injury that would hamper him through the playoffs. Despite the Jagr injury, Lemieux was optimistic about himself and the team heading into the post-season.

"I feel better and I am moving more easily, the best I've felt through my whole career,"
he said at season's end. "The new program was
good for my overall strength and keeping my
back loose. I feel very strong on my skates,
especially in handling the puck.

"I know what a great feeling it was to win
the Stanley Cup twice. Another one now would
be even better. The big reason I came back was
the playoffs and the fact that we have a good
shot at making it to the final."

While Mario, the player, was buoyed by
what happened on the ice, Lemieux, the owner,
was ecstatic with what had transpired at the box
office, where every ticket was sold after his
return — 24 straight sellouts in the regular
season. His presence in the lineup boosted the
team's revenue by $3.5 million.

Mario Lemieux scores a goal and a pair of
assists as Pittsburgh races ahead to a 3-0 first-
period lead, only to have the hometown Flyers win
the game in overtime on a goal by JOHN LECLAIR.
It is the second power-play score of the game
for the rangy winger who had spent most of
the season on the injury list.

PITTSBURGH **3**   PHILADELPHIA **4** | OT

Playoff tickets were snapped up, too, as
the Penguins prepared to face familiar rival
Washington in the first round. It was the sixth
playoff meeting between the clubs since 1991.

*Ivan Hlinka has been a low-key presence
behind the Pittsburgh bench.*

Lemieux did not have a shot on goal in the opener as strong checking stifled the Penguins, and a goal by sniper Peter Bondra gave the Capitals a 1-0 win. In his post-game comments, Lemieux said that he wasn't frustrated by the strong defensive work, but he was frustrated by repeated questions about being frustrated. He also lauded the work of goalie Hedberg, brilliant in giving his team a chance to win, although they had been outplayed solidly.

The second game was a Lemieux effort staged many times in his career, a goal and an assist in a 2-1 win, all goals in the first period. The Penguins checked as strongly as the Caps had in the opener. A Lemieux shot, going wide of the net, struck Stevens' arm and went into the net. After Bondra tied the score, Lemieux's forechecking forced a turnover, and he made it to the front of the net to backhand in a Jagr pass.

"Through my career, I've always been determined to bounce back and give a big effort in the next game against a team that shuts me down," Lemieux said.

Hedberg caught on in a big way with the Pittsburgh fans in a Game 3 shutout. He acquired the nickname Moose because he wore a blue mask from his previous IHL team, not wanting to change his luck by wearing a new mask in Penguin colors. That caliber of play continued in the sixth game, with Pittsburgh a win away from advancing. An exceptional piece of Super Mario legerdemain with a hockey stick produced the important first goal. Lemieux controlled a bouncing puck, pulled it to his backhand to elude a poke-check by goalie Olaf Kolzig, fought off a hook by Calle Johansson, and executed a small dance move over Johansson's stick to tuck the puck in the net.

PITTSBURGH 6   4 CAROLINA

For the second consecutive game Pittsburgh races ahead to a 3-0 first-period lead, only to have the opposition tie the game. This time, however, the Pens prevail, as ALEXEI MOROZOV leads the way with two goals and rookie netminder Johan Hedberg turns aside 27 shots.

202

46 APRIL 8, 2001 GAME 82

A goal by Martin Straka gave the Pens a 4-3 overtime win and sent them to the second round. Hedberg established himself as a quality major league goalie, allowing only 10 scores in the six games while Lemieux finished with four goals and seven points, two of the goals game-winners. He played 31 minutes and 42 seconds in the clinching game, strong in all areas of the ice through the overtime, an indication that his newfound approach to conditioning had paid off.

Pittsburgh is Moose City: a special promotion had Pens fans "howling for Hedberg" during the playoffs.

That moved the Penguins into the second round against the Buffalo Sabres, who had eliminated the Philadelphia Flyers in a six-game series, wrapping up the set with an 8-0 victory. Rookie Hedberg was matched against the Sabres' Dominik Hasek, twice the NHL's most valuable player and three times the top goalie.

Pittsburgh and Buffalo would battle ferociously to Game Seven overtime to settle the series, but it was a Human Highlight move by 66 with the Penguins seconds away from elimination in Game Six, that told the tale.

Despite his shoulder injury, Jagr was the center of attention in the opener. First, he made a brilliant offensive move, pulling three Sabres to one side of the ice, then feeding a long backhand pass to Lemieux to send 66 in for the opening—and winning—goal. In the second period, however, the rangy Czech left the game in the second period after a check by Alexander Zhitnik of the Sabres. That set off several days of controversy about the nature of the injury. Because NHL teams, Penguins included, do not want opponents to know the location, even the existence, of players' injuries, no details of Jagr's ills were announced. Speculation ranged from a charley horse to a knee injury to a separated shoulder.

Jagr missed the second game, won, 3-1, by the Penguins when the Sabres made an assortment of attempts to belt Lemieux.

Big Sabre defenseman Jay McKee discovered that colliding with the large Lemieux was a risky task. In the second period, McKee had Lemieux lined up for a hard hit and, while Lemieux spent several seconds on his knees, shaking out the cobwebs, McKee was forced out of the game with a concussion. Lemieux's head glanced off McKee's helmet and struck the Sabre on the cheek.

"The McKee hit came out of nowhere," Lemieux said. *"I was carrying the puck at center, and I was going to dump it in anyway. He looked as if he would continue going back, and he came around sideways at me. After that, I don't remember because I was knocked out for a couple of seconds. As soon as I realized he was down, I got up and went to the bench. I didn't want to show I was hurt at all."*

Although Jagr returned for the third game, the Sabres won the next three, taking 4-1 and 5-2 wins at Pittsburgh and a 3-2 win in Buffalo on an overtime goal by ex-Pen Stu Barnes. They then held a 2-1 lead in the sixth game with less than two minutes to play when the miracle worker showed he still had a trick or two in his bag. Lemieux twice needed on-ice visits by the trainer when felled by blows to his head with the knee and the stick of Sabres' Vaclav Varada.

THROUGH MY CAREER, I'VE ALWAYS BEEN DETERMINED TO BOUNCE BACK

|Mario Lemieux|

The "miracle" came with goalie Hedberg on the bench for an extra attacker as time ran out on the Penguins' season. Lemieux was parked off the right edge of Hasek's crease when a shot from the point by the Pens' Alexei Kovalev struck the skate of the Sabres Curtis Brown and was deflected high in the air. Hasek and the other players on the ice lost track of it, Lemieux didn't, and when it landed with a bounce in the crease at his feet, Lemieux needed two whacks at it to gain control and push it into the net.

"I saw the puck in the air all along and I think I was the only one who knew where it was," Lemieux said. *"I just picked it up coming down, and I was waiting for the last second when it would hit the ice—not showing where the puck was. It was just instinct to wait and wait until the last second, but I was surprised no one else saw it and I was able to get it by Hasek."*

Straka's second overtime winner of the playoffs after 11:29 of extra time sent the series to a seventh game, which was won on an overtime goal by defenseman Darius Kasparaitis.

Although Pittsburgh claimed victory in the second game of the series in New Jersey, the Penguins were never really in it and succumbed in five games, done in by the superior depth of the Devils, who used four lines and three defense pairs in a regular rotation. Head coach Larry Robinson never was forced to shorten his bench to stay competitive, a luxury that the Penguins' Ivan Hlinka did not have.

Lemieux admitted that he was out of gas during the series against the Devils. That admission, plus Lemieux's revelation that Jagr played with a separated shoulder, was a big part of the story.

"I think I played too much in key situations against Washington and Buffalo, and killing penalties and playing hard defense really took a lot out of me," he said. *"I think that hurt our chances of going to the final. If Jagr had not been injured, he would have carried more of the load and I might have had a little more left at the end.*

Mario shares a word with Martin Brodeur of the New Jersey Devils.

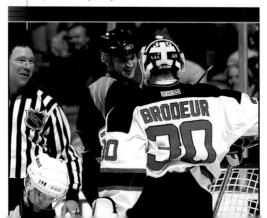

"Jagr's shoulder was separated and that really affected his play, even the way he skated. The way he plays at his best means going into the corner with two guys on him and holding them off with his arm. But he couldn't do it because the strength just wasn't there."

For Lemieux, who looked at the situation from two different viewpoints as owner and player, the overall emotion was elation at the team's success in moving into the NHL's version of The Final Four. Other positives were the development of good young players such as goalie Hedberg and Andrew Ference—an aggressive and skilled defender—his own good health and the boost to the team's financial situation by his comeback and the playoff success.

"I took a heavy workload in the playoffs with no pain whatsoever because the new training and preparation program I started a couple of months ago has really helped," Lemieux said. "But I can't deny I hit a wall physically and did not produce the offensive numbers I wanted and the team needed all the way through the playoffs.

"But the playoffs are difficult at the best of times because you play every second day and after being out more than three years, to play around 26 minutes a game was tough. I have no excuses, absolutely none. I was part of a team and we all tried our best to get us to that Cup. I'm proud of the good shot we took at it."

Lemieux, who had dominated the playoffs during the 1991 and 1992 Stanley Cup years, discovered that things had changed. Depth and the total team game was the key to playoff success in the new millennium.

"No one dominates the playoffs now and the best player can be a defensive defenseman or a checking forward," he said. "You're not going to win on a big shooter, a 60-goal scorer, or a rushing defenseman. The game has changed in the past few years, a move to much more of a team game. A team must have a system of play strongly in place, stick to it and take pride in it."

Finally, the big question: How had the Lemieux comeback turned out?

"I think it has been a success," the player replied.

Did he think the team's CEO would have the same conclusion in his season's post mortem, a day or two hence?

Mario laughed out loud.

"Yeah, I'm pretty sure he'll agree with me."

He paused for effect: "I think I might even ask him for a raise."

JUNE 9, 1984 At the NHL Amateur Entry draft held in Montreal, the Penguins use the No. 1 pick overall to select Mario Lemieux.

OCTOBER 11, 1984 In his first NHL game, on his first shift, and on his first shot, rookie Mario Lemieux scores his first NHL goal. He adds an assist, but the Penguins lose 4-3 to the Bruins in their season opener at Boston.

APRIL 7, 1985 Mario Lemieux becomes the third NHL rookie to register 100 points, when he scores a goal in a 7-3 loss to the Capitals at Washington.

DECEMBER 31, 1985 Mario Lemieux scores four goals (his first career hat trick) and adds two assists (for his first six-point game) in an 8-4 win at St. Louis.

MAY 26, 1986 He wins the Lester Pearson Award as the Outstanding Player in the NHL, in a vote by the NHL Player's Association members.

MARCH 12, 1987 Mario Lemieux scores his seventh career hat trick and adds two assists as the Penguins beat Quebec 6-3. He becomes the fifth player in club history to record 50 goals in a season.

SEPTEMBER 13, 1987 His goal at 10:07 of the second overtime gives Team Canada a 6-5 win over the Soviet Union, and ties their best-of-three Canada Cup final. Two nights later, he scores the series' winner with 1:26 remaining in the third period.

JANUARY 12, 1988 Mario Lemieux has a pair of goals in a 5-5 tie with the Islanders to move past Wayne Gretzky into first place in the NHL scoring race. He goes on to win the Art Ross Trophy with 168 points, breaking Gretzky's eight-year stranglehold.

APRIL 3, 1988 Mario Lemieux becomes the fourth player in NHL history to score 70 goals in a season, in a 4-2 win over Hartford.

JUNE 8, 1988 Mario Lemieux wins the Art Ross (scoring) and Hart (MVP) trophies, becoming the first Penguins' player to win either award.

OCTOBER 15, 1988 Mario Lemieux scores twice and adds six assists, for eight points, as the Penguins defeat the Blues, 9-2.

DECEMBER 31, 1988 Another NHL first; Lemieux scores five goals in five different ways (power play, shorthanded, even-strength, penalty shot, and empty net) in an 8-6 win over New Jersey.

FEBRUARY 26, 1989 His three assists allow him to join select company, Bobby Orr and Wayne Gretzky, as the third NHL player to reach 100 assists in a season.

MARCH 30, 1989 Mario Lemieux sets an NHL record with a 13th shorthanded goal of the season, and adds three more goals in Pittsburgh's 9-5 loss to the visiting Whalers.

APRIL 25, 1989 Mario Lemieux ties five NHL playoff records with five goals and three assists in a 10-7 win over Philadelphia, in Game Five of the Patrick Division finals. Lemieux scores four goals in the first period, including three in seven minutes.

FEBRUARY 19, 1990 Penguins announce that Mario Lemieux, the NHL's leading scorer, will miss the rest of the regular season (six weeks) while undergoing therapy for a herniated disk in his lower back.

JULY 11, 1990 Mario Lemieux undergoes back surgery to repair a herniated (fourth lumbar vertebra) disk. He would eventually miss the first 50 games of the 1990-91 season when an infection/inflammation (diskitis) would result.

MAY 25, 1991 Mario Lemieux scores a goal and three assists as the Penguins defeat the North Stars, 8-0, at Minnesota, in Game Six of the Stanley Cup final. The win gives Pittsburgh its first Stanley Cup championship, and Lemieux is awarded the Conn Smythe Trophy as playoffs MVP.

JUNE 1, 1992 Pittsburgh beats Chicago, 6-5, in Game Four of the Cup final to win a second straight championship. Lemieux becomes the second player in NHL history to win the Conn Smythe Trophy two years in a row.

MARCH 2, 1993 Mario Lemieux has a goal and an assist in his first game back in almost two months since undergoing radiation treatment for Hodgkin's disease, in Pittsburgh's 5-4 loss in Philadelphia.

APRIL 9, 1993 Mario Lemieux scores five goals to lead Pittsburgh to a 10-4 win over the Rangers at New York. The Penguins set an NHL record with their 16th consecutive victory.

JUNE 17, 1993 Lemieux strikes the mother-lode in silverware as winner of the Art Ross, Hart, Masterton and Lester B. Pearson awards.

AUGUST 29, 1994 Mario Lemieux announces that he will sit out the 1994-95 NHL season, due to fatigue from his previous illnesses.

OCTOBER 26, 1995 Mario Lemieux scores three times to become the first Penguin (and 20th NHL player) to score 500 career goals.

JANUARY 26, 1997 Mario Lemieux ties an NHL record with four goals in the third period as Pittsburgh wins 5-2 at Montreal. It is his 13 career four-goal game, tying the NHL record shared by Wayne Gretzky and Mike Bossy.

FEBRUARY 4, 1997 Mario Lemieux scores his 600' goal (in his 719' game, one more than it took Gretzky), as the Penguins defeat Vancouver, 6-4. Lemieux becomes the first player to score 600 goals while spending his entire career with one team.

APRIL 5, 1997 Mario Lemieux formally announces that he will retire at the end of the 1996-97 season. At the time of his announcement, he leads the NHL in scoring with 117 points.

NOVEMBER 17, 1997 Mario Lemieux, Bryan Trottier and Glen Sather are inducted into the Hockey Hall of Fame, in Toronto. Lemieux becomes the seventh player to gain immediate induction, without having to wait three years after retirement.

NOVEMBER 19, 1997 Pittsburgh Penguins retire jersey No. 66 in honor of Mario Lemieux, in a pre-game ceremony before a 3-3 tie against the Boston Bruins.

SEPTEMBER 3, 1999 Lemieux's ownership group takes control of the Pittsburgh Penguins.

DECEMBER 11, 2000 Mario Lemieux announces that he is coming out of retirement to play for the Penguins.

DECEMBER 27, 2000 After a three-and-a-half-year layoff, Lemieux picks up a point on his first shift, finishing the night with a goal and two assists in Pittsburgh's 5-0 win over the visiting Toronto Maple Leafs.

DECEMBER 30, 2000 Mario Lemieux scores a goal and adds three assists to become the 10 NHL player to amass 1,500 career points.

MARCH 23, 2001 Mario Lemieux is named team captain when Canada announces the selection of the first eight players on its 2002 Olympic hockey team, in Salt Lake City.

MARCH 29, 2001 Mario Lemieux scores twice to set an NHL record for most career goals by a player who has spent his entire career with one team. He moves ahead of Detroit's Steve Yzerman (645 goals) in a 5-2 win over the visiting Chicago Blackhawks.

648 REGULAR SEASON GOALS – BREAKDOWN

#	DATE	OPPONENT	ASSISTS	PD	TIME	GOALIE	SCORE
SEASON 1984-85 (43)							
1	10/11/84	at Boston	UNASSISTED	1	2:59	Pete Peeters	3-4
2	10/31/84	at New Jersey	UNASSISTED	1	7:32	Glenn Resch	7-6
3	11/14/84	at Winnipeg	Mantha, Warren Young	OT	3:54	Marc Behrend	4-3
4	11/16/84	at Vancouver	Warren Young, Hillier	3	16:18	Frank Caprice	6-7
5	11/17/84	at Los Angeles	Babych, Bodger	1	6:11	Daren Eliot	3-5
6	12/12/84	vs. NY Islanders	Warren Young, Babych	2	4:35	Kelly Hrudey	4-3
7	12/19/84	vs. New Jersey	Warren Young, Bullard	2	19:34	Glenn Resch	2-3
8	12/22/84	at NY Islanders	Mantha, Bullard (PPG)	2	19:00	Billy Smith	2-5
9	12/26/84	vs. NY Islanders	Warren Young, Belanger	2	11:00	Kelly Hrudey	6-5
10	12/26/84	vs. NY Islanders	Bullard, Warren Young	2	19:35	Kelly Hrudey	6-5
11	12/29/84	at Quebec	PENALTY SHOT	2	13:39	Mario Gosselin	2-10
12	1/12/85	vs. Edmonton	Warren Young, Babych	1	0:36	Andy Moog	4-3
13	1/12/85	vs. Edmonton	Warren Young, Babych (PPG)	3	7:30	Andy Moog	4-3
14	1/16/85	vs. Washington	Maxwell	2	12:25	Pat Riggin	4-5
15	1/16/85	vs. Washington	McDonnell, Chabot (PPG)	3	14:58	Pat Riggin	4-5
16	1/17/85	at Washington	Shedden, McDonnell (PPG)	3	9:59	Bob Mason	2-6
17	1/19/85	vs. Chicago	Shedden, Loney (PPG)	2	8:22	Murray Bannerman	5-4
18	1/25/85	at Calgary	Charlesworth, Babych	1	16:45	Don Edwards	6-6
19	1/25/85	at Calgary	Babych, Mantha	2	1:30	Rejean Lemelin	6-6
20	1/26/85	at Edmonton	Babych, Maxwell	3	1:52	Grant Fuhr	3-6
21	1/30/85	vs. Toronto	Babych, Buskas	1	1:19	Tim Bernhardt	5-6
22	2/7/85	at New Jersey	McCarthy	1	11:27	Glenn Resch	3-6
23	2/14/85	at Chicago	McCarthy, Warren Young	1	15:41	Murray Bannerman	4-5
24	2/14/85	at Chicago	Buskas, Warren Young	2	5:05	Murray Bannerman	4-5
25	2/20/85	vs. Calgary	Warren Young	1	5:11	Rejean Lemelin	6-3
26	2/20/85	vs. Calgary	Gatzos (PPG)	3	16:46	Rejean Lemelin	6-3
27	2/22/85	vs. NY Rangers	Loney	3	15:07	J. Vanbiesbrouck	3-8
28	2/23/85	at Minnesota	Maxwell	1	2:51	Don Beaupre	3-1
29	2/25/85	vs. Minnesota	McDonnell, Bodger (PPG)	3	0:35	Gilles Meloche	5-4
30	3/2/85	vs. NY Rangers	Shedden (PPG)	1	8:41	Glen Hanlon	5-4
31	3/3/85	at NY Rangers	Warren Young	2	4:16	J.Vanbiesbrouck	3-7
32	3/9/85	at Boston	Rissling, Bodger (PPG)	1	5:52	Pete Peeters	6-5 (OT)
33	3/13/85	vs. Boston	Shedden	3	11:32	Pete Peeters	3-7
34	3/16/85	vs. NY Rangers	UNASSISTED	1	15:11	J. Vanbiesbrouck	5-0
35	3/17/85	at Hartford	McGeough, Babych	3	17:37	Mike Liut	3-4
36	3/19/85	vs. Philadelphia	McCarthy, Fox	1	4:55	Pelle Lindbergh	3-5
37	3/26/85	at NY Rangers	McDonnell, Bullard	2	16:03	Glen Hanlon	4-5
38	3/27/85	vs. New Jersey	Hannan	1	0:39	Glenn Resch	4-3
39	3/30/85	at New Jersey	Mantha, Bullard (PPG)	2	10:49	Ron Low	4-6
40	3/30/85	at New Jersey	UNASSISTED	3	0:11	Ron Low	4-6
41	4/2/85	at NY Islanders	Mantha, Bullard (PPG)	1	7:54	Kelly Hrudey	3-4
42	4/3/85	vs. Detroit	Weir, Warren Young	1	18:33	Greg Stefan	2-3
43	4/7/85	at Washington	Babych, Warren Young	2	16:08	Pat Riggin	3-7
SEASON 1985-86 (48)							
44	10/10/85	vs. Montreal	Shedden, Cunneyworth	1	5:18	Patrick Roy	3-5
45	10/16/85	at Chicago	Mantha, Johnson (PPG)	1	10:29	Murray Bannerman	5-5
46	10/16/85	at Chicago	Johnson (PPG)	3	13:59	Murray Bannerman	5-5
47	10/23/85	at Toronto	Bullard, Lindstrom	1	8:49	Don Edwards	5-4
48	10/23/85	at Toronto	Buskas	3	15:01	Don Edwards	5-4
49	10/24/85	vs. Toronto	Lindstrom, Johnson (PPG)	2	5:38	Tim Bernhardt	6-4
50	10/24/85	vs. Toronto	Shedden, Ruskowski	3	19:08	Tim Bernhardt	6-4
51	10/26/85	vs. Quebec	Bodger, Buskas	2	8:16	Mario Gosselin	4-4
52	11/2/85	at Montreal	Mantha	2	3:16	Doug Soetaert	4-4
53	11/9/85	vs. Chicago	UNASSISTED (PPG)	3	15:51	Murray Bannerman	3-1
54	11/13/85	at Vancouver	UNASSISTED	3	0:55	Richard Brodeur	6-3
55	11/16/85	at Los Angeles	Bodger, Mantha (PPG)	2	1:45	Bob Janecyk	3-4 (OT)
56	11/22/85	vs. Winnipeg	UNASSISTED (PPG)	1	19:12	Brian Hayward	8-1
57	11/24/85	at Philadelphia	Shedden, Errey	1	6:03	Darren Jensen	4-7
58	12/4/85	vs. Detroit	Ruskowski, Mantha (PPG)	3	7:31	Greg Stefan	5-2
59	12/6/85	at Buffalo	Shedden, Schmidt	3	6:48	Tom Barrasso	3-1
60	12/10/85	at NY Islanders	Simpson, Mantha (PPG)	1	5:13	Kelly Hrudey	4-7
61	12/11/85	vs. NY Islanders	Errey, Siren	2	3:26	Billy Smith	4-4
62	12/15/85	at NY Rangers	Simpson	2	10:40	J. Vanbiesbrouck	5-2
63	12/22/85	at Philadelphia	Ruskowski, Blaisdell	1	11:26	Bob Froese	2-3 (OT)
64	12/31/85	at St. Louis	Dahlquist, Ruskowski	1	4:18	Rick Wamsley	8-4
65	12/31/85	at St. Louis	UNASSISTED	1	9:40	Rick Wamsley	8-4
66	12/31/85	at St. Louis	Mantha, Bullard (PPG)	2	1:20	Rick Wamsley	8-4
67	12/31/85	at St. Louis	Mantha, Bodger (PPG)	3	4:53	Rick Wamsley	8-4

#	DATE	OPPONENT	ASSISTS	PD	TIME	GOALIE	SCORE
68	1/11/86	vs. Buffalo	Ruskowski, Mantha	1	15:37	Tom Barrasso	3-3
69	1/18/86	at St. Louis	UNASSISTED	2	2:52	Rick Wamsley	5-2
70	1/24/86	at Vancouver	UNASSISTED	2	15:03	Richard Brodeur	3-4
71	2/1/86	at NY Islanders	Ruskowski, Mantha	3	19:08	Kelly Hrudey	3-4
72	2/8/86	vs. New Jersey	Bodger	2	4:50	Alain Chevrier	4-0
73	2/8/86	vs. New Jersey	Bodger	3	16:37	Alain Chevrier	4-0
74	2/12/86	vs. Washington	Shedden, Buskas	1	6:20	Pete Peeters	8-1
75	2/15/86	vs. Vancouver	Mantha, Bullard (PPG)	2	15:55	Richard Brodeur	9-4
76	2/15/86	vs. Vancouver	Bullard, Frawley (PPG)	3	4:09	Wendell Young	9-4
77	2/16/86	at New Jersey	Loney, Simpson	3	13:30	Craig Billington	5-5
78	2/19/86	vs. Winnipeg	UNASSISTED	1	6:02	Marc Behrend	5-2
79	2/19/86	vs. Winnipeg	Bullard, Blaisdell (PPG)	3	7:52	Marc Behrend	5-2
80	2/21/86	at Detroit	Siren, Hannan (PPG)	2	11:11	Mark LaForest	7-3
81	2/21/86	at Detroit	Shedden, Ruskowski	3	10:43	Mark LaForest	7-3
82	2/26/86	vs. Buffalo	Bullard, Bodger	1	9:39	Tom Barrasso	5-2
83	2/26/86	vs. Buffalo	Bullard, Frawley (PPG)	2	1:38	Tom Barrasso	5-2
84	3/4/86	at Calgary	Shedden, Ruskowski	2	4:00	Rejean Lemelin	3-6
85	3/9/86	at Winnipeg	Bodger, Shedden	1	13:17	Dan Bouchard	3-5
86	3/9/86	at Winnipeg	Ruskowski	2	17:27	Dan Bouchard	3-5
87	3/12/86	vs. Boston	Duguay, Ruskowski	3	13:39	Pat Riggin	2-5
88	3/15/86	vs. NY Rangers	Duguay, Ruskowski (PPG)	2	3:23	J. Vanbiesbrouck	2-2
89	3/22/86	at Quebec	Siren, Ruskowski	1	12:01	Clint Malarchuk	7-4
90	3/22/86	at Quebec	Ruskowski, Duguay	3	9:42	Clint Malarchuk	7-4
91	4/6/86	at NY Rangers	Duguay, Simpson (PPG)	OT	0:25	Glen Hanlon	5-4 (OT)
SEASON 1986-87 (54)							
92	10/9/86	vs. Washington	Duguay, Bullard (PPG)	2	15:26	Al Jensen	5-4
93	10/11/86	vs. NY Rangers	Frawley, Johnson	1	18:54	J. Vanbiesbrouck	6-5 (OT)
94	10/12/86	at Chicago	UNASSISTED	2	16:20	Murray Bannerman	4-1
95	10/14/86	vs. Los Angeles	Ruskowski, Duguay	3	7:59	Roland Melanson	4-3 (OT)
96	10/14/86	vs. Los Angeles	Warren Young, Siren	OT	3:40	Roland Melanson	4-3 (OT)
97	10/17/86	at Buffalo	Duguay, Ruskowski	1	15:30	Tom Barrasso	7-3
98	10/17/86	at Buffalo	Simpson, Warren Young (PPG)	2	16:58	Tom Barrasso	7-3
99	10/17/86	at Buffalo	Bodger	3	7:09	Tom Barrasso	7-3
100	10/22/86	vs. Buffalo	Mantha, LaVallee (PPG)	3	14:53	Jacques Cloutier	5-4 (OT)
101	10/22/86	vs. Buffalo	Ruskowski, Siren (PPG)	3	16:02	Jacques Cloutier	5-4 (OT)
102	10/23/86	at Philadelphia	Mantha	3	8:11	Bob Froese	3-5
103	10/25/86	vs. Philadelphia	Warren Young, Mantha (PPG)	1	6:54	Ron Hextall	4-2
104	10/28/86	at Hartford	Ruskowski, Bodger (PPG)	1	19:17	Mike Liut	2-5
105	10/28/86	at Hartford	Simpson, Errey	3	1:56	Mike Liut	2-5
106	10/29/86	vs. New Jersey	Ruskowski, LaVallee (PPG)	3	14:43	Alain Chevrier	6-8
107	11/1/86	at St. Louis	LaVallee, Ruskowski (PPG)	3	6:45	Greg Millen	3-3
108	11/4/86	vs. Vancouver	Frawley, Bodger	3	10:21	Wendell Young	2-2
109	11/14/86	at New Jersey	Mantha, Bodger (PPG)	1	10:14	Alain Chevrier	4-5
110	11/15/86	vs. Quebec	Simpson, Mantha	2	2:38	Mario Gosselin	5-2
111	11/20/86	at Calgary	Simpson, Siren	3	7:25	Mike Vernon	5-2
112	11/29/86	vs. NY Rangers	Belland	1	7:30	Doug Soetaert	5-5
113	12/10/86	vs. Calgary	Bodger (PPG)	2	1:57	Mike Vernon	4-6
114	12/12/86	vs. Toronto	Mantha, Bodger (PPG)	1	5:01	Ken Wregget	8-3
115	12/12/86	vs. Toronto	Ruskowski, Bodger	1	9:35	Ken Wregget	8-3
116	12/12/86	vs. Toronto	LaVallee, Mantha (PPG)	1	13:42	Ken Wregget	8-3
117	12/12/86	vs. Toronto	Simpson, Bodger (PPG)	2	14:16	Allan Bester	8-3
118	12/20/86	vs. Philadelphia	LaVallee, Mantha (PPG)	2	15:55	Ron Hextall	4-6
119	1/21/87	at Los Angeles	Errey, Buskas	1	5:39	Roland Melanson	5-10
120	1/23/87	at Vancouver	Bodger	2	17:07	Frank Caprice	6-0
121	1/23/87	at Vancouver	McGeough, Cunneyworth	2	19:23	Frank Caprice	6-0
122	1/23/87	at Vancouver	Buskas	3	19:33	Frank Caprice	6-0
123	1/27/87	vs. Washington	UNASSISTED	2	15:58	Bob Mason	7-5
124	1/29/87	at Philadelphia	Bourque (PPG)	3	4:36	Ron Hextall	3-5
125	2/1/87	vs. Hartford	Cunneyworth, Quinn	1	19:45	Mike Liut	6-8
126	2/1/87	vs. Hartford	Ruskowski	3	16:42	Mike Liut	6-8
127	2/4/87	at Boston	Bodger, Ruskowski (PPG)	2	5:39	Bill Ranford	5-6
128	2/4/87	at Boston	Ruskowski, Quinn	2	9:54	Bill Ranford	5-6
129	2/4/87	at Boston	Buskas, Ruskowski	3	9:14	Bill Ranford	5-6
130	2/14/87	vs. Vancouver	Ruskowski, Mantha	2	6:18	Richard Brodeur	3-3
131	2/26/87	at NY Islanders	UNASSISTED	2	19:07	Kelly Hrudey	4-5
132	3/1/87	vs. St. Louis	Loney, Kontos	2	10:39	Greg Millen	5-5
133	3/3/87	at Quebec	UNASSISTED	1	15:38	Mario Gosselin	8-1
134	3/3/87	at Quebec	Bodger	2	5:21	Mario Gosselin	8-1
135	3/7/87	at Minnesota	Cunneyworth	1	0:49	Don Beaupre	7-3
136	3/7/87	at Minnesota	Siren, Buskas (PPG)	3	2:24	Kari Takko	7-3
137	3/8/87	at Winnipeg	Kontos, Buskas (PPG)	2	10:27	Eldon Reddick	5-3
138	3/8/87	at Winnipeg	UNASSISTED	3	6:30	Eldon Reddick	5-3
139	3/8/87	at Winnipeg	Cunneyworth	3	19:59	ENG	5-3
140	3/12/87	vs. Quebec	Errey	2	19:21	Mario Gosselin	6-3
141	3/12/87	vs. Quebec	Mantha, Quinn	3	18:51	ENG	6-3
142	3/12/87	vs. Quebec	UNASSISTED	3	19:28	ENG	6-3
143	3/18/87	vs. St. Louis	Schmidt, Johnson (PPG)	1	4:07	Greg Millen	5-4
144	3/28/87	at Hartford	Simpson, Schofield	2	13:33	Mike Liut	4-5
145	4/4/87	vs. Detroit	Hillier	OT	1:26	Glen Hanlon	4-3 (OT)
SEASON 1987-88 (70)							
146	10/15/87	vs. NY Rangers	Simpson (SHG)	1	14:15	Bob Froese	6-6
147	10/15/87	vs. NY Rangers	Quinn, Simmer (PPG)	2	7:32	Bob Froese	6-6
148	10/15/87	vs. NY Rangers	Cunneyworth, Quinn (PPG)	3	15:33	Bob Froese	6-6
149	10/17/87	at Montreal	UNASSISTED	3	3:20	Patrick Roy	2-3

#	DATE	OPPONENT	ASSISTS	PD	TIME	GOALIE	SCORE
150	10/21/87	vs. New Jersey	Simmer, Simpson	1	6:41	Alain Chevrier	4-5
151	10/23/87	at Detroit	Mantha, Simpson (PPG)	3	3:22	Glen Hanlon	2-5
152	10/24/87	vs. Buffalo	Joseph, Simpson (PPG)	3	10:26	Jacques Cloutier	5-3
153	10/24/87	vs. Buffalo	Simpson, Joseph (PPG)	3	1:34	Jacques Cloutier	5-3
154	10/24/87	vs. Buffalo	Hannan	3	18:55	ENG	5-3
155	10/27/87	vs. Los Angeles	Paiment	1	2:17	Roland Melanson	4-4
156	10/27/87	vs. Los Angeles	Frawley	1	17:19	Roland Melanson	4-4
157	10/31/87	at Quebec	Paiment, Siren	1	8:36	Mario Brunetta	5-4 (OT)
158	10/31/87	at Quebec	Bodger, Mantha (PPG)	2	15:09	Mario Brunetta	5-4 (OT)
159	11/3/87	vs. Philadelphia	Hannan	1	12:18	Ron Hextall	5-1
160	11/3/87	vs. Philadelphia	Bodger	2	13:22	Ron Hextall	5-1
161	11/14/87	vs. NY Rangers	Simpson	2	14:03	J. Vanbiesbrouck	3-2 (OT)
162	11/17/87	at Vancouver	UNASSISTED	2	5:14	Richard Brodeur	4-6
163	11/21/87	at Calgary	Simpson	3	14:07	Doug Dadswell	4-4
164	11/25/87	vs. Quebec	UNASSISTED	3	10:16	Mario Brunetta	6-4
165	11/25/87	vs. Quebec	Quinn (PPG)	3	19:53	ENG	6-4
166	11/28/87	vs. Washington	Coffey, Callander (PPG)	1	17:41	Pete Peeters	5-5
167	12/5/87	vs. Vancouver	Coffey, Callander	2	10:12	Kirk McLean	6-3
168	12/5/87	vs. Vancouver	Coffey	3	19:12	ENG	6-3
169	12/9/87	vs. Calgary	Cunneyworth, Callander	3	1:45	Doug Dadswell	5-2
170	12/11/87	vs. NY Islanders	Coffey, Cunneyworth (PPG)	1	13:49	Billy Smith	6-4
171	12/17/87	at New Jersey	Hillier (PPG)	2	5:28	Alain Chevrier	7-4
172	12/17/87	at New Jersey	UNASSISTED (SHG)	2	18:34	Alain Chevrier	7-4
173	12/19/87	vs. NY Rangers	Bourque, Coffey (PPG)	2	1:47	Bob Froese	4-3
174	12/20/87	at NY Rangers	Cunneyworth (PPG)	1	14:16	J. Vanbiesbrouck	8-4
175	12/20/87	at NY Rangers	Callander, Cunneyworth (PPG)	1	19:10	J. Vanbiesbrouck	8-4
176	12/26/87	vs. Detroit	Callander, Bourque (PPG)	2	8:18	Greg Stefan	6-3
177	1/2/88	at NY Islanders	Hunter, Hillier (SHG)	2	3:11	Billy Smith	2-3
178	1/5/88	vs. Los Angeles	Cunneyworth, Hillier (PPG)	1	2:11	Glenn Healy	4-4
179	1/5/88	vs. Los Angeles	Hillier	1	19:17	Glenn Healy	4-4
180	1/5/88	vs. Los Angeles	Bodger, Cunneyworth	2	5:15	Glenn Healy	4-4
181	1/9/88	at Hartford	Simmer, Bourque	3	19:39	Mike Liut	4-5 (OT)
182	1/10/88	at Detroit	Dahlquist, Cunneyworth	1	4:31	Glen Hanlon	5-7
183	1/10/88	at Detroit	Cunneyworth, Dahlquist	1	15:14	Glen Hanlon	5-7
184	1/10/88	at Detroit	Cunneyworth	2	4:38	Glen Hanlon	5-7
185	1/10/88	at Detroit	Cunneyworth, Dahlquist (PPG)	3	16:18	Glen Hanlon	5-7
186	1/12/88	vs. NY Islanders	Cunneyworth, Bourque	3	12:15	Billy Smith	5-5
187	1/12/88	vs. NY Islanders	Quinn, Brown	3	19:53	Billy Smith	5-5
188	1/15/88	vs. Philadelphia	Hunter	1	7:23	Ron Hextall	4-5
189	1/15/88	vs. Philadelphia	Hunter (SHG)	3	6:33	Ron Hextall	4-5
190	1/16/88	at Toronto	Simmer	2	10:44	Allan Bester	4-3
191	1/19/88	at NY Islanders	PENALTY SHOT	2	13:38	Kelly Hrudey	6-4
192	1/20/88	at Chicago	Hunter, Siren	2	1:37	Bob Mason	8-3
193	1/27/88	vs. Winnipeg	Coffey, Pietrangelo (PPG)	1	9:17	Daniel Berthiaume	1-4
194	2/2/88	vs. Washington	Siren, Coffey (PPG)	1	10:55	Pete Peeters	3-2 (OT)
195	2/2/88	vs. Washington	Giffin, Coffey	OT	4:11	Pete Peeters	3-2 (OT)
196	2/6/88	vs. Hartford	Buskas, Cunneyworth	1	11:03	Mike Liut	5-4
197	2/6/88	vs. Hartford	Johnson	2	5:54	Mike Liut	5-4
198	2/13/88	at Los Angeles	Coffey (SHG)	1	11:33	Roland Melanson	7-5
199	2/21/88	vs. St. Louis	Erickson, Siren	3	3:28	Greg Millen	4-5
200	3/1/88	vs. Minnesota	Coffey	1	3:03	Don Beaupre	8-3
201	3/1/88	vs. Minnesota	Stevens, Cunneyworth (PPG)	3	14:27	Don Beaupre	8-3
202	3/7/88	at Calgary	Brown, Coffey	1	16:32	Mike Vernon	5-4
203	3/16/88	vs. Toronto	Zalapski	1	0:56	Ken Wregget	5-2
204	3/19/88	vs. Philadelphia	Stevens, Zalapski	1	10:33	Ron Hextall	7-0
205	3/20/88	at Philadelphia	Coffey, Quinn (PPG)	2	1:38	Mark LaForest	2-4
206	3/23/88	vs. Washington	Coffey, Bodger (PPG)	3	8:07	Clint Malarchuk	7-1
207	3/25/88	vs. Montreal	Brown	1	14:22	Patrick Roy	5-2
208	3/25/88	vs. Montreal	UNASSISTED (SHG)	2	13:47	Patrick Roy	5-2
209	3/27/88	at Quebec	UNASSISTED (SHG)	1	16:23	Mario Gosselin	6-3
210	3/27/88	at Quebec	UNASSISTED (SHG)	2	2:18	Mario Gosselin	6-3
211	4/2/88	at Washington	Errey (SHG)	1	9:57	Clint Malarchuk	7-6 (OT)
212	4/2/88	at Washington	Zalapski (SHG)	1	13:18	Clint Malarchuk	7-6 (OT)
213	4/2/88	at Washington	Cunneyworth, Bodger (PPG)	1	19:06	Clint Malarchuk	7-6 (OT)
214	4/2/88	at Washington	Bodger, Cunneyworth	OT	4:02	Clint Malarchuk	7-6 (OT)
215	4/3/88	vs. Hartford	Hunter, Bodger	3	19:26	ENG	4-2
SEASON 1988-89 (85)							
216	10/11/88	vs. Washington	Buskas, Brown	1	3:15	Pete Peeters	8-7
217	10/11/88	vs. Washington	Errey (SHG)	2	3:08	Pete Peeters	8-7
218	10/11/88	vs. Washington	Errey (SHG)	3	12:34	Clint Malarchuk	8-7
219	10/12/88	at Buffalo	Coffey (PPG)	1	12:35	Tom Barrasso	5-8
220	10/15/88	vs. St. Louis	Bodger, Zalapski	2	1:54	Vincent Riendeau	9-2
221	10/15/88	vs. St. Louis	Brown, Dykstra	2	8:59	Vincent Riendeau	9-2
222	10/18/88	vs. Philadelphia	Cullen, Bodger (PPG)	2	5:17	Ron Hextall	4-2
223	10/18/88	vs. Philadelphia	Brown	2	12:33	Ron Hextall	4-2
224	10/18/88	vs. Philadelphia	UNASSISTED	3	19:55	ENG	4-2
225	10/21/88	at New Jersey	Coffey, Errey	2	9:29	Sean Burke	4-6
226	10/21/88	at New Jersey	Brown, Hillier	2	16:53	Sean Burke	4-6
227	10/22/88	vs. Chicago	Coffey, Brown (PPG)	1	3:29	Ed Belfour	7-4
228	10/22/88	vs. Chicago	Brown, Errey	3	9:25	Ed Belfour	7-4
229	10/25/88	vs. Calgary	Brown, Quinn (PPG)	1	9:31	Mike Vernon	6-1
230	10/25/88	vs. Calgary	Brown, Errey	3	1:53	Mike Vernon	6-1
231	10/29/88	at Montreal	Brown, Errey	3	10:46	Brian Hayward	5-4
232	11/1/88	vs. Vancouver	UNASSISTED	3	8:59	Steve Weeks	5-3

#	DATE	OPPONENT	ASSISTS	PD	TIME	GOALIE	SCORE
233	11/1/88	vs. Vancouver	Bodger, Guenette (SHG)	3	19:59	ENG	5-3
234	11/12/88	at Los Angeles	Coffey (PPG)	3	6:53	Glenn Healy	7-2
235	11/13/88	at Vancouver	Quinn, Cullen	3	15:34	Steve Weeks	4-2
236	11/16/88	at Toronto	Coffey, Cullen (PPG)	2	15:38	Ken Wregget	5-8
237	11/23/88	vs. NY Rangers	Zalapski, Brown (PPG)	3	19:15	J. Vanbiesbrouck	8-2
238	11/25/88	at Washington	Errey (SHG)	1	19:57	Clint Malarchuk	5-3
239	11/30/88	vs. Washington	Bourque, Brown (PPG)	2	19:57	Clint Malarchuk	6-4
240	12/6/88	vs. Chicago	Brown, Errey	1	1:28	Darren Pang	7-6
241	12/8/88	at Philadelphia	Errey (SHG)	3	19:21	Ron Hextall	3-4
242	12/10/88	vs. New Jersey	Quinn, Zalapski (PPG)	3	10:12	Sean Burke	4-4
243	12/10/88	vs. New Jersey	Brown	3	10:51	Sean Burke	4-4
244	12/14/88	vs. Los Angeles	Errey (SHG)	2	1:10	Mark Fitzpatrick	5-4
245	12/14/88	vs. Los Angeles	Bourque	3	19:30	ENG	5-4
246	12/15/88	at NY Islanders	Coffey, Cullen (PPG)	3	9:36	Kelly Hrudey	5-2
247	12/20/88	vs. NY Islanders	Johnson, Brown	2	10:29	Kelly Hrudey	5-3
248	12/20/88	vs. NY Islanders	Errey, Quinn	3	14:09	Kelly Hrudey	5-3
249	12/21/88	at Toronto	Brown, Cullen	1	10:39	Ken Wregget	6-1
250	12/21/88	at Toronto	Errey, Quinn	1	18:06	Ken Wregget	6-1
251	12/21/88	at Toronto	Coffey, Zalapski (PPG)	3	5:09	Ken Wregget	6-1
252	12/26/88	at Hartford	Zalapski, Cullen (PPG)	3	4:44	Mike Liut	4-3 (OT)
253	12/29/88	vs. Philadelphia	Brown, Dahlquist	1	16:54	Ron Hextall	2-3
254	12/31/88	vs. New Jersey	Brown	1	4:17	Bob Sauve	8-6
255	12/31/88	vs. New Jersey	Hillier (SHG)	1	7:50	Bob Sauve	8-6
256	12/31/88	vs. New Jersey	Coffey, Dineen (PPG)	1	10:59	Bob Sauve	8-6
257	12/31/88	vs. New Jersey	PENALTY SHOT (SHG)	2	11:14	Chris Terreri	8-6
258	12/31/88	vs. New Jersey	Caufield	3	19:59	ENG	8-6
259	1/10/89	vs. NY Islanders	Coffey, Bourque (PPG)	1	18:55	Kelly Hrudey	5-3
260	1/10/89	vs. NY Islanders	Coffey, Quinn (PPG)	2	5:56	Kelly Hrudey	5-3
261	1/10/89	vs. NY Islanders	Errey	3	19:45	ENG	5-3
262	1/12/89	at Minnesota	Brown, Coffey	2	0:17	Jon Casey	9-2
263	1/15/89	at NY Rangers	Cullen, Cunneyworth (PPG)	1	10:01	J. Vanbiesbrouck	4-6
264	1/15/89	at NY Rangers	Brown, Coffey (PPG)	1	12:27	J. Vanbiesbrouck	4-6
265	1/20/89	at Winnipeg	Brown, Errey	1	1:18	Eldon Reddick	3-7
266	1/21/89	at Edmonton	Quinn, Brown (PPG)	2	10:15	Bill Ranford	7-4
267	1/21/89	at Edmonton	Bourque	3	13:21	Bill Ranford	7-4
268	1/25/89	vs. Winnipeg	Quinn, Hillier	1	4:29	Daniel Berthiaume	5-4
269	1/28/89	vs. Detroit	Coffey (PPG)	3	16:12	Greg Stefan	10-5
270	2/3/89	vs. St. Louis	Coffey, Barrasso (PPG)	3	4:21	Greg Millen	3-3
271	2/9/89	vs. Quebec	Coffey, Bourque (PPG)	1	13:35	Mario Gosselin	5-2
272	2/11/89	at Quebec	Coffey	2	7:15	Ron Tugnutt	1-8
273	2/12/89	vs. Calgary	UNASSISTED (SHG)	2	13:44	Mike Vernon	2-4
274	2/14/89	vs. Buffalo	Cullen, Quinn (PPG)	1	15:55	Jacques Cloutier	7-3
275	2/14/89	vs. Buffalo	Coffey, Errey	3	6:39	Jacques Cloutier	7-3
276	2/14/89	vs. Buffalo	Cullen, Coffey (PPG)	3	8:36	Jacques Cloutier	7-3
277	2/17/89	at Buffalo	Coffey, Zalapski (PPG)	2	3:20	Jacques Cloutier	1-5
278	2/25/89	at NY Islanders	Coffey, Johnson	1	8:07	Mark Fitzpatrick	5-5
279	2/25/89	at NY Islanders	Coffey, Quinn (PPG)	3	6:07	Mark Fitzpatrick	5-5
280	2/26/89	at Hartford	UNASSISTED (SHG)	1	17:07	Mike Liut	6-8
281	3/7/89	at Los Angeles	PENALTY SHOT (SHG)	1	15:41	Kelly Hrudey	2-3
282	3/10/89	at Winnipeg	Bourque, Coffey	3	8:40	Tom Draper	5-1
283	3/12/89	at Chicago	Coffey, Quinn (PPG)	1	1:57	Alain Chevrier	6-5
284	3/12/89	at Chicago	Coffey, Zalapski (PPG)	2	9:39	Alain Chevrier	6-5
285	3/12/89	at Chicago	UNASSISTED (SHG)	2	10:29	Alain Chevrier	6-5
286	3/14/89	vs. Boston	Coffey, Bourque (PPG)	2	6:30	Rejean Lemelin	2-8
287	3/14/89	vs. Boston	Zalapski, Quinn (PPG)	3	10:11	Rejean Lemelin	2-8
288	3/22/89	vs. Washington	Hannan, Brown	2	12:58	Pete Peeters	4-5
289	3/22/89	vs. Washington	Coffey, Zalapski (PPG)	3	19:00	Pete Peeters	4-5
290	3/25/89	vs. New Jersey	UNASSISTED	2	2:59	Bob Sauve	5-4
291	3/25/89	vs. New Jersey	Brown, Coffey	2	3:54	Bob Sauve	5-4
292	3/25/89	vs. New Jersey	Quinn, Zalapski	3	19:55	Sean Burke	5-4
293	3/26/89	at NY Rangers	Coffey, Hillier	3	3:24	J. Vanbiesbrouck	6-4
294	3/26/89	at NY Rangers	Errey, Loney	3	19:43	ENG	6-4
295	3/30/89	vs. Hartford	Brown, Zalapski	1	7:34	Kay Whitmore	5-9
296	3/30/89	vs. Hartford	Brown, Johnson	2	14:54	Kay Whitmore	5-9
297	3/30/89	vs. Hartford	UNASSISTED (SHG)	3	11:25	Kay Whitmore	5-9
298	3/30/89	vs. Hartford	Coffey, Zalapski (PPG)	3	19:29	Kay Whitmore	5-9
299	4/2/89	at Philadelphia	Brown, Errey	2	1:24	Ron Hextall	6-5 (OT)
300	4/2/89	at Philadelphia	Loney	OT	3:38	ENG	6-5 (OT)
SEASON 1989-90 (45)							
301	10/15/89	at NY Rangers	McBain, Gilhen	2	19:14	Bob Froese	2-4
302	10/17/89	vs. Toronto	Stevens, McBain	2	14:21	Allan Bester	7-5
303	10/17/89	vs. Toronto	Gilhen, Errey	3	19:17	ENG	7-5
304	10/17/89	vs. Toronto	Johnson, Gilhen	3	19:47	ENG	7-5
305	10/26/89	at Detroit	Errey, Brown	1	10:55	Glen Hanlon	3-3
306	11/2/89	vs. NY Islanders	Errey, Callander	1	2:23	Glenn Healy	5-2
307	11/5/89	at Vancouver	Quinn, Brown (PPG)	3	14:00	Steve Weeks	3-5
308	11/9/89	at Chicago	Brown, Errey	1	4:54	Jacques Cloutier	3-4
309	11/11/89	at St. Louis	Cullen (PPG)	3	13:12	Greg Millen	3-8
310	11/14/89	vs. NY Rangers	Stevens, Errey	3	1:57	Bob Froese	6-0
311	11/16/89	vs. Quebec	Stevens, Quinn (PPG)	1	10:33	Stephane Fiset	8-2
312	11/24/89	at Washington	PENALTY SHOT (SHG)	3	4:19	Bob Mason	7-4
313	11/25/89	vs. Washington	UNASSISTED (SHG)	3	8:10	Don Beaupre	1-4
314	12/2/89	at Quebec	Errey, Stevens	1	1:20	Ron Tugnutt	7-4
315	12/2/89	at Quebec	Brown, Dineen	1	5:54	Ron Tugnutt	7-4

#	DATE	OPPONENT	ASSISTS	PD	TIME	GOALIE	SCORE
316	12/2/89	at Quebec	Stevens, Coffey	3	4:12	Ron Tugnutt	7-4
317	12/6/89	vs. Washington	Coffey, Brown (PPG)	1	2:04	Bob Mason	5-3
318	12/8/89	at New Jersey	Stevens, Hillier	3	1:54	Sean Burke	3-2
319	12/9/89	vs. Chicago	Coffey, Stevens	2	1:18	Alain Chevrier	4-6
320	12/12/89	vs. Boston	Stevens, Hillier	3	17:15	Rejean Lemelin	7-5
321	12/21/89	vs. Washington	Brown, Stevens	2	12:04	Don Beaupre	5-2
322	12/26/89	at Washington	Coffey	1	2:32	Don Beaupre	3-6
323	12/27/89	vs. NY Rangers	Errey, Coffey	1	11:39	J. Vanbiesbrouck	7-4
324	12/27/89	vs. NY Rangers	Dahlquist	3	10:48	J. Vanbiesbrouck	7-4
325	12/31/89	at NY Rangers	Coffey	3	14:10	Bob Froese	5-4
326	1/2/90	vs. Boston	Errey, Hillier	3	14:39	Rejean Lemelin	2-5
327	1/6/90	vs. Winnipeg	Coffey, Gilhen	1	2:54	Bob Essensa	5-3
328	1/8/90	at NY Rangers	UNASSISTED	1	3:25	Bob Froese	7-5
329	1/8/90	at NY Rangers	Brown, Errey	1	17:40	Bob Froese	7-5
330	1/8/90	at NY Rangers	Coffey (SHG)	2	3:19	J. Vanbiesbrouck	7-5
331	1/8/90	at NY Rangers	Zalapski, Coffey (PPG)	2	4:41	J. Vanbiesbrouck	7-5
332	1/12/90	at Washington	Brown	1	12:31	Don Beaupre	6-4
333	1/18/90	vs. NY Rangers	Tanti, Coffey (PPG)	1	6:23	Mike Richter	3-3
334	1/18/90	vs. NY Rangers	Zalapski, Coffey	3	17:03	Mike Richter	3-3
335	1/25/90	at Detroit	Brown, Coffey	1	5:49	Sam St. Laurent	5-3
336	1/28/90	at Buffalo	Stevens, Coffey (PPG)	3	10:41	Daren Puppa	2-7
337	2/2/90	vs. Edmonton	Cullen, Coffey (PPG)	2	11:18	Randy Exelby	6-3
338	2/2/90	vs. Edmonton	Coffey, Stevens (PPG)	2	18:04	Randy Exelby	6-3
339	2/2/90	vs. Edmonton	Tanti	3	19:27	Randy Exelby	6-3
340	2/3/90	at Toronto	Coffey, Zalapski (PPG)	3	0:51	Jeff Reese	4-8
341	2/6/90	vs. NY Islanders	Coffey, Cullen (PPG)	3	3:23	Mark Fitzpatrick	7-8
342	2/6/90	vs. NY Islanders	Brown, Coffey (PPG)	3	4:45	Mark Fitzpatrick	7-8
343	2/8/90	vs. Washington	Coffey, Cullen (PPG)	1	16:21	Jim Hrivnak	7-5
344	2/11/90	at Philadelphia	Recchi, Cullen	2	1:59	Ken Wregget	4-1
345	3/31/90	vs. Buffalo	Coffey, Pederson (PPG)	3	3:38	Clint Malarchuk	2-3 (OT)
SEASON 1990-91 (19)							
346	1/28/91	vs. Washington	Jagr	3	14:39	Don Beaupre	3-2 (OT)
347	1/31/91	at Philadelphia	Jiri Hrdina, Coffey (PPG)	2	15:52	Ron Hextall	2-4
348	2/8/91	at Winnipeg	Roberts, Recchi	3	12:42	Bob Essensa	2-6
349	2/11/91	at Edmonton	Coffey, Barrasso	3	6:30	Bill Ranford	5-7
350	2/14/91	vs. NY Islanders	Errey, Jagr	3	15:00	Glenn Healy	5-2
351	2/16/91	at NY Islanders	Recchi, Jagr	1	7:41	Glenn Healy	3-4
352	2/21/91	vs. Toronto	Recchi, Errey	2	12:36	Jeff Reese	11-4
353	2/24/91	at Washington	Coffey, Recchi	3	9:28	Jim Hrivnak	5-5
354	3/1/91	at Calgary	Jagr, Recchi (PPG)	2	5:30	Rick Wamsley	2-6
355	3/5/91	vs. Vancouver	Coffey, Scott Young (PPG)	1	14:12	Troy Gamble	4-1
356	3/9/91	at Hartford	Stevens	1	1:29	Kay Whitmore	5-2
357	3/12/91	vs. Montreal	Stevens, Taglianetti	1	4:58	Patrick Roy	4-4
358	3/17/91	at NY Rangers	Recchi, Errey	1	18:02	Mike Richter	4-2
359	3/17/91	at NY Rangers	Stevens, Recchi (PPG)	2	19:57	Mike Richter	4-2
360	3/19/91	at New Jersey	Errey, Roberts	2	16:39	Chris Terreri	4-5
361	3/23/91	vs. Chicago	Errey, Taglianetti	2	8:33	Dominik Hasek	5-7
362	3/26/91	at Philadelphia	Murphy (PPG)	1	9:35	Pete Peeters	3-1
363	3/26/91	at Philadelphia	UNASSISTED (SHG)	1	12:15	Pete Peeters	3-1
364	3/26/91	at Philadelphia	Murphy, Coffey (PPG)	2	10:30	Pete Peeters	3-1
SEASON 1991-92 (44)							
365	10/4/91	at Buffalo	Jagr, Stevens	3	6:18	Daren Puppa	5-4
366	10/10/91	at Philadelphia	Coffey, Recchi	3	14:10	Ken Wregget	6-3
367	10/15/91	at NY Islanders	Jagr, Jiri Hrdina	1	17:56	Glenn Healy	7-6
368	10/15/91	at NY Islanders	Stevens, Recchi (PPG)	3	9:17	Glenn Healy	7-6
369	10/15/91	at NY Islanders	Stevens, Murphy (PPG)	3	10:26	Glenn Healy	7-6
370	10/31/91	vs. Minnesota	Coffey, Recchi (PPG)	1	1:56	Darcy Wakaluk	8-1
371	10/31/91	vs. Minnesota	Jagr, Stevens	3	6:28	Darcy Wakaluk	8-1
372	11/2/91	vs. Hartford	Mullen, Stevens	1	19:47	Peter Sidorkiewicz	6-5
373	11/2/91	vs. Hartford	Mullen, Roberts	2	8:17	Peter Sidorkiewicz	6-5
374	11/8/91	at Winnipeg	Stevens, Loney	3	12:39	Rick Tabaracci	3-1
375	11/9/91	at Minnesota	Stevens, Jagr	3	10:00	Jon Casey	3-2
376	11/11/91	at NY Rangers	Mullen, Stevens	1	15:46	J. Vanbiesbrouck	1-3
377	11/13/91	vs. Edmonton	Stevens, Jagr	2	1:30	Bill Ranford	5-4
378	11/27/91	vs. New Jersey	Coffey (SHG)	3	15:39	Chris Terreri	8-4
379	11/29/91	at Philadelphia	Jagr, Coffey	2	15:48	Dominic Roussel	9-3
380	11/29/91	at Philadelphia	Jagr, Stevens	3	12:59	Dominic Roussel	9-3
381	11/30/91	vs. Philadelphia	Stevens, Jagr	1	5:33	Ken Wregget	5-1
382	12/5/91	at San Jose	Francis (PPG)	1	11:53	Jeff Hackett	8-0
383	12/5/91	at San Jose	Coffey, Recchi (PPG)	2	11:43	Arturs Irbe	8-0
384	12/10/91	vs. NY Rangers	Stevens, Mullen	2	10:59	Mike Richter	5-3
385	12/17/91	vs. San Jose	Roberts (SHG)	1	12:37	Jarmo Myllys	10-2
386	12/17/91	vs. San Jose	Recchi, Jagr (PPG)	2	9:56	Jarmo Myllys	10-2
387	12/21/91	vs. NY Rangers	UNASSISTED	1	8:08	J. Vanbiesbrouck	5-7
388	12/23/91	at NY Islanders	Murphy, U.Samuelsson (PPG)	3	13:46	Glenn Healy	6-3
389	12/26/91	vs. Toronto	Mullen, Stevens	2	16:16	Grant Fuhr	12-1
390	12/26/91	vs. Toronto	Murphy, Francis (PPG)	3	1:55	Grant Fuhr	12-1
391	12/29/91	at NY Rangers	Stevens, Jagr	3	5:51	Mike Richter	6-3
392	12/31/91	vs. New Jersey	Francis, Murphy (PPG)	2	11:00	Craig Billington	4-7
393	1/25/92	at NY Islanders	Jagr, Stevens	3	19:04	Mark Fitzpatrick	5-3
394	2/25/92	at Washington	Stevens, Mullen (PPG)	3	10:20	Don Beaupre	3-5
395	2/29/92	vs. Buffalo	Tocchet, Stevens	2	10:02	Tom Draper	5-2
396	2/29/92	vs. Buffalo	Jagr, Errey	3	16:54	Tom Draper	5-2
397	3/6/92	at San Jose	Taglianetti	1	9:47	Jarmo Myllys	7-3
398	3/10/92	vs. Calgary	Errey, Roberts	3	19:50	ENG	5-2
399	3/12/92	vs. NY Islanders	Tocchet, Errey	3	19:25	ENG	6-4
400	3/14/92	at Toronto	Stevens, Francis (PPG)	2	8:01	Grant Fuhr	3-6
401	3/19/92	vs. Quebec	UNASSISTED	1	2:23	Stephane Fiset	6-3
402	3/19/92	vs. Quebec	Francis (SHG)	2	8:15	Stephane Fiset	6-3
403	3/22/92	at Hartford	Francis, Barrasso (SHG)	2	18:21	Peter Sidorkiewicz	2-2
404	3/24/92	at Detroit	Tocchet, Stevens	2	4:50	Tim Cheveldae	3-4
405	3/26/92	vs. Vancouver	Tocchet	1	17:27	Troy Gamble	7-3
406	3/26/92	vs. Vancouver	Tocchet, Stevens	3	9:35	Troy Gamble	7-3
407	3/28/92	vs. Montreal	Stevens, Tocchet	3	0:53	Andre Racicot	6-3
408	3/31/92	vs. Philadelphia	UNASSISTED (PPG)	3	7:33	Ron Hextall	6-5
SEASON 1992-93 (69)							
409	10/6/92	vs. Philadelphia	U.Samuelsson	1	0:46	Dominic Roussel	3-3
410	10/8/92	vs. NY Islanders	K.Samuelsson	3	8:38	Mark Fitzpatrick	7-3
411	10/8/92	vs. NY Islanders	Jagr, Jennings	3	11:44	Mark Fitzpatrick	7-3
412	10/10/92	at Montreal	Tocchet, K.Samuelsson (PPG)	2	17:32	Patrick Roy	3-3
413	10/13/92	vs. Buffalo	Francis, McEachern (PPG)	2	1:36	Daren Puppa	6-5
414	10/15/92	vs. Montreal	Loney, Fogarty	2	5:52	Patrick Roy	5-2
415	10/17/92	at Hartford	Barrasso	1	16:15	Sean Burke	7-3
416	10/20/92	vs. Vancouver	Murphy, Stevens (PPG)	1	17:35	Kirk McLean	5-1
417	10/22/92	vs. Detroit	Jagr, Stevens (PPG)	1	17:02	Tim Cheveldae	9-6
418	10/22/92	vs. Detroit	Murphy	1	19:15	Tim Cheveldae	9-6
419	10/22/92	vs. Detroit	Tocchet, Stevens	3	18:28	Tim Cheveldae	9-6
420	10/24/92	at New Jersey	Francis, Tocchet (PPG)	2	18:56	Craig Billington	4-3
421	10/27/92	at Ottawa	Stevens	2	1:19	Peter Sidorkiewicz	7-2
422	10/27/92	at Ottawa	Stevens, Tocchet	2	13:16	Peter Sidorkiewicz	7-2
423	10/29/92	at St. Louis	Stevens, Stanton	1	9:35	Guy Hebert	4-6
424	10/29/92	at St. Louis	Stevens, Tocchet	2	18:54	Guy Hebert	4-6
425	11/1/92	at Tampa Bay	Jagr, McEachern	1	1:25	Wendell Young	5-4
426	11/1/92	at Tampa Bay	Stevens, Francis (PPG)	2	14:43	Wendell Young	5-4
427	11/5/92	vs. St. Louis	Tocchet, U.Samuelsson	3	5:12	Guy Hebert	8-4
428	11/7/92	at Toronto	Mullen	1	3:16	Felix Potvin	2-4
429	11/8/92	at Chicago	Tocchet, Murphy	1	4:18	Ed Belfour	2-7
430	11/10/92	at Minnesota	UNASSISTED (SHG)	3	18:39	ENG	4-1
431	11/17/92	vs. Buffalo	Murphy	2	7:01	Dominik Hasek	4-2
432	11/23/92	at NY Rangers	UNASSISTED	2	6:11	Mike Richter	5-2
433	11/23/92	at NY Rangers	Tocchet	3	18:32	J. Vanbiesbrouck	5-2
434	11/25/92	vs. NY Rangers	Paek, Jagr	1	0:14	J. Vanbiesbrouck	3-11
435	11/27/92	at Washington	Stevens	2	0:43	Jim Hrivnak	4-6
436	11/28/92	vs. Washington	Francis, Murphy (PPG)	2	13:02	Don Beaupre	5-3
437	11/28/92	vs. Washington	Tocchet	3	19:50	ENG	5-3
438	12/1/92	at NY Islanders	Mullen, Jagr	2	5:05	Mark Fitzpatrick	7-3
439	12/5/92	at San Jose	U.Samuelsson, Barrasso (PPG)	3	14:11	Brian Hayward	9-4
440	12/8/92	vs. Winnipeg	Mullen, Jagr	2	17:31	Bob Essensa	5-2
441	12/12/92	vs. New Jersey	Mullen	3	16:31	Chris Terreri	6-5
442	12/15/92	vs. Philadelphia	Tocchet, Stevens	3	11:29	Step. Beauregard	6-2
443	12/23/92	at Philadelphia	Stevens, Tocchet	1	0:41	Tommy Soderstrom	4-0
444	12/23/92	at Philadelphia	Stanton, Tippett	2	2:06	Tommy Soderstrom	4-0
445	12/31/92	vs. Toronto	Francis (SHG)	1	17:20	Grant Fuhr	3-3
446	1/2/93	vs. NY Rangers	Francis (SHG)	1	4:16	J. Vanbiesbrouck	5-2
447	1/2/93	vs. NY Rangers	Stevens, Tocchet (PPG)	3	12:06	J. Vanbiesbrouck	5-2
448	3/2/93	at Philadelphia	K.Samuelsson, Tocchet	2	1:54	Dominic Roussel	4-5
449	3/11/93	vs. Los Angeles	Francis, Mullen	2	13:41	Robb Stauber	4-3
450	3/18/93	vs. Washington	Stevens, Murphy	1	1:00	Don Beaupre	7-5
451	3/18/93	vs. Washington	UNASSISTED	1	4:28	Don Beaupre	7-5
452	3/18/93	vs. Washington	Jagr, Stevens	2	3:30	Don Beaupre	7-5
453	3/18/93	vs. Washington	Murphy (PPG)	3	5:35	Jim Hrivnak	7-5
454	3/20/93	vs. Philadelphia	Jagr, Stevens (PPG)	1	15:08	Tommy Soderstrom	9-3
455	3/20/93	vs. Philadelphia	Francis, Murphy (PPG)	2	11:13	Tommy Soderstrom	9-3
456	3/20/93	vs. Philadelphia	Stevens, Francis (PPG)	2	19:21	Tommy Soderstrom	9-3
457	3/20/93	vs. Philadelphia	Murphy, Francis (PPG)	3	16:11	Dominic Roussel	9-3
458	3/21/93	vs. Edm. (Cleveland)	Mullen, Murphy (PPG)	1	2:32	Ron Tugnutt	6-4
459	3/23/93	vs. San Jose	Stevens, Tocchet	2	14:02	Arturs Irbe	7-2
460	3/23/93	vs. San Jose	U.Samuelsson, Tocchet	3	14:08	Arturs Irbe	7-2
461	3/25/93	vs. New Jersey	UNASSISTED (SHG)	2	13:39	Chris Terreri	4-3
462	3/27/93	at Boston	Taglianetti	3	2:12	Andy Moog	5-3
463	3/27/93	at Boston	Francis, Jagr	3	10:13	Andy Moog	5-3
464	3/28/93	at Washington	Tocchet, Tippett	3	18:50	ENG	4-1
465	3/30/93	vs. Ottawa	Tocchet	3	6:57	Peter Sidorkiewicz	6-4
466	4/1/93	vs. Hartford	Murphy, Ramsey	1	3:12	Mario Gosselin	10-2
467	4/1/93	vs. Hartford	UNASSISTED	3	9:39	Mario Gosselin	10-2
468	4/3/93	at Quebec	Tocchet, K.Samuelsson	2	5:07	Ron Hextall	5-3
469	4/3/93	at Quebec	Tocchet, Stevens	2	8:12	Ron Hextall	5-3
470	4/4/93	at New Jersey	Jagr	3	19:51	ENG	5-2
471	4/9/93	at NY Rangers	U.Samuelsson	2	4:43	Corey Hirsch	10-4
472	4/9/93	at NY Rangers	Francis, Tocchet (PPG)	2	8:09	Corey Hirsch	10-4
473	4/9/93	at NY Rangers	Barrasso (SHG)	2	16:05	Corey Hirsch	10-4
474	4/9/93	at NY Rangers	Tocchet, Stevens	3	4:14	Mike Richter	10-4
475	4/9/93	at NY Rangers	Stevens, Jennings	3	11:15	Mike Richter	10-4
476	4/14/93	at New Jersey	Murphy, Tocchet	2	1:42	Craig Billington	6-6
477	4/14/93	at New Jersey	UNASSISTED (SHG)	2	12:40	Craig Billington	6-6
SEASON 1993-1994 (17)							
478	11/2/93	at San Jose	Stevens, Tocchet (PPG)	2	14:35	Arturs Irbe	3-3
479	2/12/94	vs. Dallas	Murphy, Francis (PPG)	2	5:06	Darcy Wakaluk	3-9
480	2/13/94	at Philadelphia	Francis, Stevens	3	0:34	Dominic Roussel	3-0
481	2/13/94	at Philadelphia	Stevens	3	6:13	Dominic Roussel	3-0

#	DATE	OPPONENT	ASSISTS	PD	TIME	GOALIE	SCORE
482	2/26/94	vs. Buffalo	U.Samuelsson, Francis	2	6:42	Grant Fuhr	4-3
483	2/28/94	at Florida	Greg Brown, Stevens	2	14:40	J. Vanbiesbrouck	4-3
484	3/8/94	vs. Boston	Murphy, Doug Brown	2	9:06	Vincent Riendeau	7-3
485	3/12/94	vs. NY Rangers	Murphy, Francis (PPG)	1	16:47	Glenn Healy	6-2
486	3/12/94	vs. NY Rangers	Jagr, Sandstrom	2	0:22	Glenn Healy	6-2
487	3/22/94	vs. San Jose	Jagr, Sandstrom	3	6:05	Arturs Irbe	2-2
488	3/24/94	vs. Ottawa	Sandstrom, U.Samuelsson	1	10:23	Craig Billington	5-1
489	3/26/94	at Calgary	Jagr	1	2:07	Mike Vernon	3-5
490	4/3/94	vs. Bos.(Cleveland)	Francis, Murphy (PPG)	1	16:49	Jon Casey	6-2
491	4/3/94	vs. Bos.(Cleveland)	Tocchet, Francis (PPG)	2	13:56	Vincent Riendeau	6-2
492	4/6/94	vs. New Jersey	Stevens, Murphy (PPG)	2	0:21	Martin Brodeur	3-1
493	4/6/94	vs. New Jersey	Stevens, Taglianetti	2	16:43	Martin Brodeur	3-1
494	4/11/94	vs. Ottawa	Stevens, Jagr (PPG)	2	7:01	Craig Billington	4-0
SEASON 1995-96 (69)							
495	10/8/95	at Colorado	Jagr, Zubov (PPG)	2	2:25	Jocelyn Thibault	6-6
496	10/8/95	at Colorado	Jagr, Francis (PPG)	2	19:15	Stephane Fiset	6-6
497	10/12/95	at Chicago	Sandstrom, Mironov (SHG)	3	11:49	Ed Belfour	1-5
498	10/26/95	at NY Islanders	Maciver, Jagr (PPG)	1	18:04	Tommy Soderstrom	7-5
499	10/26/95	at NY Islanders	Naslund, Maciver	3	0:19	Tommy Soderstrom	7-5
500	10/26/95	at NY Islanders	Sandstrom, Mironov	3	17:12	Tommy Soderstrom	7-5
501	10/28/95	at New Jersey	Sandstrom, Jagr (PPG)	2	7:49	Martin Brodeur	5-3
502	10/28/95	at New Jersey	Sandstrom, Naslund	2	16:34	Martin Brodeur	5-3
503	10/28/95	at New Jersey	Francis, Jagr (PPG)	2	17:34	Martin Brodeur	5-3
504	11/1/95	vs. Tampa Bay	UNASSISTED	3	14:04	J.C. Bergeron	10-0
505	11/4/95	vs. Philadelphia	Maciver, Naslund	1	16:22	Dominic Roussel	7-4
506	11/4/95	vs. Philadelphia	Jagr, Francis	3	19:36	ENG	7-4
507	11/8/95	at Ottawa	Jagr, Francis (PPG)	3	16:31	Don Beaupre	7-1
508	11/10/95	at San Jose	Sandstrom, Maciver	3	10:31	Wade Flaherty	9-1
509	11/14/95	vs. Dallas	Naslund, Francis (PPG)	1	9:43	Darcy Wakaluk	4-2
510	11/14/95	vs. Dallas	Mironov, Maciver	3	2:32	Darcy Wakaluk	4-2
511	11/18/95	vs. Washington	Jagr, Sandstrom (PPG)	2	9:36	Jim Carey	3-0
512	11/22/95	vs. NY Rangers	Francis, Jagr (PPG)	3	9:08	Mike Richter	3-4
513	11/30/95	at Boston	Naslund	1	13:21	Scott Bailey	9-6
514	11/30/95	at Boston	Naslund, Mironov	2	7:02	Scott Bailey	9-6
515	11/30/95	at Boston	Jagr, Mironov (PPG)	3	8:11	Craig Billington	9-6
516	11/30/95	at Boston	Naslund, Maciver (PPG)	3	12:24	Craig Billington	9-6
517	12/5/95	at NY Islanders	Sandstrom, Naslund	2	2:22	Tommy Soderstrom	6-3
518	12/7/95	at Montreal	UNASSISTED	2	15:56	Pat Jablonski	7-5
519	12/7/95	at Montreal	Naslund, Jagr	3	12:35	Pat Jablonski	7-5
520	12/9/95	vs. Hartford	Francis (PPG)	2	12:00	Sean Burke	6-0
521	12/13/95	at Anaheim	Smolinski, Zubov (PPG)	3	15:22	Mikhail Shtalenkhov	3-6
522	12/15/95	at Dallas	Sandstrom, Naslund	3	1:38	Darcy Wakaluk	5-1
523	12/19/95	vs. Calgary	Francis, Jagr (PPG)	1	19:45	Trevor Kidd	7-1
524	12/26/95	vs. Buffalo	Francis, Zubov	2	11:03	Steve Shields	6-3
525	12/28/95	vs. Hartford	Sandstrom, Francis (PPG)	3	1:02	Jason Muzzatti	9-4
526	12/30/95	vs. Florida	Sandstrom, Wilkinson	1	0:36	J. Vanbiesbrouck	6-5
527	12/30/95	vs. Florida	Sandstrom, Jagr (PPG)	1	7:04	J. Vanbiesbrouck	6-5
528	12/30/95	vs. Florida	UNASSISTED (SHG)	2	6:06	J. Vanbiesbrouck	6-5
529	1/5/96	vs. Detroit	Wells	2	11:43	Chris Osgood	5-2
530	1/8/96	vs. Vancouver	Jagr	3	19:53	ENG	8-5
531	1/12/96	vs. Montreal	Francis, Naslund (PPG)	2	9:10	Jocelyn Thibault	5-6
532	1/13/96	vs. San Jose	Sandstrom, Mironov (SHG)	1	1:26	Chris Terreri	8-10
533	1/13/96	vs. San Jose	Smolinski	3	13:26	Wade Flaherty	8-10
534	1/16/96	vs. Colorado	UNASSISTED (SHG)	2	15:49	Patrick Roy	2-5
535	1/22/96	vs. Boston	Zubov, Francis (PPG)	1	4:16	Bill Ranford	7-6 (OT)
536	1/22/96	vs. Boston	UNASSISTED (SHG)	OT	1:54	Bill Ranford	7-6 (OT)
537	1/27/96	vs. Philadelphia	Francis, Zubov (PPG)	1	14:35	Garth Snow	7-4
538	1/27/96	vs. Philadelphia	Murray, Sandstrom	2	4:14	Garth Snow	7-4
539	1/27/96	vs. Philadelphia	Sandstrom, Leroux	3	8:30	Ron Hextall	7-4
540	2/6/96	vs. Boston	Jagr, Sandstrom (PPG)	3	10:37	Bill Ranford	6-5
541	2/10/96	vs. Chicago	Sandstrom, Tamer (SHG)	1	6:25	Ed Belfour	6-3
542	2/18/96	vs. NY Rangers	Sandstrom, Smolinski	OT	2:17	Glenn Healy	4-3 (OT)
543	2/23/96	vs. Hartford	Smolinski, Francis (PPG)	1	7:49	Sean Burke	5-4
544	2/23/96	vs. Hartford	Francis, Zubov (PPG)	3	5:37	Sean Burke	5-4
545	2/24/96	at Montreal	Nedved, Zubov (PPG)	2	5:33	Jocelyn Thibault	3-7
546	2/27/96	at Vancouver	Jagr, Zubov (PPG)	1	1:43	Kirk McLean	7-4
547	2/27/96	at Vancouver	Naslund, Dziedzic	1	7:29	Kirk McLean	7-4
548	3/7/96	vs. Ottawa	McLlwain, Francis	1	0:18	Damian Rhodes	5-1
549	3/9/96	vs. New Jersey	Francis, Mironov	1	6:19	Martin Brodeur	3-4 (OT)
550	3/13/96	at Hartford	Francis, Mironov (PPG)	2	4:19	Sean Burke	2-3
551	3/16/96	vs. NY Islanders	Zubov, Foster (PPG)	3	18:44	Eric Fichaud	4-2
552	3/23/96	vs. Buffalo	Tamer, Leroux	2	6:00	Andre Trefilov	5-7
553	3/26/96	vs. St. Louis	Nedved, Leroux	1	3:35	Grant Fuhr	8-4
554	3/26/96	vs. St. Louis	Francis, Zubov (PPG)	1	15:37	Jon Casey	8-4
555	3/26/96	vs. St. Louis	Nedved, Jagr (PPG)	2	8:43	Jon Casey	8-4
556	3/26/96	vs. St. Louis	UNASSISTED (SHG)	2	11:15	Jon Casey	8-4
557	3/26/96	vs. St. Louis	Francis, McLlwain	3	6:08	Jon Casey	8-4
558	3/28/96	at Florida	Zubov, Daigneault (PPG)	1	18:53	Mark Fitzpatrick	3-2
559	4/4/96	vs. Washington	Kevin Miller, Leroux	2	11:56	Jim Carey	4-2
560	4/4/96	vs. Washington	Smolinski, Foster	3	18:05	Jim Carey	4-2
561	4/10/96	vs. NY Islanders	Jagr, Nedved (PPG)	3	2:34	Tommy Soderstrom	2-6
562	4/11/96	at Ottawa	UNASSISTED (SHG)	2	10:42	Damian Rhodes	5-3
563	4/14/96	at Boston	Nedved, Jagr (PPG)	1	10:58	Bill Ranford	5-6
SEASON 1996-97 (50)							
564	10/5/96	vs. Tampa Bay	Hatcher, Nedved	3	19:56	Daren Puppa	3-4 (OT)

#	DATE	OPPONENT	ASSISTS	PD	TIME	GOALIE	SCORE
565	10/8/96	at Hartford	Sandstrom, Francis (PPG)	2	9:05	Sean Burke	3-7
566	10/11/96	at Ottawa	Tamer, Sandstrom	1	10:51	Damian Rhodes	2-3
567	10/12/96	vs. Ottawa	UNASSISTED	3	12:02	Ron Tugnutt	3-2
568	10/22/96	at Edmonton	Jagr, Dziedzic	2	10:57	Curtis Joseph	2-5
569	11/1/96	at Washington	Hatcher, Klima (PPG)	3	4:11	Olaf Kolzig	2-4
570	11/6/96	vs. Edmonton	Nedved (PPG)	3	12:23	Bob Essensa	5-2
571	11/8/96	at Tampa Bay	Jagr, Francis (PPG)	1	19:07	Corey Schwab	5-5
572	11/21/96	at Philadelphia	Woolley, Olausson	3	16:20	Ron Hextall	3-7
573	11/30/96	vs. Boston	Jagr, Francis	2	1:57	Bill Ranford	6-2
574	12/6/96	at Washington	Johansson, Barnes	3	3:13	Olaf Kolzig	5-3
575	12/7/96	vs. Anaheim	Hatcher	2	16:26	Mikhail Shtalenkov	5-3
576	12/10/96	at Los Angeles	Hatcher, Woolley (PPG)	1	18:58	Byron Dafoe	5-3
577	12/11/96	at Anaheim	Francis, Hatcher (PPG)	1	3:10	Mikhail Shtalenkov	7-3
578	12/11/96	at Anaheim	Francis, Jagr	3	2:04	Mike O'Neill	7-3
579	12/17/96	vs. Boston	Daigneault, Olausson (PPG)	1	5:05	Bill Ranford	4-6
580	12/17/96	vs. Boston	Jagr	2	10:39	Bill Ranford	4-6
581	12/19/96	at St. Louis	Jagr, Kasparaitis	2	5:04	Jon Casey	4-0
582	12/19/96	at. St. Louis	Francis, Jagr (PPG)	2	14:18	Jon Casey	4-0
583	12/19/96	at St. Louis	Jagr	2	14:50	Jon Casey	4-0
584	12/21/96	vs. San Jose	Francis, Olausson	2	8:12	Chris Terreri	3-1
585	12/23/96	at Toronto	Jagr, Roche	1	15:28	Felix Potvin	6-5
586	12/23/96	at Toronto	Kasparaitis, Jagr	2	5:09	Felix Potvin	6-5
587	12/26/96	vs. Montreal	Nedved, Murray	3	14:35	Jocelyn Thibault	3-3
588	12/28/96	vs. Buffalo	Hatcher, Francis (PPG)	3	5:35	Dominik Hasek	2-0
589	12/30/96	vs. Washington	Jagr, Leroux	2	3:59	Olaf Kolzig	5-3
590	12/30/96	vs. Washington	UNASSISTED	3	19:43	ENG	5-3
591	1/4/97	vs. Tampa Bay	Woolley (PPG)	1	11:45	Corey Schwab	7-3
592	1/4/97	vs. Tampa Bay	Olausson, Francis (PPG)	2	17:40	Corey Schwab	7-3
593	1/21/97	vs. Calgary	Woolley	1	8:13	Trevor Kidd	4-2
594	1/26/97	at Montreal	Francis, Jagr	3	4:35	Jocelyn Thibault	5-2
595	1/26/97	at Montreal	Mullen, Jagr	3	9:06	Jocelyn Thibault	5-2
596	1/26/97	at Montreal	Francis	3	16:54	Jocelyn Thibault	5-2
597	1/26/97	at Montreal	UNASSISTED	3	19:29	ENG	5-2
598	2/1/97	vs. Phoenix	Moran	1	1:18	Nikolai Khabibulin	4-1
599	2/1/97	vs. Phoenix	Nedved, Woolley	1	11:30	Nikolai Khabibulin	4-1
600	2/4/97	vs. Vancouver	Francis, Jagr	3	19:04	ENG	6-4
601	2/8/97	vs. Detroit	Francis, Jagr	1	5:39	Mike Vernon	5-6 (OT)
602	2/8/97	vs. Detroit	Jagr, Woolley	1	17:20	Mike Vernon	5-6 (OT)
603	2/18/97	vs. Florida	Woolley, Hatcher	3	13:33	J. Vanbiesbrouck	4-2
604	2/18/97	vs. Florida	Nedved, Tamer	3	19:02	ENG	4-2
605	2/22/97	vs. Chicago	Hatcher, Greg Johnson	2	13:50	Jeff Hackett	2-5
606	2/22/97	vs. Chicago	Woolley, Nedved (PPG)	2	17:38	Jeff Hackett	2-5
607	3/1/97	at New Jersey	Hatcher, Mullen (PPG)	2	15:22	Martin Brodeur	3-6
608	3/26/97	at Montreal	Francis, Hatcher	3	15:59	Jocelyn Thibault	5-8
609	3/26/97	at Montreal	Francis, Olczyk (PPG)	3	19:08	Jocelyn Thibault	5-8
610	3/31/97	vs. Florida	Francis, Jagr (PPG)	2	18:30	J. Vanbiesbrouck	4-3
611	4/3/97	vs. Hartford	Jagr, Olausson	3	5:28	Sean Burke	5-5
612	4/5/97	vs. Ottawa	Jagr, Kasparaitis (SHG)	2	15:22	Ron Tugnutt	5-2
613	4/11/97	at Florida	PENALTY SHOT	3	2:28	J. Vanbiesbrouck	2-4
SEASON 2000-2001 (35)							
614	12/27/00	vs. Toronto	Jagr, Kasparaitis	2	10:33	Curtis Joseph	5-0
615	12/30/00	vs. Ottawa	Jagr, Jan Hrdina	3	19:47	ENG	5-3
616	1/3/01	vs. Washington	Jagr, Straka (PPG)	1	6:35	Olaf Kolzig	3-2
617	1/5/01	vs. Montreal	Jagr, Bergevin	3	4:56	Jose Theodore	3-4
618	1/9/01	at Boston	Jagr, Lang (PPG)	1	4:00	Byron Dafoe	2-5
619	1/9/01	at Boston	Jagr, Jan Hrdina	3	11:17	Byron Dafoe	2-5
620	1/12/01	vs. NY Islanders	Lang, Jagr (PPG)	1	2:14	Wade Flaherty	4-3
621	1/13/01	at NY Islanders	Jagr, Kovalev	1	12:28	J. Vanbiesbrouck	5-6
622	1/13/01	at NY Islanders	Corbet, Kasparaitis	2	2:25	J. Vanbiesbrouck	5-6
623	1/19/01	at Dallas	Jagr, Stevens	1	13:02	Ed Belfour	5-6 (OT)
624	1/21/01	at Chicago	Stevens, Jagr	2	19:28	Jocelyn Thibault	4-0
625	1/24/01	vs. Montreal	Stevens, Jagr	1	16:36	Jose Theodore	3-1
626	1/24/01	vs. Montreal	Jagr	2	17:28	Jose Theodore	3-1
627	1/24/01	vs. Montreal	Kovalev, Straka (PPG)	3	1:27	Jose Theodore	3-1
628	1/30/01	at Atlanta	UNASSISTED (PPG)	2	19:34	Damian Rhodes	6-3
629	1/31/01	vs. Philadelphia	Stevens, Jagr (PPG)	1	7:35	Roman Cechmanek	1-5
630	2/7/01	vs. Philadelphia	Jagr, Kovalev (PPG)	2	8:42	Brian Boucher	9-4
631	2/14/01	vs. Minnesota	Jonsson, Laukkanen	3	7:30	Manny Fernandez	2-1
632	2/14/01	vs. Minnesota	Jagr	3	16:25	Manny Fernandez	2-1
633	2/16/01	at New Jersey	Stevens, Jagr	3	4:34	Martin Brodeur	4-4
634	2/21/01	vs. Florida	Straka, Kovalev (PPG)	OT	2:10	Roberto Luongo	3-2 (OT)
635	2/23/01	vs. NY Rangers	Kovalev, Straka (PPG)	2	3:50	Vitali Yeremeyev	6-4
636	3/2/01	at NY Rangers	UNASSISTED	2	3:56	Kirk McLean	7-5
637	3/2/01	at NY Rangers	Jagr, Straka (PPG)	3	15:34	Kirk McLean	7-5
638	3/7/01	vs. Washington	Straka, Stevens (PPG)	3	13:57	Olaf Kolzig	3-4
639	3/10/01	vs. Calgary	Straka, Jagr (PPG)	2	13:47	Mike Vernon	6-3
640	3/12/01	at NY Rangers	Ference, Jagr (SHG)	3	4:43	Guy Hebert	3-3
641	3/14/01	vs. NY Islanders	Straka (PPG)	2	8:39	Chris Terreri	1-3
642	3/16/01	at Florida	Jagr, Beranek (PPG)	1	8:17	Roberto Luongo	6-3
643	3/16/01	at Florida	Straka, Jonsson	2	9:34	Roberto Luongo	6-3
644	3/17/01	at Tampa Bay	Ference, Jonsson	2	0:48	Kevin Weekes	1-5
645	3/29/01	vs. Chicago	Jagr, Jonsson	3	16:16	Jocelyn Thibault	5-2
646	3/29/01	vs. Chicago	Jagr, Jan Hrdina	3	19:26	ENG	5-2
647	3/31/01	vs. St. Louis	Kovalev, Jagr (PPG)	3	18:48	Brent Johnson	5-3
648	4/7/01	at Philadelphia	Lang, Jagr (PPG)	1	13:15	Roman Cechmanek	3-4 (OT)

PHOTOGRAPH CREDITS

Editor's Note

We have made every effort to trace the ownership of copyrighted photos. If we have failed to give adequate credit, we will be pleased to make changes in future printings.

Photos are detailed from left to right, top to bottom on the page they appear.

Photographer's name is listed in italics. Source of photo, if differing from author or copyright publication, appears in parentheses.

Year photo taken is listed, if known.

Sources abbreviations

AP	Associated Press
BBS	Bruce Bennett Studios
HHOF	Hockey Hall of Fame
JMTL	Journal de Montréal
PENS	Pittsburgh Penguins
PPG	Pittsburgh Post-Gazette
RPM	Reich Publishing & Marketing
TPP	Team Power Publishing

p. 2-3 PLAYING HOCKEY WITH AUSTIN, 2001, *Normand Pichette,* ©JMTL

p. 4 MARIO LEMIEUX IN HERITAGE SWEATER, 2001, ©Nike Hockey

p. 8 LEMIEUX FAMILY, 2000, *©Matt Polk*

p. 9 MARIO SALUTING THE CROWD, 2000, *©Matt Polk*

CHAPTER 1

p.10-11 MARIO LEMIEUX & TEAMMATES, 1984, ©BBS

MARIO RESTING ON STICK, *Bernard Brault,* ©La Presse

MARIO SHOOTS, 1984, ©BBS

PITTSBURGH VS. BOSTON, 1984, ©BBS

p.12 BANNER COMING DOWN, 2000, *©Matt Polk*

p. 13 AUSTIN & BANNER, 2000, *©Matt Polk*

p. 14 3 CHEERS FOR AUSTIN, 2000, *©Matt Polk*

MARIO FOR PRESIDENT, 2000, ©Reuters

MARIO SIGN, 2000, *©Matt Polk*

p.15 MARIO WALKING IN RINK, 2001, *©Matt Polk*

p. 16 WAYNE GRETZKY'S RETIREMENT, 1999, *Jim McIsaac,* ©BBS

p. 17 MARIO & PARENTS WITH GUY LAFLEUR, ©Lemieux Collection

p. 19 MARIO LEMIEUX WATCHING GAME, 1999, *John Heller,* ©PPG

p. 20 AGENT TOM REICH, ©Lemieux Collection

MARIO TALKING TO MEDIA, 2000, *©Matt Polk*

p.21 MARIO LAUGHING, 2000, *©Matt Polk*

MEDIA AT PRESS CONFERENCE, 2000, *©Matt Polk*

p. 22 MELLON ARENA, 2000, *©Jason Cohn*

p. 23 MARIO READY FOR ACTION, 2001, *©Matt Polk*

MARIO AT GOLF TOURNAMENT, 2001, ©Mario Lemieux Foundation

p. 24 MARIO & MICHAEL JORDAN, 2001, *Peter Diana,* ©PPG

MARIO'S SKATES, 2001, ©Nike Hockey

p. 25 DARIUS KASPARAITIS, 2001, ©BBS

p. 26 JAROMIR JAGR, 2001, ©BBS

p. 27 AUSTIN LEMIEUX, 2000, *©Matt Polk*

p. 28 MARIO KNEELING, 2000, *©Jason Cohn*

MARIO BENDING, 2000, *©Jason Cohn*

TEAM SKATING, 2000, *Jason Cohn,* ©Reuters

MARIO HEADSHOT, 2000, *Keith Srakocic,* ©AP

p. 30 MARIO TRAINING WITH JAY CAUFIELD, 2001, *©Matt Polk*

CAUFIELD & LEMIEUX TAKING A BREAK, 2001, *©Matt Polk*

p. 31 MARIO SCORING, 2000, *Jason Cohn,* ©Reuters

p. 32 TEAMMATES CELEBRATING, 2000, *©Matt Polk*

p. 33 AFTER A GOAL, 2000, *©Jason Cohn*

CHAPTER 2

p. 34 MARIO LYING ON ICE, ©Lemieux Collection

p. 35 MARIO IN HURRICANES UNIFORM, ©Lemieux Collection

p. 36 ACTION 1 & 2, ©Lemieux Collection

ACTION 3, 1978, ©Lemieux Collection

p. 37 YOUNG MARIO CELEBRATING, 1972, ©Lemieux Collection

ST. JEAN DE MATHA ICE RINK, ©Dilallo Collection

p. 38 MARIO'S 1500TH POINT, 2000, ©PENS

p. 39 PIERRETTE & JEAN-GUY LEMIEUX, 2001, *Guy Tessier,* ©TPP

ALAIN LEMIEUX AS ST. LOUIS BLUES, ©BBS

p. 40 PIERRETTE & MARIO LEMIEUX, ©Lemieux Collection

p. 41 CHRISTMAS AT LEMIEUX HOUSE, ©LemieuxBilllection

JAROMIR JAGR, 2001, *Jim McIsaac,* ©BBS

p. 42 CHAMPIONS TEAM PICTURE, 1973, ©Lemieux Collection

MOSQUITO TEAM PICTURE, ©Lemieux Collection

MARIO WITH TWO TEAMMATES, ©Fernand Fichaud

TEAM CELEBRATION, 1978, ©Lemieux Collection

p. 43 ERIC WEINRICH, 2000, *Len Redkoles,* ©BBS

HURRICANES JEAN FICHAUD & MARIO LEMIEUX, ©Fernand Fichaud

p. 44 MARTIN STRAKA, 2001, *Bruce Bennett,* ©BBS

p. 45 MARIO & FERNAND FICHAUD, 1991, ©Fernand Fichaud

p. 46 YOUNG MARIO & MARC BERGEVIN, ©Lemieux Collection

p. 47 TEAM PICTURE, ©Lemieux Collection

ANDREI KOVALENKO, 2000, ©BBS

JEAN-JACQUES DAIGNEAULT, 1989, *Bernard Brault,* ©La Presse

p. 48 YOUNG WAYNE GRETZKY, ©HHOF

ALEXEI KOVALEV, 2001, ©BBS

p. 49 MARIO SHOWING TROPHIES, ©Lemieux Collection

MARIO WITH JEAN BÉLIVEAU, ©Lemieux Collection

MARIO & YVON LAMBERT, ©Lemieux Collection

MARIO WITH PIERRE BOUCHARD & MARCEL BONIN, ©Lemieux Collection

p. 50 *6700 RUE JOGUES,* VILLE EMARD, ©HHOF

MARIO'S SKATES, 2001, *Guy Tessier,* ©TPP

CHRISTMAS SETTING, 2001, *Guy Tessier,* ©TPP

VILLE EMARD BASEMENT, 2001, *Guy Tessier,* ©TPP

MARIO'S SWEATERS, 2001, *Guy Tessier,* ©TPP

CHAPTER 3

p. 52 MARIO AS JUNIOR WITH LAVAL, ©HHOF

p. 53 MARIO LAUGHING, 1984, *Pierre Côté,* ©La Presse

p. 54 MARIO WITH JOURNALISTS, 1984, *Armand Trottier,* ©La Presse

p. 55 WAYNE GRETZKY & MARIO, 1990, *Peter Diana,* ©PPG

p. 56 MARIO IN TRAINING, 1984, *Bernard Brault,* ©La Presse

p. 57 MARIUSZ CZERKAWSKI, 2001, *Jim McIsaac,* ©BBS

p.58 ALEXEI KOVALEV, 2000, ©BBS

p.59 MARIO WITH ALBERT MANDANICI, 1984, *Bernard Brault,* ©La Presse

p. 60 JUNIOR MARIO & PAT LaFONTAINE, 1983, *Pierre Côté,* ©La Presse

p. 61 GUY LAFLEUR & JUNIOR PAT LaFONTAINE, 1983, *P.-H. Talbot,* ©La Presse

p. 62 MARIO WITH MIKE BOSSY, 1984, ©Lemieux Collection

MARIO WITH TEAM CANADA, 1983, ©Lemieux Collection

p. 63 ACTION WITH TEAM CANADA, 1983, ©Lemieux Collection

p. 64 KEITH TKACHUK, 2000, ©BBS

p. 65 MARIO ON BENCH, 1984, *Bernard Brault,* ©La Presse

p. 66 DARRYL SYDOR, 2000, ©BBS

MARIO WITH GUY LAFLEUR, 1984, ©Lemieux Collection

p. 67 EDDIE JOHNSTON BEHIND BENCH, ©BBS

YOUNG BOBBY ORR, ©BBS

p. 68 EDDIE JOHNSTON, ©PENS

p. 69 COVER *JOURNAL DE MONTRÉAL* WITH GRETZKY & LEMIEUX, March 15, 1984, *Pierre Vidricaire,* ©JMTL

p. 70 MARIO CARRYING PRESIDENT CUP, 1984, *Armand Trottier,* ©Lemieux Collection

LAVAL VOISINS ACTION 1, 1984, *Pierre Côté,* ©La Presse

LAVAL VOISINS ACTION 2, 1983, *Robert Nadon,* ©La Presse

LAVAL VOISINS ACTION 3, 1983, *Robert Nadon,* ©La Presse

p. 71 GARTH SNOW, 2001, *Bruce Bennett,* ©BBS

p. 72 TEAMMATES CARRYING MARIO, ©HHOF

p. 73 EDDIE JOHNSTON & MARIO, 1997, *©Marc Serota*

p. 74 MARIO WITH GUS BADALI, 1984, *Pierre Vidricaire,* ©JMTL

MARIO NERVOUS, 1984, ©La Presse

MARIO RUBBING HIS EYES, 1984, ©La Presse

p. 75 MARIO AT NHL DRAFT, 1984, *Armand Trottier,* ©La Presse

MARIO SCORING AGAINST MONTREAL CANADIENS, 2001, *Peter Diana,* ©PPG

CHAPTER 4

p. 76 MARIO WITH STICK & SKATES, 1984, ©HHOF

p. 77 YOUNG MARIO AS PENGUIN, 1984, ©BBS

p. 78 MARIO WITH TEAMMATES, 1984, ©BBS

p. 79 MARIO READY FOR ACTION, ©HHOF

JAN HRDINA, 2000, *Jim McIsaac,* ©BBS

p. 80 BOSTON BRUINS VS. NEW YORK RANGERS, ©BBS

p. 81 ACTION AGAINST NEW JERSEY DEVILS, 1984, ©BBS

p. 82 MARIO IN PENGUINS UNIFORM, 1984, *Bernard Brault,* ©La Presse

p. 83 MARIO ARRIVES IN PITTSBURGH, 1984, ©HHOF

MARIO LEMIEUX PLACE, 1997, *©Marc Serota*

p. 84 THE LEMIEUX FAMILY, 1997, *©Marc Serota*

PAUL STEIGERWALD, 1991, ©PENS

p. 85 MARIO & JEAN-GUY LEMIEUX, *Luc Laforce,* ©JMTL

MARIO LEMIEUX, ©HHOF

p. 86 CLASS OF '84 BROCHURE, ©PENS

MARIO IN FRONT OF CIVIC ARENA, 1984, *Pierre-Yvon Pelletier,* ©JMTL

p. 87 MARK RECCHI, 2001, *Brian Winkler,* ©BBS

MARIO BETWEEN 2 PENGUINS, 1985, ©PENS

p. 88 PIERRE LAROUCHE, 1977, ©BBS

ALEXEI KOVALEV, 2001, *Len Redkoles,* ©BBS

p. 89 MARIO WITH THE MATTHEWS, 1985, *Marlene Karas,* ©PPG

p. 90 PIERRETTE & LAUREN LEMIEUX WITH NANCY MATTHEWS, ©Lemieux Collection

p. 91 PIERRETTE & JEAN-GUY LEMIEUX, ©Lemieux Collection

ALEXEI KOVALEV, 2001, ©BBS

p. 92 MARIO LEMIEUX, 1984, ©Fred Vuich/Allsport

p. 93 DOUG SHEDDEN, 1984, ©BBS

p. 94 JAMIE McLENNAN, 2001, *Bruce Bennett,* ©BBS

p. 95 LEMIEUX VS. LUPUL, 1984, ©PENS

CHAPTER 5

p. 96 RENDEZ-VOUS '87, 1987, *Bruce Bennett,* ©PENS

p. 97 FACE-OFF GRETZKY-LEMIEUX, ©BBS

p. 98 ACTION MARIO LEMIEUX, 1985, *Fred Vuich,* ©PENS

p. 99 PENGUINS CELEBRATING, *Bruce Bennett,* ©BBS

p. 100 ACTION MARIO LEMIEUX, 2001, *©Matt Polk*

MARIO WITH VOTING BOX, ©PENS

p. 101 READY FOR ACTION, 1985, ©PENS

MARIO STEPPING ON THE ICE, 1990, *Marlene Karas,* ©PPG

MARIO VS. DETROIT RED WINGS, ©Lemieux Collection

ACTION VS. MONTREAL CANADIENS, 1985, *Marlene Karas,* ©PPG

p. 102 LEMIEUX IN ACTION, *Mark Murphy,* ©PPG

p. 103 GUY CARBONNEAU, *Robert Laberge,* ©BBS

BOB GAINEY & DENIS POTVIN, *Bruce Bennett,* ©BBS

p. 104 BUFFALO SABRES MIKE PECA, 1999, *Jim McIsaac,* ©BBS

LEMIEUX VS. CARBONNEAU, 1989, *Bernard Brault,* ©La Presse

p. 105 TERRY RUSKOWSKI, 1986, ©BBS

BILLY TIBBETTS, 2001, *Bruce Bennett,* ©BBS

p. 106 LEMIEUX & GRETZKY, 1987, *Bruce Bennett,* BBS

ROBERT LANG, 2001, ©BBS

p. 107 LEMIEUX & GRETZKY, 1987, *Bruce Bennett,* ©BBS

p. 108 LEMIEUX & SOVIET PLAYER, ©PENS

LEMIEUX-GRETZKY CELEBRATING A GOAL 1-2-3, 1987, *Bruce Bennett,* ©BBS

p. 109 PETER FORSBERG, 2001, ©BBS

MARIO LEMIEUX & MARK MESSIER, ©PENS

214

ACKNOWLEDGEMENTS

We wish to thank the following for their special participation and contributions: Albert Barbusci, Bruce Bennett, Bob Borgen, Bernard Brisset, Doug Campbell, Jay Caufield, Jason Cohn, Peter Diana, Denis Dion, Jean-Luc Duguay, Louise Fagnan, Joe Fava, Fernand and Sylvia Fichaud, Roland Forget, Anne Fotheringham, Jon Goyens, Tom Grealish, Sylvain Guimond, Jean-Guy and Pierrette Lemieux, Glenn Levy, Nancy and Tom Matthews, Tom McMillan, Barbara Pilarski, Tom Plasko, Matt Polk, Steve Reich, Tom Reich, Marc Serota, Doug Shedden, Paul Steigerwald, Duke Stump and Tyler Wolosewich.

As well, a special thank you to Mike Reisinger for his precious help throughout the production of this project.

And then, the design division of Team Power Publishing, without whom this project would never have seen the light of day: Julie Desilets, Geneviève Desrosiers, Nathalie Michaud and Brigitte Boudrias, who slaved during the hot summer months, sometimes even without air conditioning.

BIBLIOGRAPHY

Bobby Orr and the Big, Bad Bruins, by Stan Fischler, Dell, New York, 1969.

Boss, The Mike Bossy Story, by Mike Bossy and Barry Meisel, McGraw-Hill Ryerson Limited, Scarborough, Ont., 1988.

Fire on Ice, Hockey's Greatest Series, by Scott Morrison, Pulse Books Inc., Goddard & Kamin, Downsview, Ont. 1987.

The Game of Our Lives, by Peter Gzowski, McLelland & Stewart, Toronto, 1981.

Gretzky, An Autobiography, with Rick Reilly, Harper Collins Publishers Inc. Toronto, 1990.

Hockey, The Official Book of the Game, Hamlyn Publishing, London, 1980.

In the Crease, Goaltenders Look at Life in the NHL, by Dick Irvin, McClelland & Stewart Inc., Toronto, 1995.

Los Angeles Kings, Hockeywood, by Rick Sadowski, Sagamore Publishing, Champaign, IL, 1993.

Mario Lemieux, Best There Ever Was, Pittsburgh Post-Gazette & Michael J. Bynum, Macmillan Canada, Toronto, 1997.

Mario Lemieux, The Final Period, Photography by Marc Serota, Edited by Tom McMillan, Reich, Brisson and Reich Publishing Inc. & Rare Air Ltd., a Mark Vancil Company, Pittsburgh, 1997.

National Hockey League 75th Anniversary Commemorative Book, Edited by Dan Diamond, McLelland & Stewart, Toronto, 1991.

The Official National Hockey League Stanley Cup Centennial Book, Edited by Dan Diamond, McLelland & Stewart, Toronto, 1992.

100 Great Moments in Hockey, by Brian Kendall, Viking (Penguin Books Canada Ltd.), Toronto, 1994.

One Hundred Years of Hockey, by Brian McFarlane, Deneau Publishers, Toronto, 1989.

Scotty Bowman, A Life in Hockey, by Douglas Hunter, Penguin Books, Toronto, 1998.

Stanley Cup Fever, 100 Years of Hockey Greatness, by Brian McFarlane, Stoddart Publishing, Toronto, 1992.

Total Hockey, The Official Encyclopedia of the National Hockey League, Edited by Dan Diamond, Toronto, 1998.

Total Stanley Cup, The Official Encyclopedia of the Stanley Cup, Edited by Dan Diamond, Editor, Toronto, 2000.

Official Guide & Record Book, 1998-99; 1999-2000, National Hockey League Publications, Toronto & New York, 1998, 1999.

Le Journal de Montréal, Montreal

La Presse Archives, Montreal

The Gazette Library, Montreal

The Hockey News, Toronto

City of Montreal Public Library

Pittsburgh Post-Gazette, Pittsburgh

Saturday Night Magazine (The National Post), Toronto

Sports Illustrated, New York

The Toronto Star, Toronto

HE'S AN EQUIPMENT MANAGER'S DREAM.

HE'S NOT PARTICULAR ABOUT ANYTHING. **HE'S WEARING THE SAME SHIN PADS HE WORE IN '97.**

PEOPLE THINK HE WORKS ON HIS STICKS FOR HOURS.

HE JUST TAKES THEM OUT OF THE BOX.

I MAKE SURE THE SHAFTS AREN'T WARPED, HE TAPES THEM UP.

HE'S GOING TO PLAY IN **THE OLYMPICS.** THEY'RE WORRIED ABOUT HAVING HIM.

THEY'RE CALLING ME ASKING WHAT TO DO TO MAKE SURE HE'S HAPPY.

I SAY, 'HE WALKS IN, HE PUTS IT ON, AND OFF HE GOES.

I CAN'T STRESS ENOUGH, **HE WILL BE THE EASIEST SUPERSTAR YOU'LL EVER WORK WITH.**

SOURCE: STEVE LATIN, PENGUINS EQUIPMENT MANAGER / ALEC WILKINSON, ESPN.COM - ESPN THE MAGAZINE

MARIO HAD IT ALL, MORE THAN ANYONE I EVER PLAYED AGAINST,

ESPECIALLY HIS NATURAL **SPEED** AND **POWER,**

ALL DONE WITH SUCH **FINESSE,** HE WAS SO ELEGANT

THAT YOU DIDN'T REALIZE JUST **HOW MUCH POWER HE HAD UNTIL YOU HAD TO DEAL WITH HIM ONE-ON-ONE.** MARIO AND WAYNE WERE PART OF AN ERA

OF GREAT HOCKEY IN THE '80S WHEN THERE WERE SOME

EXCEPTIONAL TEAMS, THE KIND WE MAYBE WON'T SEE AGAIN

VERY OFTEN BECAUSE OF THE SALARY AND BUDGET LIMITS

SOURCE: MARK MESSIER, CE YNTER NEWORK RANGERS

CAN YOU IMAGINE MARIO FROM THE START WITH AN OFFENSIVE TEAM

LIKE THE OILERS WERE AT THAT TIME, PLAYING WITH SO MANY SKILLED PLAYERS?

IN THEIR PRIME, **IF YOU HAD BEEN OFFERED YOUR CHOICE OF 99 OR 66**

IT WOULD HAVE BEEN THE TOUGHEST DECISION POSSIBLE TO MAKE

BECAUSE **THEY BROUGHT SO MUCH TO THE TABLE.**

MARIO WAS THE BETTER PURE GOAL SCORER, AS GOOD AS I SAW.

WAYNE WAS THE MASTER OF USING THE PLAYERS WITH HIM, MAKING THEM BETTER.

SOURCE: RON LOW, COACH NEW YORK RANG